MOVE YOUR BODY (2 THE 90's)

UNLIMITED EURODANCE

Juha Soininen

MOVE YOUR BODY (2 THE 90's)

UNLIMITED EURODANCE

Cover design: Juha Soininen
This is a revised and international version of the book Move Your Body -
Rajaton eurodance (ISBN 9789515683137, BOD, 2019)

Kustantaja: BoD – Books on Demand, Helsinki, Suomi

Valmistaja: BoD – Books on Demand, Norderstedt, Saksa

ISBN: 9789528026303

CONTENTS

℘

INTRO

" I've got this feeling
Somebody dance with me..."

...echoed out of of my tape recorder, which I had inherited from my sister. What was this melodic goodness from heaven, I wondered? Previously I had only been exposed to schlager (which my parents were always listening), but this was something else entirely. Fierce and deep male voice rapped in between and a lady with an amazing voice blasted out the catchy refrain. This was accompanied by an enchanting bassline and a piano.

The year was 1993.

For me it started from there. I started to buy audio cassettes and when I got a CD player for Christmas, I started to collect CD's. Many dance collections and albums refined my taste and got me to hunger for this European electronic sound more and more.

The previously mentioned first eurodance song I heard was DJ Bobo's *Somebody Dance With Me.* It was followed by a bunch of other artists who tried to grab my attention: Culture Beat, Haddaway, 2 Unlimited, Pandora, Flexx, Rob'n'Raz etc. Eurodance was here to stay.

Or so it seemed.

Years went by and eventually the genre faded and started to change its shape. Around the millennium, I started to get interested in anonymous DJ's and their instrumental trance songs and started to forget eurodance...

At the moment about 25 years has passed since eurodance's golden age. Eurodance was at its best during 1992-1996. When a new century was approaching, new dance music genres started to appear in the mainstream. For example trance, dream dance and bubblegum (which developed from euro) started to take over the charts so much that you could basically declare eurodance dead.

Although there are a lot of books about music, there seems to be a marginal number of books written about electronic music, especially electronic pop. One of the reasons I'm writing this book, is that there has never been a single book concentrating just in classical eurodance, even worldwide (and in English).

However, there are books that have some eurodance artists. American James Arena has done several interview books about 70's and 80's dance music artists. He has written one book, *Stars Of 90's Dance Pop: Hitmakers Discuss Their Careers,* which has interviews from the likes of Dr. Alban, Haddaway, La Bouche etc. Although it has a wider spectrum of 90's dance artists, it's a good steppingstone for this book. In addition to Arenas book, there has been a couple books written about this genre in in German and in French. They are a little undetailed and call almost all 90's dance music eurodance (I'm going to prove that eurodance and 90's dance music are not one and the same) and they don't approach the subject on a larger scale as I have. Talking about eurodance is mainly concentrated on the Internet, where there are a lot of pages devoted to the genre. These sites mainly have a different views of what eurodance is.

One of my objectives with this book is to define the genre more clearly. The term eurodance is used for vain and too often in connection with many other electronic music genres. When talking about eurodance (for short euro) usually people include all dance music made in Europe. Euro or in sometimes the term classical eurodance is a standout style which has its own characteristics.

Especially in Finland, national discussion about euro has negative or condescending nuances as if to show that it is subordinate to other more appreciated dance music genres like house and techno. One example is to add nickname *eurohumppa* to it.

With my book, I want to give respect to the genre and go into it more deeply than any one has gone before. I'm going beyond the stage performers (which were always not the ones who sang the songs) and the most famous hits. There are interesting stories behind the songs and song writers, which usually don't get the visibility they deserve. Media's interest usually doesn't go beyond the leading figures. I want to give voice also to those artists and producers, which the large audience have never even heard of. One of my main missions is to offer new information and surprising connections especially to eurodance aficionados.

I have no education in music, but I've been a buff for over 25 years, so my approach is largely subjective. My perspective is of a listener. My apologies for the reader if I use wrong musical terms in some point. My focus is on the music itself, how does it sound, but I won't talk a lot about the technical side.

If you happen to be Finnish, this book is a revised version of my eurodance book released in Finland in 2019. The main differences are that most of the Finnish artists have been removed and several new interviews added. I have also corrected some errors of the first edition. Also, my excuses for grammar mistakes in this book, my native language is Finnish.

This book is my tribute to the greatest electronic music genre. It's hedonistic and feverish rhythm and strong production have helped me to carry on in the midst of all my personal problems.

So welcome to the world of eurodance and:

MOVE YOUR BODY!

ABOUT THE SOURCES

I have used many sources in making this book. The ones I've used the most are Eurokdj, Wikipedia and Discogs. In addition, I have used my music collection and interviewed artists and producers, if that option has been available to me. In many cased I have had to rely on information published in the web.

I have intentionally left out all the artist discographies because they would have taken too much space in the book. You can check the credits and other information from www.discogs.com.

The pictures are from my own personal CD collection, if not mentioned otherwise. The photographer is Henri Kumlander.

WHAT IS EURODANCE?

First we must define what eurodance really is. There are probably as many definitions as there are euro fans. For me it has always been a genre which lived in the 90's and it's golden age was 1992-1996. Usually it's a European song, which is quite energetic and fast, *120-150 bpm* (hits/beats per minute) and it comprises of a woman singing the catchy refrain and the man (usually colored) rapping in between. Sometimes rap parts are performed in raggamuffin (heavy Jamaican accent) style. It could sometimes be also a song performed by one man or woman with no raps. Lyrics are usually quite simple, only a one sentence repeating over and over again.

Yle reporter Heidi Sommar states in an article that eurodance used synth riffs and simple melodies. Music magazine Rumba's reporter Anton Vanha-Majamaa defines it like this: synth riff, male rapper, women singing sharply but he considers the beat being slower, 110-130 bpm.

Usually eurodance songs are melancholic but on the other hand lots of cheerful songs were also made. Bubblegum dance and eurodance are often considered one and the same, although that is not the case. Bubblegum is really naive and has lighter sound and vocals. On the other hand, artists like Scatman John and Me & My are something in between those two genres.

Eurodance is NOT any European dance music. Usually euro house and eurodance are considered to be the same thing. In my opinion eurohouse is a like a second cousin to eurodance: although it incorporates some of the characteristics of it, it has lighter feel to it, relying more on house and soulful vocals. Artists like Livin' Joy, Whigfield and Robin S represent eurohouse. Also dance-pop is basically eurohouse, for example boybands like East 17.

Eurodance is still being made today but not in the same extent that most people think. Contemporary artists who make euro are bands like Digital Base Project and Acting Lovers who make authentic 1990's sound with today's technology. Eurodance is music of the 90's and or its made with 90's sounds. For example, when Culture Beat released *Mr.Vain* in 2003 with a reloaded sound, it wasn't anymore eurodance. It was a reproduction made in hard trance style (and quite fantastic I might say).

Karine Sanche, who is behind the biggest eurodance encyclopedia in Web, sees it otherwise. In her opinion eurodance is (addition to classical euro) bubblegum, happy hardcore, trance, dream dance and hands up. My definition is a whole lot narrower. Although the genres Karine mentioned have traces of euro, I wouldn't use that word in connection with these genres.

People behind the upcoming eurodance movie *Neverending Dream* have even larger view of the genre. In the project's homepage has been described that it's 90's dance music, music of your childhood; music that moves you and begets deep emotions.. This definition is based strongly on the feeling, not caring too much about genre boundaries.

ॐ

BIRTH

Eurodance was born "squashed" in between many genres. Many songs, artists and styles laid the groundwork for euro. Elements for example of house, techno and hip hop were mixed together to be able to create radio friendly hits.

70's disco music has a big meaning for eurodance because it created the basis for all electronic dance music. Style born in gay and black peoples' underground clubs created the DJ. DJ (disc jockey), aka the man behind the turntables, got to be on the center stage and he/she could create hits by choosing what to play in the clubs. Disco developed from Motown, funk and Philadelphia soul into its own genre. For example, Gloria Gaynor, Donna Summer, The Salsoul Orchestra and Tavares were famous disco performers.

In the beginning of the 70's American record producer Tom Moulton developed so called disco mix, a long mix which extended the original song. In addition to vocals it contained a long instrumental part, "disco break", which utilized songs more catchy string parts. With these remixes the party people would go into ecstasy on the dance floor. Moulton is the grandfather of remix, without him there wouldn't be so many variations of songs to play in clubs or in radios. That's one thing that disco brought straight to eurodance, euro songs were remixed a lot to bring different interpretations for the dance floor or to those who didn't like the original. Other famous disco mixers were for example Walter Gibbons, Bobby "DJ" Guttadaro and Larry Levan.

Disco made its way into Europe too. Producers like Jean-Marc Cerrone, Henri Belolo and Jacques Morali got inspiration from the dark Philadelphia sound. When thinking about electronic dance music in general, the biggest influencer has to be Giorgio Moroder who made disco sound more electronic. He made *I Feel Love* (1977) for Donna Summer with Pete Bellotte. That song is, I think, the grandfather to all modern electronic music. With its synthesized sound it was a revelation for many artists. David Bowie remembers that his partner Brian Eno declared (after hearing the song) that this single was to change the club sound for the next 15 years. The song continues to influence music makers even further to this day and it has a big meaning for commercial dance music, which eurodance basically was.

After Donnas *I Feel Love*, disco music started to develop and so a faster version of disco was born, hi-NRG. That genres gift to eurodance was a hectic and fast rhythm. Artists like Sylvester, Weather Girls, Kelly Marie and Evelyn Thomas represented this subgenre. Later, in the 1980's, production team SAW (Stock, Aitken & Waterman) were heavily inspired by hi-NRG sound and got a massive amount of hits with their energetic sound. Like disco, also hi-NRG, flourished in gay and black clubs.

Hi-NRG itself influenced the birth of a totally electronic genre of disco music, italo disco in the 80's. I think that the italo disco was direct predecessor of eurodance. It laid the groundwork for euro with its catchy and wishful melodies and refrains. The connection just strengthened when many italo artist made eurodance songs in the 1990's, like Ken Laszlo, Sabrina and Radiorama. In Sabrina's outrageous hit *Boys* (1987) there was even a rap part which would be quite common in eurodance songs.

Also, house music had its part to play in creation of eurodance. House was born as a combination from many genres in the US. Like disco, it was born in the underground clubs. When disco died, DJ's didn't have any newer songs to play in clubs. Then they started to emulate the disco sound by using a drum machine and using samples and melodies on top of that. For example, Frankie Knuckles made a long remix of Michael Jackson's *Rock With You* by replacing live drums with a drum machine. Knuckles became so popular that he was asked to DJ in a club called Warehouse. Warehouse became so popular, that people were starting to ask about the music being played there and finally the prefix "ware" was left out and all that remained was house. House music was born.

Hip house developed from house and was a one step closer to eurodance. It was born as a mix between house and hip hop, rhyming and rapping was attached to house rhythms. Genre used a lot of samples and pieces from other songs. Rap musicians wanted a piece of house music's success and in return house DJ's wanted rappers to feature in their own productions. These coalitions produced bands like Technotronic and Snap!, which were a kind of prototypes for eurodance bands. These were projects where producers were in control and the performers and singers could be changed even between songs. Many eurodance acts started with hip house like M.C. Sar & Real McCoy, B.G. The Prince Of Rap, 2 Brothers On The 4th Floor, Twenty 4 Seven and Cartouche.

Techno was born out of house, or it was more European style of house music. It took the monotony and the sound volume to the maximum. Besides the beat, also low frequencies that effect the dancers physically, are considered important in the genre. Big contrasts, variation in speed, surprise pauses and samples (borrowed rhythms and or vocals, spoken word) are also some of characteristics of techno. The term techno (as well as eurodance) has been used falsely starting from the 1990's. Laymen have used it to call any music made with computers from eurodance to happy hardcore.

All these musical ingredients from techno to rap were added to the soup called eurodance.

CHARACTERISTICS OF EURODANCE

Eurodance has many common characteristics. One thing what euro inherited from techno was reiterated, short vocals. The lyrics sometimes consisted of even just one repetition of a sentence like "let the rhythm move you", "move your body" or "dance to the beat". Usually lyrics had no deeper meaning, just dance, love and party. Verbal gimmicks were mostly absent in eurodance, rhythm and melody were the most important thing in these songs.

Rap parts (inherited from hip hop), which were performed between refrains, were not even trying to be something that people would remember or have some kind of deeper meaning. It was just rhyming with words that fit together. They sounded more like intermediate phrases than opinions or thoughts of the writer. Rap parts main function was to stimulate the listener before getting into the melody and the refrain. Eurodance songs had mainly one to three rap parts, although in some cases the rap was absent, and the lead singer sang the whole song.

Jumpin', jumpin' up and down
From the top right to the ground
Free your soul and free your mind.
Now set you free, right on time
It's weekend and it's party-time
Feel the heat and free your mind

(Masterboy: Feel The Heat Of The Night -excerpt)

Drive me crazy all night long
Till my grandma sings this song
Drive me crazy, take it down now
Squeeze me baby, take my hand now

(U.S.U.R.A.: Drive Me Crazy –excerpt)

There were still exceptions to the rule concerning the depth of the lyrics, e.g. Dr. Alban. His lyrics have dealt with issues like drug use, racism, and the price of fame. Also, one-time-project Lovemessage (which assembled many famous eurodance acts) rapped about sex education. Also, E-Rotic, which was a part of that coalition, could be considered to have pushed the safe sex agenda.

My opinion is that the vocals in eurodance are like instruments: their main mission is to support the music and melody. Sometimes the singers were so bad that the songs great melody compensated the lack of singing skills. The catchy melody played the leading part.

Everybody's walking
Everybody's talking
Talk to me baby

(Redcat: Everybody's Walking – excerpt)

Dance to the beat, to the beat
Dance to the beat, to the beat
Dance to the beat, you can't stop it

(Bass Expanders: Beats Go -excerpt)

Although called *euro*dance, it wasn't strictly limited to Europe. Projects sprouted like mushrooms after the rain. The most peculiar euro countries were Mexico, USA and Japan. The origin country of the project wasn't an important thing, sometimes the band was comprised of people from many countries. Eurodance collected all nations under the same dance beat.

Eurodance acts fates were heavily in the hands of their producers, leading figures could change fast, or they could stay on board as long as they proved to be successful in that incarnation. Although the bands were personified in those who performed live and in music videos, the producers were in charge. They managed their projects like companies, changing staff as they pleased, even after one single or album. Sometimes the studio singer stayed the same although the figureheads changed, like in E-Rotic. It was very common that the studio singer was a different person who performed them live. Lip-syncing was very obvious in many cases, like in Corona project, where Sandy Chambers sang most of the songs and Olga de Souza mimed to the lyrics in public events. Cappella took this to another level: for example, *U Got 2 Know* album (1994) has several singers, most of them were not even credited. In addition to that, all of the songs on the album contain a lot of samples from various songs.

Live performers were usually chosen because of their good looks, sometimes even models were used. The use of beautiful front ladies was a very common habit in dance music industry before the millennium. For example, euro house project Black Box hired the French model Katrine to perform *Ride On Time* (1989), but later it was revealed that the song used disco diva Loleatta Holloway's vocal from the song *Love Sensation*. After the millennium there hasn't been a lot of these kind hoaxes, maybe because the public has become more aware and the strong presence of musicians in the social media has brought transparency.

In dance music the popular genres change really fast, and it has become even faster in current Spotify-obsessed climate. The constant change was fast also in the 90's, whenever one artist got a hit with a certain sound, dozens of imitators were born to grab their share of the success. These kind of songs were for example Robert Miles *Children* and Sash!'s *Encore Une Fois*. Also, the popularity of happy hardcore influenced eurodance artists as the beats started to get faster and faster.

Because of this constant fishing for a big hit, many artists who made eurodance, eventually changed their style into something else. You had to live on the cutting edge, or you were out and forgotten. For instance : the only single released after Maxx's one and only album was called *Move Your* Body (1995), which was from another world compared to Maxx's typical euro style, this was a replica from the sound of American Reel 2 Real. Also, the Swedish Look Twice dumped eurodance after two albums and transformed into a hip hop / funk band. Many project went through a similar metamorphosis after the best eurodance days were over.

As a fan and a listener, you felt betrayed, if your own favorite artists changed their style entirely. Although there are cases where bands have returned to their original style. Case in point: Basic Element. They did a really light disco music influenced album *Tracks* (1996) but returned hard as a rock with their *Earthquake* album after two years. Especially many solo artists started to lose interest in eurodance very fast, when they had achieved success with the current euro sound. Alexia was one of those who almost completely gave up on euro on her second album. Usually their interests laid in some other genres, although gaining the public success by singing euro.

Artists also tried to repeat the success of their previous hits with the same sound. Alexia got hits with songs like *Summer Is Crazy* and *Number One* but *Uh La La La* (1997) was the song that made here rise to mega stardom. *Uh La La La* is a slow, reggaeish downtempo. She decided to offer more of that in the following albums, suffice to say that dance songs were scarce after the debut album... A great singer was lost in the midst of boring ballads and euro reggae.

Only a handful eurodance acts made albums which were entirely in eurodance style. It was usual to include euro reggae or even ballads to the mix, in order to attract a larger audience. The album with the most eurodance, have grown into the biggest classics.

As in dance music in general, sampling (aka taking parts from other songs) was very common in euro. The master of sampling was Italian Gianfranco Bortolotti who took pieces from various sources and attached them together with a unique touch, the downside to this was that sometimes he "forgot" to ask permissions from the original artists. Covering hit songs in eurodance style was also a typical way to make yourself a hit. Sometimes the original slow song needed upgrading for the club people in euro form. For example, the project Urgent C made an eurodance version of Rednex's *Wish You Were Here* ballad. Sometimes the song was remixed into several different versions according to the country where the single was released, different countries had different tastes.

Producers behind the projects did remixes for other artists under the name of their project. For example, La Bouche, E-Rotic, Damage Control and Pharao have mixed many songs, there was even a Scatman John remix. In these cases, songs were remixed with the familiar sound of the projects.

VISUAL STYLE

The music videos seemed like they were done with little money. Background could be a storage hall or an abandoned warehouse. In some cases, the artists could be filmed on the streets, fields or even in railway stations miming to their songs. Usually there were primitive props, or an environment made completely with computer graphics (like Cymurai ft. Thea Austin : *Magic Touch*). With the use of computer graphics, they tried to go for the futuristic feel. That iconography was inherited from 80's synth pop and italo disco aesthetics. After 25 plus years later, these graphics used in eurodance videos look like relics.

Project's own unique style was of course reflected in the videos. For example, in Imperio's videos ancient Rome was introduced, while Pharao danced in Egypt. Magic Affairs videos were a bit more serious and gloomy projecting the bands mystical and magical side.

In majority of these videos, professional dancers were present, sometimes a whole auditorium, sometimes only a couple. If the artist in question had dancing skills, he or she performed them on video, like Kelly Overett in Cappella's *U Got 2 Let The Music*. If the project wanted to stay more anonymous, the video could feature only dancers

Videos were usually very colorful, although some black and white videos were made. I prefer colored because it reflects better eurodance's ideology of partying and dancing.

Projects success also had a big meaning in the quality of the music videos. For example, bands like La Bouche or Real McCoy, who had big hits in USA, made better looking videos, because there were usually bigger record labels involved and they had deeper pockets.

So, did eurodance have its own kind of style in fashion? Well some could be observed through music videos or live performances. In my opinion the style of euro has been vastly copied from rave/techno culture. Many artists wore outfits made of PVC plastic, especially black. In many cases the rappers took their style from hip hop, preferring loose clothes. Round and dark sunglasses were also present to emphasize the rappers "cool" look.

Both female and male singers showed some bare skin, although not equally. Male singer or rapper could keep their shirt open or if the artist was considered "good-looking". Women wore short skirts or shorts. Skimpy wear was a must for projects like E-Rotic, who sang mostly about sex. Women liked to wear wigs or dreadlocks, the more colorful the better. Also, the theme chosen for the project determined the style of clothes.

Overall, the visual style of eurodance was a mix of techno and other dance music aesthetics. As the music, it was a blend of many genres and styles.

RHYTHM IS A DANCER – THE INFLUENCERS OF EURODANCE

Some bands have been elemental in the development of eurodance by bringing different elements to the genre. In this next part I introduce some of the most famous ones.

▶ *Snap!* *(Germany)*

Snap! is one of the first bands to release a eurodance song. Although they did a lot of euro hip hop, they influenced many euro bands.

The journey of Maurice Durron Butler (b. 1967) toward Snap! started from unusual settings: he was a drummer in his hometown's heavy metal band. He joined the US Army where he specialized in bomb disposal. One personal bomb waited him around the corner, because after leaving the Army he moved to Germany where he met two producers, Michael Münzing (aka Benito Benites) and Luca Anzilotti (aka John Virgo Garrett III). They were producing a project called Snap!, which had gotten its name from a sequencer hardware. Before Snap! the producers had gotten their slice of fame with an act Off *(Electrica Salsa)*.

When they met Maurice, the producers were working on a song called *Power* (1990), which was constructed from various vocal samples: songs by Chaka Khan, Jocelyn Brown, and Chill Rob G. Actually, there are several versions of the song due to obscurities concerning the samples that were used. In the beginning the song was released with Chill's original rap, but when problems started to emerge, the producers recruited Maurice to replace the original rap part. (Around these times Maurice took an artist name, Turbo B.). Penny Ford (b.1964) was chosen to replace Jocelyn Brown vocal sample *"I've Got The Power!"*. Penny was Chaka Khan's back-up singer and a roommate. Originally Chaka was asked to perform the vocals, but she didn't have the time, so she delegated this gig to Penny. When the new version was released with Penny's and Turbo B's vocals, it started to gather success all over the world. Also, the video (where Jackie Harris lip-syncing to Penny's vocals) caused more buzz.

Turbo B. and Penny Ford

From the first album, *World Power* (1990), big hits were released, like *Ooops Up*, which sampled Gap Band. In this stage Snap! -sound was mainly hip hop and hip house, but eurodance was waiting around the corner.

Penny has revealed that hers and Turbo B's work relationship wasn't that good. Bands fast rise to the top and obscurities concerning samples affected Penny's decision to leave Snap! and embark on a solo career.

A new female voice was needed, and the American Thea Austin was chosen for this job. She was transported to Germany to begin a whole new chapter for the project with Turbo B. First single with Thea, *Colour Of Love*, was a typical downtempo but the next single *Rhythm Is A Dancer* (1992)would going to be as meaningful to eurodance as Donna Summer's *Feel Love* was to the whole dance music genre.

The rhythm danced people around the world. It was the bestselling single in UK, number 5 in USA Billboard Hot 100 and in addition to that it fared greatly all over Europe. The song gave form to the typical eurodance convention: woman sings catchy refrain; man raps and the song features a straight techno beat and a clear melody. Dozens of remixes and cover versions tell a story about how meaningful this song has been for the genre. It has stood the test of time, even after 30 years.

It also gathered some notoriety for being a song which contains the worst lyrics of all time (or at least that was being claimed). The lyrics "*I'm serious as cancer, when I say rhythm is a dancer*" were just too much for some people, although the metaphor in question had been used in hip hop since 1980's.

The popularity gained with *Rhythm Is A Dancer* guaranteed that the second album *The Madman's Return* (1992) was a hit. The album was even released in three different versions, the first version didn't contain the mega hit. Turbo B wanted to have more influence in the project and therefore he would have liked the leading single to be *The Colour Of Love*, but it failed to perform in the charts. The album on the other hand was a harder dance album than the previous one.

Turbo B's discontent made him to yearn for a solo career although Snap! was going well. In addition to that, Thea was also trying to make it as a solo act. New single released from second album, *Exterminate*, featured yet another singer, Niki Haris (b.1962), who was Madonna's former background singer. Niki provided vocals also for another song, *Do You See The Light*.

The next album changed the sound of Snap! completely. *Welcome To Tomorrow* (1994) came out in the midst of the busiest eurodance era, so the band took strong ingredients from the genre. After all they have been involved in the creation of and development of eurodance genre. Now the figurehead was one person, Paula Brown aka Summer, who had for instance acted in Spike Lee movie School Daze. Songs like *Welcome To Tomorrow* and *The First The Last Eternity (Till The End)* were harder, but at the same time lighter sound. They were more clearly eurodance than the previous efforts, but the darker aspect of Snap! sound was absent and replaced with a happier vibe.

In 1996, when the fire of eurodance was slowly waning, the band tried to reheat their old hits, like *The Power'96* but they didn't catch the same fire as the previous hits. The next new song was a reminiscent of the very first hits called *Gimme A Thrill* (2000). Turbo B. was once again onboard with a singer Paulette Parker (aka Maxayn Lewis). According to Discogs Snap! was planning to release a new album at that time called *One Day On Earth*, but didn't because the single was a flop.

The new millennium was a turning point for the project. Around 2002-2003 the old 90's projects started to make new harder versions of their original hits mainly in hard trance style. Snap! was among the first to turn their *Rhythm Is A Dancer* into a harder sound in the hands of Andreas Litterscheid aka CJ Stone in 2002. The new version introduced Snap! to a whole new generation and turned out to be quite a hit, at least in Europe. Next year the remix was modified to include Turbo B's raps, with a quite clumsy added segment. Remix was followed by a collection called *The Cult Of Snap! -1990>>2003*, where artists like Fragma, Tom Novy and Finnish Fu-Tourist made their own versions and remixes of the Snap! classics. The oddest one was definitely Motivo's take on *The Power*, an Indian bhangra version.

After these remakes, a totally new promo single, *Beauty Queen*, was released. It had nothing that would remind of Snap!, it was just a trendy house song. There were a couple of other songs, but they didn't even get a proper release.

After these failed attempts, Snap! tried once again cash in with the old hits, although not much time had gone by since the last remix album. *The Power (Greatest Hits)*

(2009) used producers and artists like Armand Van Helden and Jens Kindervater, but the results were disastrous. A major part of the new versions were worthless electro house, seemed like the remixers didn't invest much to the project.

TURBO B, THEA AUSTIN, NIKI HARIS

After leaving Snap! in unpleasant circumstances, Turbo B. started his solo career. In 1992 he released a song called *I'm Not Dead* with his old band mate, Thea Austin. It was like a copy of Snap's biggest hits, apparently Turbo B. wanted to remind people where he had come from.

The album, *Make Way For The Maniac*, followed a little bit later. Content wise it was all over the place and even on the album he wanted to make Snap! -references, like with a song *Lyrical Jesse James*.

Apparently solo career didn't go as planned, because after this Butler was in a eurodance band called Centory as a frontman. Centory used many different female vocalists like Lori Glori and Christiane Eiben. Production was done by Trime'n'Delgado (Alex Trime and Sven Jordan).

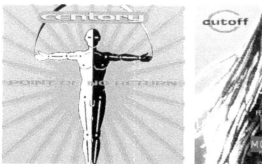

Centory was short-lived, but it managed to create some classic euro songs like *Point Of No Return* and *Eye In The Sky*. Having said that, the album *Alpha Centory* (1994) didn't offer anything worth your while excluding the single hits.

After fading out, the project released a really weird cover of Milli Vanilli song *Girl You Know It's True*. Turbo B. had gone and been replaced with Trey D (Keith McGuffey) and the song was done in euro hip hop style.

Turbo B. continued his solo career after Centory, mainly visiting as a guest rapper in other people's projects, he was even involved with bombshell Victoria Silvstedt's song *Rocksteady Love*.

Meanwhile Turbo was struggling with his solo efforts, Thea was faring better. She was the leading lady in a project called Cutoff, although the project started with other singers' vocals, the first   song *Life Is A Game* was sung by Rachel Steel. *Don't Stop* (which was downtempo) was the first song sung by Thea. *Move* released Thea's inner dance diva, although the song was just a little above average. Still it's worth noticing that *Move* featured also raps by hip hop all-female trio B.O.Y (Jackie,

Angel and Tina Harris) who were sisters and addition to that, cousins to Turbo B.! Jackie had also done some vocals for Snap! and the other two sisters had been back-up dancers. Later, Tina was the lead singer of the hip hop /dance -project Sweetbox.

Cutoff album called *Don't Stop* was released with a name Cutoff feat. Thea Austin. Although Thea was thus highlighted, previously mentioned Rachel sang some of the songs. Last single from this group was *Celebrate* (1994).

After Cutoff Thea was once again offered to be part of another project, this time it was Cymurai, which was a brainchild of two Koppehele brothers, Giorgio and Marvin. The first single *Magic Touch* (1995) is a great eurodance song, although it has a little bit generic melody. The song was accompanied by a music video, in which Thea got to sway her beautiful dreadlocks in between takes of out-of-date computer graphics. Cymurai`s next efforts like *Let Go* and *Vibe (Sending* Messages) didn't have the same kind of energy as the first one.

As the 90's sound changed into other genres, also Thea tried to do something different. Producer David Brandes's (E-Rotic) eurodance project Heart Attack had done a couple of melodic euro songs, but the last single released from it was a house cover, *Eye Of The Tiger*. Theas vocals in that one was the only redeeming factor..

Thea has mainly sung house music after the 90's. Hits like Soulsearcher's *I Can't Get Enough* gave her new recognition and she earned the title "queen of house music". But 90's dance was the genre that brought her back to the arenas. For instance, she performed in Justin Timberlake's charity event in Las Vegas. According to Thea's home page, Justin told Thea there that "he grew up listening to *Rhythm Is A Dancer*".

Niki Haris was maybe the quietest one of these three former Snap! vocalists after the time spent on the project. She made a house single called *Total Love* and featured on other artists projects like Perry Twins *(Bad, Bad Boy)*.

At the moment Snap! consists of the original singer Penny Ford and rapper Jesse Kolb. In addition to that, Turbo B. performs in 90's events rapping to Snap's biggest hits.

▶ *Technotronic* *(Belgium)*

Another major band for development of eurodance besides Snap! was Technotronic. In the 80's it started a fusion of techno and house music, which created a foundation for the tremendous energy of eurodance. At the time, that fusion wasn't called euro, but hip house.

Belgian producer Jo Bogaert was looking for a female rapper to rhyme on top of instrumental song he had made. He met Manuela Kamosi (aka Ya Kid K), who was from Zaire. At the time she was a part of Antwerpian rap group called Fresh Beat. Manuela had moved to Belgium at the age of 11 and she had visited in Chicago to absorb influences from the local techno and house culture. So Bogaert's request to perform in his track didn't feel so unfamiliar to Manuela. The result of this collaboration was *Pump Up The Jam* (1989), which would remain in dance music history as one of the biggest dance songs. Including its many merits was number two in UK single chart. The music video did also good promotion to the song, it summarized the end of the 80's perfectly with its neon colors and fanny packs.

Although Ya Kid K sang the song, she didn't get to perform it on gigs, instead of her a model called Felly Kilingi lip-synced in the video and in live performances. But when more hits started to appear with Ya Kid K on the vocals (like *Get Up! (Before The Night Is Over)* and *This Beat Is Technotronic*) Manuel got more recognition and visibility in the project. An album called *Pump Up The Jam,* which was recorded in three weeks, followed the hit singles. It sold so massively that a remix album called *Trip On* This was put out. It also contained a couple of new songs and a Ya Kid's collaboration with Hi Tek 3, *Spin That Wheel.*

Pump Up The Jam has been one of the biggest influencers of eurodance.

Black Diamond, Ya Kid K and Daisy Dee from the pages of Recall LP leaflet.

The new sound that Technotronic introduced wasn't so surprising to the public when it was time to release the next album. Although the second *Body To Body* (1991) managed to gain some hits, the success wasn't as vast as on the first album. Ya Kid K had been left out and a new singer called Reggie (aka Réjane Magloire) replaced her. Singles like *Work* and the soulful *Money Makes The World Go Round* were released from this LP. The overall look of the album was more pop and less club than the previous one.

For a couple of years after this, the project followed from the sidelines when the eurodance sound started to become the dominant sound. In 1993 Ya Kid K returned and the magnificent single *Hey Yoh, Here We Go* was released. This was Technotronic but reloaded to a more heavier euro sound. The next song *One Plus One* didn't even get near to that ethereal euro sound that the previous one had.

But in 1994 they came back with a bang: the song *Move It To The Rhythm* conquered the charts and was followed by a new album, *Recall*. Bogaert had ensured the success by hiring Phil Wilde and Peter Bauwens, who had had hits with 2 Unlimited. The album was divided between vocalists Ya Kid K and Black Diamond (aka Charles Fitzgerald Davis), which resulted in the album being uneven. It should have contained more eurodance, but a major part of the LP was lighter house music. It featured also a major eurodance singer called Daisy Dee.

Recall has been projects last album, after that just individual songs have dropped. They have updated their songs many times, for example with the project D.O.N.S. But Technotronic is still touring, with Ya Kid K. According to bands Facebook page, their records have sold over 14 million copies.

In The Spotlight

▶️⏸

Jo Bogaert producer

Published with the permission of Jo Bogaert.

Could you tell me a little about your musical background?

I'm was born in 1956.

In the early 70's I played electric guitar in a blues rock band, then progressive rock, late 70's I played in new wave bands and by halfway of the 80's I was busy with synths and sequencers, which finally resulted in me making dance music. So I consider myself a blues rocker with a computer, so to speak.

How did Technotronic was born, how did you come up with the idea to add raps to a thumping techno beat?

In 1989 I heard *Big Fun* by Inner City. That was a revelation: soulful vocals on a techno tune! Hip hop was happening at that time, so I thought that would be a good combination as well.

When I met Manuela Kamosi (Ya Kid K) the picture was complete: she was a rapper who could sing. So, I asked her to do both: rap and sing.

Pump Up The Jam is a song that's definitely one of the songs that influenced 90's eurodance, how do you see that song after 30 years?

Yes, it is exactly that: a song. People sing along, they know the lyrics. Well, not all the lyrics. Most think Manuela sings ' *I want, a place to stay'*, but she sings '*Awa, a place to stay.*' Awa is swahili (or lingala, I'm not sure) for 'a place to stay, a home'.

Beyond all expectations PUTJ still sounds fresh, I am told.

There's a big change between the first two albums and the last one, *Recall*. Did you feel pressure to make eurodance because it was so popular? Would you have wanted to take the band to another direction musically?

I should never have made that 2nd and 3rd album. It is complicated to explain, but pressure and stress played an important role, yes.

In your opinion, which of the bands did best eurodance in the 90's, and why?

I prefer Snap!: good songs, good vocals, good sounds and more than one.

And then there are the one offs: Jam & Spoon, Black Box

Have you been involved in other projects that could be considered eurodance? If so, tell me a little about them.

Well I was involved in new beat, which was the Belgian electronic dance music right before the whole eurodance thing took off. Nux Nemo and Acts of Madmen where my main projects.

After many years as a producer, how do you still challenge yourself ?

Well, my problem is finding vocalists. I have loads of tracks, but I don't seem to find good singers. But my activities have changed: I have written a few books and I paint.

Your thoughts about modern dance music, like EDM etc.?

Some of it is good, most I can't stand. I like the darker stuff, not the poppy stuff. The most intriguing thing is the evolution of the structure of songs. The way structures are in today's music is so refreshing and it happens in all musical styles: it has been going on for a while now? You find it in all kinds of music, from Thom Yorke or Burial to Kendrick Lamar and these esthetics have crossed over to dance.

The other thing is that experimentation is on with the beats: four to the floor is no longer the only option, at last!

▶ *Jam & Spoon* *(Germany)*

Published in the permission of Rolf Ellmer

The duo Jam & Spoon have been called as creators of trance, but they have influenced other electronic music genres too. Rolf Ellmer (Jam El Mar) and Markus Löffel (Mark Spoon) started their quest for success by making a remix of Alex Lee's *Age Of Love*. This work created more remix requests from artists like Moby and Frankie Goes To Hollywood. They were inspired by producer Trevor Horn's sound (who produced Frankie), so they were excited to get to remix one of their favorite producers' song. In addition to Horn, they were inspired by Tangerine Dream's synth sound.

They released their first album in 1991 called *Breaks Unit 1*, but they didn't score any hits. The situation was soon to change with the song *Stella* (1992), which has since then been hailed as one of the biggest trance classics. Although the duo was more known for making underground music than mainstream pop, that didn't prevent them from getting to the charts by releasing the eurodance song *Right In The Night (Fall In Love With Music)* (1993), in which the lovely singer Plavka Lonich (now Coleridge) gave her seductive vocals. This single led to the second album *Tripomatic Fairytales 2001*. People who loved single were surprised when they bought the album: it wasn't a pop album but a deeper experience which suited more for listening at home than partying to it in the club. The same formula was repeated in the future: single release was usually a pop song (sung by Plavka) but the albums were much deeper than your average dance album.

With the aliases Trancy Spacer and Spacy Trancer they produced Tokyo Ghetto Pussy project, which was closer to eurodance with songs like *Everybody On The Floor (Pump It)* (1994). The album formula was the same, singles were more dance pop, but the album was a deeper effort.

Before Jam & Spoon, Rolf had been in a trance project called Dance 2 Trance, who had had a major hit with *Power Of American Natives* (sung by Linda Rocco). This project, which was established with Dag Lerner, lasted for a couple of hits and two albums, until Rolf and Dag decided to put the project to sleep. Dag wanted to concentrate more on his solo career and Rolf in Jam & Spoon.

31

Unfortunately Jam & Spoon suffered a tragedy in 2006, when Markus got a heart attack in his apartment and died. But Rolf is still going strong and touring as Jam & Spoon.

In The Spotlight

▶️II

Rolf Ellmer aka *Jam El Mar* producer

Published with permission of Rolf Ellmer.

You have been involved in many dance productions. What are your favorite projects and why, or do you have favorites?

I necessarily don't have any favorites. I can say that the more ambitious projects and tracks were more for me. But basically, I loved them all.

You are a master of many dance music genres, is it more difficult to make popular music like eurodance comparing to more underground music? Or is it the other way around?

Every genre has its very own special vibe and style and the challenge is to hit that vibe. So first, you have to get into that vibe, secondly, you have to be able to hit that vibe with your production. Most important is to like what you are doing and don't force yourself into something you don't feel. It happened to me a few times and, looking back, it was lost time.

I consider Dance 2 Trances *Power of American natives* to be a precursor for eurodance. Could you tell me a little how this song was made?

I would not consider this track as eurodance. I would more see it in the genre of trance - anyway: *Power Of American Natives* was inspired by DJ Dag's inspiration by American Indians. It was the last track among the tracks of the *Moon Spirits* album, and we had to deliver a potential chart hit to the record company. After a long search we finally ended up with this pan flute melody. But still there was no vocal on it. We hired a studio and asked Linda Rocco, a great female rock singer I knew for some time, into the studio. Eventually we had a recording and the record company was super happy. It became our first ever golden record!

Tokyo Ghetto Pussy was a little more eurodance, but the album had more deeper sounds, what's the story behind this project?

This was always a fun project. The concept was: Let's do something that's just fun but finally it ended up being caught up into delivering hit records again, since the very first release, *Everybody On The Floor*, hit the charts very well. When we finally came to deliver the album we also wanted to show a different side of our creativity.

How do you remember your time with Markus, Mark Spoon?

I am not able to answer this in a few words. I could write a book about our collaboration! Mark Spoon was a phenomenon in ideas and creativity. He was also a walking contradiction and a difficult person to cope with. But our friendship - and collaboration was blind understanding. We usually had the same goal, ideas, and thoughts. I miss him dearly although it never was easy to work with him.

Right In The Night with Plavka became a massive hit, how did you find Plavka?

Mark Spoon knew Plavka from the very first Love Parade. He was clever enough to ask for her number so, when we were about to record *Right In The Night,* he opened his magic book of secret telephone numbers.

Jam & Spoon released singles that were more pop, but the albums contained deeper dance music. How the listeners reacted to your albums because they weren't full of pop songs they were accustomed to?

I am sure, some were confused, and some were disappointed. Because getting famous in the pop genre with a track like *Right In The Night* people had certain expectations about the album. But we thought to rather stay experimental and trying to not just deliver a flat pop album but something with more surprises and unheard musical secrets. Mark had the idea of a fairytale book in a musical context. This is what we tried to do. I think we did well, because to my ears, the music still sounds fresh and inspired and you can listen to it without ending up skipping track after track.

Are there other eurodance acts you would like to mention, that you have been involved with?

B.G. The Prince Of Rap was full-on eurodance - at least the second album was. With him we had our first chart success in the Hot 100 in the US. Something quite remarkable for German producers.

What's your current status in music business, are you remixing etc?

Remixing a lot, yes, and also creating new tracks. I finally ended up being a DJ, so I produce the sound that I am going for as a DJ. But it's not pop or eurodance anymore, it's more like something in the interspace between techno & trance.

▶ *U96* (Germany)

Project, which got its name from a German submarine in WWII, was established by Ingo Hauss, Hayo Lewerentz, Helmut Hoinkis and Alex Christensen in 1990. The first single *Das Boot*, was released in the midst of techno and rave era and with its highly electric techno sound it reached Germanys single chart number one position and stayed there for 13 weeks. The song itself was a cover of the movie *Das Boot*'s (1981) theme song.

The first album carried the same name as the first single and it consisted of similar techno songs. U96's sound was rough and raw. Album also succeeded in Germany so that it gained a gold record. Another single released from the album, *I Wanna Be A Kennedy*, sampled 80's synth-pop band Visage (*Fade To Grey*). In the future, big part of U96's sound would be to use melodies from other songs.

Replugged (1993) was a step closer to eurodance and also pop music. Albums name was a wordplay referring MTV's Unplugged show. The single *Love Sees No Colour* added sung male vocals, which was also going to be one of the distinctive marks of the project. A second version of this song was produced, which added a melody from an italo disco band Trans-X (*Living On Video)*. The album was recorded in France, so some of the flavor from Jean Michel-Jarre's music was introduced.

The next step would be their first big step into euro sound. *Love Religion* (1995) recruited Daisy Dee on the vocals and took its main melody from Giorgio Moroder's *The Chase*. The most peculiar single release was *Club Bizarre* (which was the name of the third album), which wasn't your average dance song. It mixed strangely ethereal trance sound and strings and added filtered vocals. In addition to that, it was released with a weird music video. In the 2000's it would receive a contemporary cover by another 90's outfit, Brooklyn Bounce.

Heaven album (1996) showed another chance in U96's sound: this album has been their most eurodance-filled yet. Singer called Dorothy Lapi (aka Dea-Li) joined the party and sang most of the songs on the album. The single *Heaven* was probably their biggest hit so far. It used the melody from Cyndi Lauper's ballad *Time After Time*, although at first the band failed to mention the source. Problems arised when was discovered that they haven't asked for permission. Later the band acknowledged the original creators. Also, two additional singles with the same sound were released, *Venus In* Chains and *Seven Wonders.*

With a collection called *Best Of 1991-2001*, U96 sealed their career, which had at that time lasted for ten years. Alex Christensen was prominently presented in the cover because he had been the frontman. Included in the collection was an old song in new form, *Das Boot 2001*, which added more trance pop feel to it with female vocals.

U96 took a breather. Alex was working on his own projects like producing the bubblegum band ATC. In addition to this he started a solo career with a singer Yasmin K. With Yasmin he released trance pop songs and naughty sex songs in the vain of E-Rotic but done in a more contemporary style (for example *Du Bist So Porno*). During this break, U96 released only one new song, *We Call It Love.*

The next twist was something that no one could have anticipated: *Put On The Red Light* single was electronic hip hop featuring Das Bo (with a little wink to the first U96 hit. Album *Out Of Wilhelmsburg* (2007) followed.

After this Christensen departed the project because he was busy with his own productions. Nowadays Alex has promoted 90's music by producing three *Classical 90's Dance* albums which were done with Berlin Orchestra.

In 2015 the original members Ingo and Hayo decided to take hold of their own project and reboot it. After some digital releases came *Reboot* (2018), album consisting of 2 CD:s. This was a slight return to the techno era of the 1990's. But it also featured pop songs, like the fantastic *Angels*, sung by Terri Bjerre. They are also releasing a new album in 2020 with Wolfgang Flür (Kraftwerk) called *Transhuman*.

This band is so versatile that you just have to acknowledge its meaning to the whole dance music genre. U96 has managed to pull off the one thing that many bands fail in: the balance between pop music and underground. They have introduced both sides with a good balance. These songs have come straight from the soul of these producers, not because the market demands something. It's no wonder that they have been a big inspiration to many eurodance bands too.

In The Spotlight

Ingo Hauss *producer, singer*

Hayo Lewerentz *producer*

published with the permission of Ingo Hauss and Hayo Lewerentz.

Your music started as more techno like *Das Boot*. Was it difficult to change your music during the 90's into more pop like *Heaven*?

Hayo:

No, we are always looking for new challenges and sounds, so it is a natural thing that your music changes throughout your career. Apart from that we had a major record label at the time and they always tried to convince us to do more "hit singles" rather than techno tracks. So, we tried to combine both worlds as you can hear on our albums. On those we also had more experimental sounds and less commercial tracks apart from the hits.

In what genre you put yourself today and in the 90's? Eurodance, dance, rave?

Ingo:

Well, we never really were a eurodance act as much as other artists, but as it happened in the 90's, we are seen as a part of that. We are more into artists such as the Chemical Brothers or Underworld who are still active and successful today.

I would still not put us in a certain genre, but we are very much influenced by today's club and festival scene too and main new influences in our music are definitely trance and psytrance. But some of our tracks are still also techno and even have a eurodance feel, I guess. We mainly listen to new music as we always did, rather than being stuck in the 90's.

U96 has a long line of hits. Which are your favorites and why?

Hayo:

Our favorites are definitely *Love Religion*, *Love Sees No Colour*, *Club Bizarre* and *Night in Motion* when we talk about the hits. Other album favorites are *Jack*, *Je Suis Selected* and *Der Kommandant*

Do you prefer instrumental tracks or vocal tracks? And why?

Ingo:

We love both. Vocal tracks are better remembered by most people, but instrumental tracks can carry nice atmospheres and sound designs better.

Why did you decided to do a new album *Reboot* after many years? Was it easy or hard work?

Hayo:

As Ingo and I decided to relaunch U96 as a live-act, we were sure to not only play our old hits on 90's festivals but also work on new material. So, we recorded a new album with all new tracks. It was easier than we thought to get back into the writing process again like we did in the 90's. You know we had a long gap, where Ingo and I didn't see each other so we were not sure if it would work again. But it did and now we are writing new material every week and we'll have more releases out this year (2019).

Looking back, which artists or producers were instrumental in the evolution of the eurodance sound? Or in a broader view, the whole European dance scene?

Hayo:

We think there were different sides of that, but artists and producers like Snap! or 2 Unlimited had a more international approach than for example artists like Mr. President. So, we think the overall success of eurodance was mainly created by the international success of those German artists/producers with native speaking singers such as Penny Ford of Snap!.

The 90's was the first time when some European producers who were not coming from England could score massive international hits. Today, thanks to the Internet and social media, this is far more normal, and we see a lot of European artists score international hits. (i.e. Avicii, Alan Walker, Armin van Buuren, Robin Schulz, Felix Jaehn and many more)

What are your thoughts about dance music nowadays?

Ingo:

We love a lot of it and also get influenced by some of it. Dance music is a global phenomenon now and this is a good thing. Of course, all of it is a matter of taste, but it was always like that;-)

▶ *2 Unlimited* (Netherlands/Belgium)

Anita and Ray, used with permission of photographer Luke Skys.

Current 2 Unlimited, Ray and Kim. Used with permission of 2 Unlimited.

Belgium-based 2 Unlimited was the first act who encapsulated the eurodance style: it was melodic and electric fusion of techno and house where a woman delivered the vocals and a man rapped.

Their first song was an instrumental *Get Ready For This* (1991), which was a brainchild of the producers Jean-Paul De Coster and Phil Wilde (Byte Records). Although the single fared quite nicely in the charts even without the vocal (English single chart position two), the men thought that the song would accomplish a bigger audience with vocals. They contacted the Dutch Raymond Slijngaard (b.1971) and gave him the task of writing the lyrics and rap them. Ray was a former chef whose hobbies were rapping and break dancing, so he was the perfect voice. Also, Anita Dels (aka Anita Doth) (b.1971) was hired to sing the refrain. Anita had had some experience in the music world, because she had been part of a girl band called Trouble Sisters, who made rap music. *Get Ready For This* with added Ray and Anita's vocals rose to new heights all over the world. The winning recipe was ready.

The next single *Twilight Zone* was even a bigger success gaining number one positions in many countries. Album *Get Ready!* was released and their success was sealed with further singles from the album like *Workaholic*. The album sold over two million copies. Album was divided in three parts: vocal songs, instrumentals, and the romantic part (ballads). At that time their sound was largely rave and techno, but the ingredients of classic eurodance were there.

Their next step would be written in history: monotonic and obnoxious, but on the other hand catchy *No Limit (1993)* was like a mating call to party people. Although the songs straightforward refrain (*No, no, no, no, no, no, no, no, no, no, no, no there's no limit*) has been used as an example to describe how simple the eurodance songs were, it was 2 Unlimited's biggest hit. It reached number one position in dozens of countries and sold over 2,5 million copies. It was also the bestselling single in Europe that year. It's up there in the canon of the biggest eurodance songs, accompanied by super hits like Haddaway's *What Is Love*.

It would have been stupid to name the next album anything else than *No Limits!*, which is a more controlled and stable album than the first one. It contained, in my opinion, even better songs than the monotonous hit, like *Tribal Dance* and *The Power Age*. But still they added ballads in the end, which were totally unnecessary.

Real Things album (1994) gave us a more tranquil band. The pace wasn't so hectic excluding the single *The Real Thing*, which incorporated organs to their typical sound quite cleverly. Lighter tones were present for instance in songs like straightforward house song *No One*. Also, *Nothing Like The Rain* was released from the album, which was their first ballad single release. This album took the charts by storm and stomped to number one in Germany and France.

There was a whiff of conclusion in 1995 when *Hits Unlimited* collection was released. In addition to hits from previous albums, it contained three new songs, which each showed a different side of the band, with *Jump For Joy* being the most typical eurodance song.

There had been drama behind the scenes so that Ray and Anita couldn't continue working together. They were tempted by their individual solo careers. To everybody's amazement, 2 Unlimited rose from the ashes in 1998 with two new female members. Blond Romy van Ooyen (who had done one eurodance single previously with the artist name Romy) and dark-haired Marjon Van Iwaarden were the projects new representatives. The first single from this new line-up was *Wanna Get Up,* which was a very boring house song indeed. Their album *II* (1998) was a totally different experience, it had various melodic songs with one feet on upcoming trance pop sound.

2U got some success with Marion and Romy, but the producers had to admit that the heydays of the band were long gone. After their contracts expired, Marion and Romy left the band. Projects active recording career was over.

Meanwhile, Anita was faring much better on the solo front than Ray. She even managed to release an album called *Reality*, while Ray released only a couple of singles (like hip hop *3 X A Day*). They both stayed away from eurodance at this point.

Although 2U didn't release any new songs, that didn't prevent the DJ's and producers retouching their old classics. In Japan, *Greatest Hits Remixes* and *Special Edition: Trance Remixes*, were released with remixes from the likes of Push. In Europe, hard trance bands like Master Blaster and DJ Digress gave their songs a harder sound like in the reloaded version of *No Limit 2.3.* In the music video of this remake, two new faces were seen, who were supposed to become the new 2 Unlimited, but they didn't last long.

After a few years in 2009, Ray and Anita started performing again in 90's festivals. This gave hope to people, who wished that the pair would start to perform actively together and make new music. However, 2U announced that they were making new song with their old producer Phil Wilde, but they couldn't use their old band name 2 Unlimited, because De Coster owned the rights to that name. Under the name Ray & Anita they released an electro house song called *In Da Name Of Love*, which was very far from their melodic eurodance songs. *Nothing 2 Lose* gave more of the same style. According to Eurokdj, an album was planned but it didn't come to fruition. Surprisingly, Marion and Romy also announced their return with the name Two, but this attempt wasn't long-lived.

Since 2012 Ray and Anita have been able to use their original name, 2 Unlimited with Jean-Paul De Coster backing their gigs and career. They toured together for a while, but in 2016 Anita stepped down and gave room for a younger generation. Kim Wergouwen replaced her as a lead singer. Kim was a familiar face from a trance pop group Dance Nation. Nowadays Ray is touring with Kim and Anita is also making solo gigs performing the greatest hits of 2U. Anita has had also some personal issues fighting against breast cancer.

FEEL THE HEAT OF THE NIGHT - GERMANY

Germany is the most important land when it comes to producing eurodance. So many acts were born there like Culture Beat, E-Rotic, Fun Factory and Pharao. With their work they paved the way for many other euro bands and artists.

There was also a downside to this Germanys horn of plenty: many projects were hastily put together, songs were derivative, sounds were weak and the singers even weaker. This was due to a fast rotation of the songs: you had to produce more hits; singles had to be released fast. Sometimes even famous production teams were guilty of this.

▶ Magic Affair

Magic Affairs saga started in the 80's, when the producer Mike Staab had a synth-pop band called Mysterious Art. They used a lot of influences from techno music and they had hits like *Das Omen* and *Carma (Omen II)*. Staab decided to update the band's sound in 1993 and so Magic Affair was born. The strangely named debut single *Omen III*, was a reference to Mysterious Art (during the first single Magic Affair was called M.A.).

Franca ja A.K. together in the album's leaflet.

Franca Morgano was chosen as the singer and A.K.Swift as the rapper. Franca had previously sung backgrounds for Mariah Carey whereas A.K. had released hip hop tracks.

With this line-up the act accomplished much: *Omen* III was Germany's single chart number one and broke into Top 10 in many countries, *Give Me All Your Love* Top 5 in Germany and Top 40 in England and *In The Middle Of The Night* Top 30 in Germany. Single *Fire* didn't create so much interest as the previous singles.

In the end of 1994 Franca and Swift fell out. A.K was replaced with another rapper, who wasn't as good as A.K. so Swift was soon asked to return. But still both, Franca and A.K, left the group the next year.

Magic Affair was reborn, this time with two new female leads: Anita Davis and Jannet De Lara. Anita's voice was familiar from example Centory's album. The first single with this line-up was *Rhythm Makes You Wanna Dance* (1995), but it wasn't a big success. The next single *Energy Of Light* is one of the best songs from eurodance era, it has such energetic feeling. After this they released Axel Breitung production *World Of Freedom,* which was followed by a second album *PhenOMENia* (1996). In addition to Staab and Breitung, the album featured contributions from vocalists Lori Glori and Daisy Dee, so it was a big gathering of eurodance mainstays. This also made the album a little bit all over the place. Also, happy and hopeful choral singing (which Breitung used heavily in his productions) didn't fit with the mystical theme of Magic Affair.

Phenomenia album's fantasy cover art.

Despite the members being in the cover,
Bohemian Rhapsody was instrumental.

Jannet got fired from the band in the same year the second album was released and was replaced with a rapper from E-Rotic, Raz-ma-taz. Her and Anita's first joint effort was a song made for *Queen Dance Traxx* collection, *Bohemian Rhapsody*. Oddly, the song is instrumental, although Anita and Raz pose visibly in the single cover. After this, another single from *PhenOMENia* was put out, *Break These Chains*. After this the project changed record company. *Night Of The Raven* (1997) was the first release with this new company, but it was going to be the last release from M.A. in the 90's. But Raz's rap was finally present in this new song..

First new song in the 2000's was *Fly Away (La Serenissima)* (2003) and now Franca returned to the project. Styles had changed over the years, so it was no surprise that this new song was more euro trance than eurodance. Fans had to wait once again for several years for a new song: *Stigmata (Of Love)*, was released in 2008. In the same year *Omen III* was remixed to a new audience, this time in the ghastly style of hands up trance, in the hands of remixers like Pussylickerz.

For the time being *Hear The Voices* (2014) has been the last new song released from Magic Affair. The song is a great reminder of their best days.

Nowadays M.A. is touring clubs with Franca and a changing rapper. A.K.Swift has also come back to eurodance: At DMN Records he has released tracks with the project J.O.Y.C.E and also covered one old M.A. song *In The Middle Of The Night* with Chrizz Morisson and Timi Kullai.

The original Mysterious Art hit *Das Omen* also got a eurodance update in the 90's. T'N'T Partyzone released this with Art's original singer Nicole Boeúf. T'N'T Partyzone was a project of Tillmann Uhrmacher, who was a member of Mysterious Art. Producer of both M.A's, Mike Staab, died in 2009.

The original singers of Magic Affair, Franca ja A.K., did also a house/hip hop track in 1996 called *Good* Times, which covered Chic's disco classic. In addition to this, Franca sang in two euro projects in the 90's: Shift and Voice.

In The Spotlight

▶ ▌▌

Franca Morgano singer

Magic Affair today, published with permission of Franca Morgano.

How did you start singing eurodance? What kind of road led you there?

Somebody recommended me. I was known as a good studio session singer. So, one day we did three tracks: *Omen*, *Give Me All Your Love*, *Fire*.

But I was always a rock-, pop and soul singer.

How was it like working with Mike Staab?

It was hard but good school! He was strict.

How would you define eurodance?

Eurodance is a combination of electric sound with a continuous bass drum. A new style of disco dance without 70's disco. It was not techno, it was pop music with electro sound – less words, it was mostly rap and singer.

Magic Affair takes its tone and style from mystery and magic. Did Staab come up with this style or was it a group effort? What's the story behind Magic Affair?

It started with a mysterious concept because it was *Omen* and omens are mystical.

It was his concept – we continued with Magic Affair.

43

Have you sung in other eurodance acts/groups?

No. I received offers from DJ Bobo and others, but I was under contract.

Today it is possible to cooperate. I would like to – I am my own boss.

Comparing 90's and today, which things in dance music industry have changed and what hasn't changed? Are the changes good or bad?

The changes are very good. Today everything is possible. You can have success with a guitar and with dance, with all kinds of styles. I love it. But eurodance is eurodance from the 90's.

Is there a public demand for new songs or even an album? Are you satisfied as an artist to keep on performing old songs or are you craving for new material?

I love the old stuff. We did *Hear The Voices in 2014. A strong song.*

We are too much on tour to make a new album.

But I prefer to go on with a next song. We will see, we need to find the right time.

But I also go as a solo act, Franca Morgano.

Do you nowadays perform with A.K. Swift or another rapper?

With another rapper. A.K. Swift is doing his own stuff now.

Do you have a feeling how kids today (millennials) see eurodance music?

I see that they love it. It is crazy.

What's the secret of eurodance that it still gets people going ?

Maybe the easiness of the music. Many new style of dance music has only a few words. Eurodance had more sounds made by voice, game of letters, words. You can sing these songs easily.

▶ La Bouche

La Bouche was one of the most popular eurodance groups. The producer, Frank Farian, had had previous success with international bands like Boney M. and Milli Vanilli. When Melanie Thornton was chosen for this band, it was soon realized that Melanie's acquaintance Lane McCray was best suited to fill the shoes of the rapper, he would complement Melanie's spectacular voice and beauty.

Sweet Dreams (1994) was duos first single and it was a success immediately: Italy, Canada and Spain number one and USA Billboard Hot 100 position 14. During the first single Melanie was balancing between La Bouche and another dance project, Le Click. She had sung *Tonight Is The Night* Le Click. Although that song was also a hit, it was nothing compared to the enormous success of *Sweet Dreams*, so she decided to devote herself to La Bouche.

La Bouche is French for „mouth"

The next single *Be My Lover* was another hit, Top 10 was achieved in many countries. Both songs got major airplay in USA, where it's usually hard to get noticed with dance music, and even harder with the European style of dance.

Superhits opened up the way for the album *Sweet Dreams*, which success is unprecedented in eurodance history. It sold double platinum in America. In addition to this they received rewards in different galas like in France earning the title for best dance music act in 1995 and 1996.

Fallin' In Love single was dramatically different from the first two singles: it was a slow r'n'b song but the next release *I Love To Love* was once again a great euro effort, which gave them good positions on the charts once again.

The success was so massive, that they released a remix album called *All Mixed Up*, which offered the hits in remixed form, but it also featured a song which Melanie had sung for Le Click.

After the first album, the band cooled down for a while, because Farian had other projects at the same time as the boyband No Mercy. In between the time of La Bouche's two albums, a weird song *Bolingo (Love Is In The Air)* was released. It showed that they weren't just a one trick pony when it came to making dance songs. According to Eurokdj, this slow dance song was an answer to a situation where musical trends had changed.

In 1997 they came back with a bang: *You Won't Forget Me* was a powerful new song which took its style from the popular dream dance sound. Once again it was a hit for the band, but it couldn't surpass the previous singles' success, that's why it was considered a flop. A very American looking music video was shot to accompany this song.

A second album *A Moment Of Love* was released in the same year (In USA with album name *SOS)*. It had your typical La Bouche sound, but with a lot lighter touch so that the Americans could digest it better. It had even a cover of Elton John's ballad *Candle In The Wind*. This second album didn't succeed as well as was expected. There were all kinds of schisms between Farian and record company BMG. And when the album didn't sell well, BMG didn't even care to invest in the band anymore.

Two other singles were released from *A Moment Of Love*: ballad, which carried the albums name and the quite catchy *S.O.S*, but the great positions were just a memory at this point. Success was waning. Melanie decided to leave the band.

MELANIE THORNTON

Melanie embarked on a solo career. Her own style was very far away from La Bouche's dance, it was mostly r'n'b.

Her solo career was sadly cut short. When she released her solo album in 2001 called *Ready To Fly*, the name was like a premonition. November that year Melanie entered a flight from Berlin to Zürich, she was supposed to market her new single on Swiss TV shows. Only four kilometers before the destination, the plane hit a mountain and fell to the ground killing almost everybody on board, including this 34-year-old eurodance legend.

Melanie's death was a big loss to music, to pop and dance both. In addition to La Bouche and Le Click, her voice was used also in smaller euro projects like Men Behind and 100%. Her voice could lift even the most mediocre song to new heights.

AFTER MELANIE

In 2000, when Melanie left for solo career, Natascha Wright (Natascha Rekelhoff) filled the spot of female singer. Natascha had singing experience for example in singing background vocals for DJ Bobo and she had made a couple of solo singles like *Lovely Lie* (1994). With La Bouche, she released a new song, *All I Want*. A new album was supposed to be released with this new singer, but Natascha released only this one song with Bouche. My opinion is, that the death of Melanie was so tragic and sudden, that the plans were put on a hold...

..until in 2002 a new collection surfaced with the title La Bouche feat. Melanie Thornton. It collected songs from La Bouche and from Melanie's solo efforts. There was also a never-before-released La Bouche song *In Your Life*, which Melanie had composed herself. The band started a tour, now with a singer from Le Click, Kayo Shekoni. *In Your Life* reached to number nine in USA Billboard Dance Chart. This was a miracle in itself, because the song was eurodance and new trends had taken over the charts by that time.

After that Lane did some touring as La Bouche with Dana Rayne, also at that time, a new album was once again planned but nothing ever came out. Nowadays Lane is touring with an impressive singer, Sophie Cairo.

Lane and Sophie have done over 400 gigs since 2016. According to bands official homepage, there has been continuous requests for new songs. In 2018 the fans got their wish: *Night After Night* came out and you could see instantly that it was a typical La Bouche song, but with a softer housier touch. Lane has also updated his old Bouche hit *Sweet Dreams 2017* with Sophie through his own record company, McCray Records.

In the Spotlight

▶ll

Lane McCray *singer*

La Bouche is still alive, published with permission of Lane McCray.

What road led you to sing eurodance ?

I came to Germany in 1991 with the USAF and quickly became immersed in the culture and especially the music, like Urban Cookie Collective, Adeva, Double You and 2 Unlimited to name a few. I began singing in a cover band called Groovin' Affairs and that led me to meet legendary music producer Frank Farian. The rest is history.

How would you define what is eurodance?

Eurodance has a specific sound, it's a combination of bassline and keyboards unique to that era. You can distinguish the sound immediately.

La Bouche is one of the biggest eurodance acts. What other acts or producers have been essential in this genre? And why?

When you think of eurodance you have to give credit to the producers from Culture Beat, Snap, U96, 2 Unlimited and Masterboy to name a few. The contributions they have made along with our producer Frank Farian and Armir Sarif defined the sound of that era.

Do you think that German eurodance has different characteristics than other countries eurodance? Is it different?

I think that a lot of the music was borrowed from and adapted so there are elements of it all in eurodance.

There are several new groups who are making eurodance in the authentic sound of the 90's like Free 2 Night and Digital Base Project. What do you think of this?

I think the biggest form of flattery is imitation while at the same time keeping the genre alive. Free 2 Night is one of my favorites.

After Melanie Thornton's passing, was it difficult to replace her? La Bouche has gone through several female lead singers.

Let me first say no one will ever be able to replace Melanie that is for sure. Fortunately, the young ladies that have graced the stage with me representing La Bouche have been very humble and always respectful of the work Melanie and I have created. Those ladies are Kayo Shekoni of Le Click, Dana Rayne and presently Sophie Cairo.

Have you gotten negative feedback because of your style of music?

Negative feedback? None whatsoever, in fact we have introduced eurodance to a whole new generation and subsequently it has kept us working all over the globe.

You are one of the acts who were also popular in the US. Did this influence your music?

Of course, selling over 12 million records is going to land us everywhere in the world and being American we brought a sense of americana with our music.

How was it working with Frank Farian?

Each of the people Frank worked with would probably tell you a different story of their working relationship but I have to say mine was like sitting next to Picasso or Albert Einstein, I just watched and learned from the best. He has an impeccable ear and knows what works to make a hit record. I would have no career if he had not given Melanie and me the opportunity he did. I am still in touch with him and have the greatest amount of respect for him.

What makes eurodance so lasting genre that people still listen to it nowadays?

I think what makes eurodance such a global sensation is that the music has stood the test of time to the point it's become its own genre like jazz in the 40's, rock'n'roll in the 50's, disco in the 70's and now the 90's.

Is dance music your favorite genre or do you prefer something else?

I love all kinds of music but if I am going to be honest I have to say I am truly a house head... old school house.

▶ *Le Click*

La Bouche's and Le Click's story is intertwined. They both had the same record company and Melanie sang one song for Le Click, before La Bouche started to flourish. *Tonight Is The Night* (1993) had some success, but when Melanie left, a new singer had to be discovered.

Swedish Kayo Shekoni (b.1964) came on board. She had had a hit in the 80's with a band called Freestyle (*Vill Ha Dig*). When she came to Le Click, she had also released a couple of solo albums too.

Robert Haynes became the rapper. The second single from the band (and first one with this line-up) was *Call Me* (1997). Two different single versions of the song were released, different in England and in USA, British version being eurodance.

Their album *Tonight Is The Night* was a mix of many styles of music: in addition to eurodance, it had house, hip hop etc. The producers were Amir Saraf and Ulli Brenner, who were the people behind La Bouche's two first hits. Also, the German Nosie Katzmann wrote songs for them. Maria Lucia Lozane sang backing vocals, she was to become Captain Jacks female vocalist after Liza Da Costa left the band.

Le Click ended their short career with the single, *Heaven's Got To Be Better*, which didn't succeed very well. In the 2000's, Kayo joined Swedish band Afro-dite and nowadays she works as a DJ and is a part owner in a club.

▶ *Pharao*

Pharao, who took its style from ancient Egypt, is one of the most recognizable eurodance projects. The producers, Alexander Hawking and Steffen Harning (aka DJ Stevie Steve) were very interested about the Egyptian era, so it was very natural a start a project with this theme.

Popularity started right away, when the debut single *I Show You Secrets* (1994) blasted straight to top positions in Germany and elsewhere in Europe. The frontmen, who guided the people into the mysteries of Egypt, were oriental singer Kyra Pharao (aka Claudia Banerjee, b.1971) and American rapper Deon Blue (aka Marcus Deon Thomas, b.1968).

Also, two other singles released from the first Pharao album were big hits (There Is A *Star* and *World Of Magic*). And the album did deliver more of the same, but it had more deeper notions like *Gold In The Pyramid* and *Dance Of The Snake*. It had also rave sounds and one of the best ballads in the 90's, *It's Your Way*.

Pharao's Egyptian theme was very much present in live performances and promo pictures. For example, their live gigs had a gladiator drummer and a mummy dancer.

There were some disagreements behind the curtains. Deon had some disputes with Kyra and one time he even left Kyra to perform on her own on a gig. For some time, Deon was replaced with Eric Thomas, who had Egyptian forefathers.

After the first album, Pharao went on a break. In 1997 Pharao was just Kyra and in the same year a new single *Once Upon A Time* came out, which wasn't eurodance anymore. It was a slower effort but still retained Pharao's unique style.

The second album *The Return* gave us a more mature sounding Pharao, there wasn't any hectic eurodance songs in this one, it was a calmer experience.

After this. a long hiatus started, which ended in 2014, when 90's festivals were sprouting up everywhere and the demand for old eurodance artists started to rise again. The band even released a collection *Best Of 1994-1998* in 2015.

In The Spotlight

▶ll

Kyra Pharao singer

Stylish Kyra Pharao, published with permission of Diamondhouse Records And Chris Sauer.

Who invented the Egyptian mythology style in your band?

It was the idea of the producers. They were looking for a female singer for the project and I was invited at the same night, after their phone call, to sing in the studio. The concept of Pharao was already existing but fitted perfectly to my look.

What made you come back from a long hiatus?

I have never been away, but I was more concentrated on other music projects and on my regular profession as an event manager. But my fans were longing for me and they wrote me a lot of messages, especially on Facebook, to return on stage with Pharao. During that time, a lot of 90's events started in different countries and I got a few booking requests.

So why not going back onstage, because this was a great time of my life.

Have you sung in other eurodance projects?

Never. After we decided to take a longer break in the end of the 90s, the music taste was changing radically and I had a few offers to sing in other producer and DJ projects, especially in house music. So, in the end it was no way back to go on with Pharao with the same eurodance sound and style. Also, the producers went on with new projects and other genres.

You have great looking music videos. Do you have some memories from making them that you would like to share?

We made most of our videos in London, which was an awesome experience for me as a young artist.

The costumes were designed especially for the video set and they were breathtaking. Especially my crowns were handmade for me.

What was the secret behind Pharao's success?

It was the right time with the right tracks and concept.

How would you define eurodance?

In my personal opinion eurodance was the music of a generation of change, after the Cold War. It was the first real electronic dance music trend from Europe, after the wall came down in Germany.

Driving beats, combined with a beautiful female chorus and raps, performed in exiting costumes.

Do you think that German eurodance had certain characteristics that other countries eurodance doesn't have?

I think It was a bit closer to techno.

Do you think that lyrics are important in eurodance?

Absolutely not. Sometimes it's a great short vocal hook, sometimes a perfect melody.

What keeps eurodance so popular?

Good memories of our youth and a lot of young people nowadays explore this sound for the first time. And they like these great melodies and vocal hooks. I see them at the festivals wearing funny outfits in crazy colors and dancing to the 90's tracks.

▶ Captain Hollywood (Project)

Tony Dawson-Harrison, who was to become one of the most legendary eurodance artists, moved from USA to Germany after his military career in 1983. He got a nick name, Captain Hollywood, because he was dancing all the time during military service, even in uniform. Before he embarked on a singing career, he was a break dancer and choreographer for many super stars like Kim Wilde and La Toya Jackson.

He started his music career with singles like *Soulsister* and *Streetjazz*, and released a hip hop album, *Do That Thang*. During this time, it was remarkable that he worked independently without the help of record company.

Tony was a part of Twenty 4 Seven in their early days (look the chapter on Twenty 4 Seven), but left after their first album, because he wanted to concentrate on his solo efforts. He had released his previous solo songs under the name Captain Hollywood, but now he wanted to stylistically stand out from those works, so he adopted the name Captain Hollywood Project. *More And More* (1992), sung with Nina Gerhard, was *that* song that would determine his career for years to come. It was one of the first euro songs and even managed to dominate USA's number one position on Billboard chart. Overall, the single has sold over seven million units worldwide. On the single, his voice had been electronically modified to sound deeper and this would later inspire the producers of M.C. Sar & The Real McCoy.

Second single under this new project name, *Only With You*, was another huge success although it sold under half the amount of the previous hit. The next single, *All I Want*, was a Top 20 hit, this time done in the vain of hip hop. *Impossible* continued the winning streak, when a much more energetic single version of it was released. According to Captain's official Facebook page, the album containing these super hits, *Love Is Not Sex*, sold 400 000 units in Germany and worldwide over seven million. Nosie Katzmann, the German hit guru, was one of the reasons that these songs rose into fame.

Although the biggest hits from the album were eurodance, the LP had also hip hop sounds, which seems to be the style that Tony is most comfortable with. This doesn't diminish the magic at all, *Love Is Not Sex* has some mystical attraction, it's darker style and Captain's deep rap put you almost into a hypnosis.

Cap's third albums sound was going to be totally electronic. Single *Flying High* (1994) was a fast and strong eurodance and bpm had risen from previous albums moderate pace. The single *Find Another Way* was weirdly perky and a little bit annoying, so it didn't fit to his more somber style, in my opinion.

Album, *Animals Or Human*, followed and without the doubt the best album from Captain and the most pleasing for eurodance fans. It has been divided into two parts: the first part has the poppy eurodance songs, while the latter has been made for club scene on mind. Songs in the club side are furious trance and the hypnotic style from the previous album has been taken into more fierce direction. Even the name of the songs, *Relax Your Mind* and *Get Hypnotized*, tell the listeners that we are in a rave now. The album is a perfect dance album. It sold well but wasn't as popular as *Love Is Not Sex*.

After the furious third album, he wanted to change his alias to just Captain Hollywood. With the new *The Afterparty* (1996) album, he continued working with Alex Belcher who had done songs for the previous LP too. Single *Over & Over* was a more light-hearted effort and there was no trace of *Animals Or Human's* hectic atmosphere. Album and singles like *Love & Pain* were moderate hits but didn't perform as great as the previous hits.

Cap took a break from his solo career but came back in 2001 with the horrible *Danger Sign*, which was hip hop made with rock sound. He corrected this mistake a couple of years later by updating synth classic *Axel F* with Murphy Brown. In the same year he remade *Flying High* with CJ Stone (who had done good job remixing Culture Beat and Snap! to a new era).

More new material has surfaced over the years, like *It Hurts With You* and *Heat*, which were trendy EDM but brought nothing new to the table. Including these he has updated diligently his old songs, like the simply awful *More & More 3000*.

In addition to his own solo career, he has produced for other artists like C.C.Catch, Ol' Dirty Bastard, DJ Bobo and Haddaway. He has also made some film score, like for the document of Muhammad Ali and TV show Making The Band.

We Love Retro, Craiova 2019 published with permission of photographer Alexander Avram.

Nowadays Captain Hollywood is touring with his wife, Shirin Amour (aka Ginette Shirin von Gehlen). Cap met Shirin on a music festival in Germany in 2000 and they soon started dating. Six years later they got married. Captain Hollywood has become couples joint project: they plan their gigs and choreographies together. In addition to this they are actively performing all over the world performing Captain Hollywood's biggest hits.

▶ *Nina*

Nina Gerhard (b.1974) jumped into stardom from being a voice in Captain Hollywood's hits, *More And More* and *Only With You*, but she also sang in Intermission's rough club banger, *Honesty*. These successes featuring for other artists paved the way for her own solo career, where she embarked with the help of Nosie Katzmann.

The Reason Is You (1994) (which was released also with Spanish vocals) was a moderately calm first single, but *Until All Your Dreams Come True* pumped up the volume! Fairly soon after the second single, and LP called *Dare!* was released. In addition to Nosie, other well-known names like Kim Sanders worked on the album.

After the album, her style changed, eurodance was mostly gone. With the single *Wanna Feel So Good* Nina collaborated with the producers from E-Rotic. In the 2000's she released a couple of songs with house DJ's.

In The Spotlight

▶II

Nina Gerhard *singer*

Published with permission of Nina Gerhard

What kind of background you have in music business? Did you sing something else before dance music?

While I was in school, at the time I was 17 years old, I was also at the musical school in Frankfurt a. Main. I also had a training for classical singing (mezzo-soprano) by a classical opera singer from the State Theater. At the same time, I met Nosie Katzmann – and our first project together was Captain Hollywood Project. I was singing *More And More* and *Only With You*. 1995 I was offered a solo contract from the record company Intercord – at that time i started to work on my own career with my own solo songs.

Before I started to sing dance songs, I was singing from the very early age. But when I was older I always liked pop, jazz, and blues. And I still perform in these genres.

You are the voice behind many eurodance classics like Intermission's *Honesty*. Do people recognize your voice from these or from your solo songs?

I think there are people, who recognize my voice from different songs, either from songs I did under a project name like Intermission and there are also people from the time while i was performing and recording solo just under my name, Nina.

Nowadays, I still get a lot of mail from all over the world, so I can see the people still love the memories and the songs from the 90`s like *The Reason Is You, Until*

All Your Dreams Come True and other songs from my solo album. Of course, songs like *More And More* (Number one in the Charts) and *Only With You,* which was listed in the dance charts on the third place, are also still favorites of many people.

How was it like working with the legendary Nosie Katzmann?

I liked working with Nosie Katzmann. I was very grateful that he believed in me and my voice and it is always interesting working together – he wrote so many good lyrics and songs and I sang them. I think it was just the right time for dance music.

Of course, it also meant, getting to know each other and everybody has a certain behavior in working in a creative way, so we also had to learn how to work together in the best way, to be satisfied with the result.

You sang for Captain Hollywood, describe how was it like working with him?

I didn't work with him because Captain Hollywood Project was a studio project, we sang it at different times and we didn't sing the song together in the studio.

But when I started to perform solo - with my own album, I met him several times at the same events.

After the album you made some housier or more mellow songs. Was it because eurodance's popularity was fading ?

No, I didn't do housier or mellow songs because the popularity of eurodance was fading. I always liked house and mellow songs and I still like a lot of electronic underground music, same as I like blues and some other genres. But when the whole music business started to change it was in a lot of chaos. The decisions which were made by the A&R's (Artist and repertoire) of the record company were very difficult. They had chosen producers, who didn't fit in the concept and I didn't believe in the producers. And I think I was right – because after some decisions – songs like *I Wanna Feel So Good* had been released and they flopped. But I had an exclusive solo contract – I wasn't allowed to work with somebody else – so I was blocked. It needed more than three years to get out of the contract.

And I didn't want to do it in the same way I did in the past. I had also changed. I think we would have needed a producer who would have been open-minded - to change the style and to go on with the right songs. It suddenly didn't make sense to go on the way we did.

So, I started to find new collaborations.

Samantha Fox has covered your song *The Reason Is You*. Have you heard it? What do you think of it?

Yes, I heard the version of *The Reason Is You,* but the lyrics of the verses are different than my song. Also, certain parts of the original melody are not the same.

To be honest, I don't like the version.

When I heard that she did a cover version I was quite amazed, because she was a known singer in my childhood. And of course, I knew her songs during that time of the 80`s, like *Touch Me* 1986. At that time, I was 12 years old.

If you have had the chance to work with any dance music producer in the 90's, who would have that been?

I don't know – it's a long time ago...I think at that time there had been producers I liked....but I can't remember anymore who was one of my favorites....sorry!!!!

What's the greatest thing you remember from the 90's ?

That`s a difficult question:

I have a lot of great memories of the 90`s. Life seemed to be more uncomplicated, of course we were all younger – but structures and the business seemed to be easier.

I remember a lot of big gigs in Spain, or Paris or Japan....and they were all very unique. I think the general feeling of the 90`s felt easy and happy...and I guess this is a memory we all share.

Published with permission of Nina Gerhard

Are you in music business right now? Are you still performing?

Yes, I`m still in the music business. Since 2016, I started to compose more electronic music and to produce it by myself. I always wanted to be independent in writing, composing, and producing the songs I want to do. Until now I have 180 new songs. It`s time to release them. And there is no better way to be free in any decision.

Now, I could work with everybody. My plan is - to open up my own label. A new project where you will find a lot of music written and produced by myself – will be project 1012.

And yes, I'm still performing. And in the future it will be even more.

▶ B.G. The Prince of Rap

Published with the permission of Bernard Greene

Despite his artist name, B.G. The Prince Of Rap aka Bernard Greene (b.1965) would be best known for his eurodance than rap. Like many other euro artist, also American Bernard's road led to Europe through army. After his military service he started to utilize his musical talent. He won several rap contests, through which music producers found him. Other half from the duo Jam & Spoon, Jam El Mar, and Stefan Benz started to produce Prince Of Rap's music.

The first single, *Rap To The World* (1990), was a minor hit in Germany club circuit. With the same euro hip hop style, he released further singles *Give Me The Music* and *Take Control Of The Party*. The biggest hit though was *This Beat Is Hot* (in the vain of Snap!), which reached number one position in Hot Dance Music / Club Play –chart. Hits and other stuff were compiled on the first album, *The Power Of Rhythm*.

The single *Can We Get Enough* (1993) was his first jump to the emerging eurodance scene. But *The Colour Of My Dreams* was the song that would stay in eurodance history, although its chart positions then don't reflect how much the song is appreciated today. The album *The Time Is Now* is almost pure eurodance album, although in the end there is a couple of hip hop songs to honor Bernard's musical roots. Female vocals were sung by different singers like Paris Red and January Ordu.

A couple of years went by and times changed. In 1996 his song, *Stomp,* sampled an old disco song from The Brothers Johnson. Bernard wanted to update his personal favorite by bringing it to the 90's. Also singles like *Take Me Through The Night* and *Jump To This* were released from *Get The Groove On* album, but almost all of them drowned into oblivion and didn't get the success they deserved. One reason for the failure to perform was because the general sound was more house in the style of Outhere Brothers.

After this third album, he started to produce and feature for other artists, but his own solo career had appeared to go into a standstill. In 2005 he was rumored to work in a museum..

But nothing holds a good eurodance artist down, because four years after he returned to the stage and has since then been active. Nowadays he is recording for DMN Records and releasing new music. He has also dueted with Lane McCray of La Bouche fame.

▶ Culture Beat

Dance project Culture Beat caused some waves in the German club scene already in the end of the 1980's. *Der Erdbeermund* (also with the name *Cherry Lips*) (1989), with actor and cabaret singer Jo Van Nelsen reciting the vocals, was their first hit. The man behind the project was Torsten Fenslau, who had started his music career at the Dorian Gray club which located at a Frankfurter airport. Gradually he began to produce songs and founded his own record company, Abfahrt Records. Torsten had had a minor hit in his homeland under the moniker Out Of The Ordinary, but a bigger success was still to be gained.

When *Der Erdbeermund* proved out to be a hit, Torsten decided to develop the project further. He recruited Lana Earl (aka Lana E.) and Jeff Carmichael (aka Jay Supreme) for vocalists. With this line-up, songs like *I Like You* and *Tell Me What You Wait* caused some commotion on the charts. During this first chapter, Culture Beats style was tranquil and ethereal euro house and house. An album called *Horizon* followed.

After this calm start, there was big success on the horizon. Lana E. was replaced with a British Tania Evans (b.1967). The first effort from Jay and Tania together would change eurodance history. By tuning the sound of Culture Beat into a more aggressive approach, Torsten had a major hit in his hands with the song *Mr. Vain* (1993). It reached number one position in many countries like England, Netherlands, Norway, and Germany. It also became that year's most sold single in Europe and in addition to that, it managed to break also into the US Billboard chart.

Mr Vain was also a steppingstone for songwriter Jürgen Katzmann (aka Nosie Katzmann) and a calling card to other artists and productions. Nosie had developed an amazing melody and refrain, which appealed to the masses. After Culture Beat he wrote songs for other eurodance artists like Captain Hollywood Project, DJ Bobo, and the hardcore band Scooter.

Serenity album contained this super hit along with other singles like *Anything* and *Got To Get It,* which were also successful. The album is one of the few that delivers what the singles promise, an album full of eurodance. It had also a slower song *World In Your Hands*, although it was updated to a dance beat when released as a single.

Mr.Vain's massive success was overshadowed by a tragedy. Projects founder Torsten got into a car accident in November 1993. He died from these wounds in hospital. He didn't get to see the full success of his band. Torsten's brother, Frank Fenslau, took up the reins of the project and carried on his brother's legacy.

After Torsten's death, the success continued, so a *The Remix Album* (1994) was released. It contained remixed versions of the singles from *Serenity* album.

The next step once again changed Culture Beat's sound. Fans were amazed, when *Inside Out* (1995) came out. The pace was slowed down and even the sounds of dolphins was added (!) Although it was a slower effort, it had shades of trance music. Also, the single *Take Me Away* was a slower house song but fortunately *Walk The Same Line* and *Crying In The Rain* were more typical eurodance sound.

The LP *Inside Out* showed in its entirety the bands musical transformation: there were even more trance sounds. It had fantastic album tracks (whichever could have been released as a single), like the breathtaking *Under My Skin.* The first single had frightened some of the fans (like me) but hearing this album you were totally satisfied. *Inside Out* is one of the best dance albums with its fiercely progressive sound while it still maintained the poppy approach. It felt like everyone involved had given their best.

Frank Fenslau had chosen five production teams to make this album. For example Doug Laurent (famous for his remix work) and Cyborg (of Loft fame) were on board. Although it had different teams, the album sounds so intact and natural.

Although Culture Beat was at the top, Tania decided to embark on a solo career and left the band. Also, Jay left. After Culture, Tania got a minor hit with the song *Prisoner Of Love (La-Da-Di)* and she featured on trance DJ Kosmonova's song *Singin' In My Mind*. Jay has continued on various hip hop projects.

Although the band lose two of its frontmen, it didn't vanish. Instead it was time for another musical rebirth. In 1998, Kim Sanders came along. Kim had done already the great eurodance songs *Show Me* and *The Ride* (both with Nosie Katzmann). In addition to this, she had sung for other projects like the classic *Hold On* for Loft. While her previous style had been very energetic, her time with Culture Beat was not. Singles like *Pay No Mind* and *Rendez-Vous* were far away from the previous energetic sound of Culture Beat. The sound pursued something deeper, but it quite frankly fell flat. Soon followed *Metamorphosis* (1998), which is definitely the projects worst album. Only the trance mixes in the singles gave artificial respiration to these half dead songs. It was no surprise that Kim left the band in 1999.

The project was put on a hold for a few years. Saucy looking Jackie Sangster came aboard in 2001 and a new single, fairly light *Insanity* was put out. The song surprisingly went to number one in Israel.

Jackie stepped up to the plate and delivered an amazing remake of the bands old hit *Mr Vain* in 2003. Called now *Mr Vain Recall*, it managed to surpass the energy of the original while staying true to the classic value of *Mr. Vain*. It was produced by half of the trance duo Cosmic Gate, Claus Terhoeven. The song was full-on hard trance. A greatly done music video reinforces the experience: Jackie performs the song in a club surrounded by massive speakers, which give out such a big bass that people are flying all around. The CD single contained also two additional new songs, *Obsession* and *Headbangers*. According to Eurokdj, there was talk around that time to release a new album called *Obsession*, but nothing came out.

Jackie is trying to keep the walls up.

The next single, *Can't Go On Like This (No, No)*, continued with the same hard trance sound, this time producers were from Bass Bumpers and ex-Culture Beat member Kim Sanders. After this song, a silence rose. It's really sad that they didn't manage to release a new album in the 2000's, it would probably have been great.

For the time being, last new song from the band is *Your Love* (2008), which is a boring house song done in the vein of Eric Prydz. In 2012 a weird collection called *Loungin'Side Of Culture Beat*, came out. It collected the acoustic, jazz and chill out versions of their hits. Same kind of acoustic feelings are available on Nosie Katzmann's solo album *Greatest Hits 1*, where he sings the hits which he has written like the CB classics *Mr. Vain, Got To Get It* and *Inside Out*.

Culture Beat's story still goes on. Jackie is touring under the band's name performing their biggest hits of the 90's (although she entered the band in the 2000's). But I couldn't think of a more suited person to carry the legacy of Torsten Fenslau, Tania and Jay.C

In The Spotlight

▶II

Frank Fenslau producer

Published with the permission of Frank Fenslau

How Culture Beat was formed?

Culture Beat was founded by Torsten Fenslau (a DJ and producer) in 1989.

You joined Culture Beat team after it had gained massive success, how did it feel? Was it pressuring to create for an established successful group and continue your brother's legacy?

It was very difficult and emotionally challenging. However, it felt like the right thing to do and with a lot of help and support from family and friends it worked out and I am glad I did it.

Inside Out album was a hard dance album. Were there signs in 1995 that the current eurodance sound was fading? There was more housier and trancier tunes in that album too..

In comparison to what was released in Germany in 1995 the title track *Inside Out* was rather slow and mellow. I guess that is what made it so successful in Germany.

Metamorphosis was a big departure from earlier sound and Tanya and Jay left the group. Why the change in sound and band members?

We wanted to move on musically. Tania wasn't the right singer for this, and Jay left later because of his own initiative. *Metamorphosis* was initially planned with him and Kim.

In the beginning of 2000's Culture Beat came back once again with a new singer, Jackie. How she was selected to join CB?

I found her through another producer. I invited her for an audition and was so impressed by her that I signed her the same day...

Mr. Vain Recall and Can't Go On Like this were done in hard trance style. Jackie is such a strong and charismatic singer that one was a little disappointed that a new album didn't show up, why was that?

Unfortunately, many misfortunate events happened which lead to that development... I was disappointed too.

What's the status of Culture Beat now, making new music, touring?

We are touring a lot, luckily there is a high demand for 90's acts/shows.

Mr. Vain and other Culture Beat's songs were massive hits; did you think that influenced lots of other eurodance artists? And if so, how?

I am convinced that Culture Beat created a sound with the *Serenity* album that influenced and inspired many other producers - the "how" you must ask them ;)

▶ Captain Jack

Old and new captain, published with permission of Udo Niebergall

(In The Spotlight section, Captain Jack's producer speaks more closely about how the project was born.)

Captain Jack's style is clearly very militaristic. In the beginning the songs consisted of a refrain sung by a woman (in the first two albums the vocals were sung by the lovely Liza Da Costa), but instead of raps the bands main singer, Francisco Alejandro Gutiérrez aka Franky Gee, performed army style commands. The songs were accompanied by a vigorous beat. The style pertains also an iconic army uniform, which is a mix of USA's and Russians military style. Also, half-naked women around the captain are part of the project's aesthetics.

Songs like *Captain Jack*, *Drill Instructor* and slower *Soldier Soldier* were huge hits, as was the debut album *The Mission* (1996). Because eurodance was slowly fading away, they wanted to put out more songs quickly. The single *Together And Forever* wasn't lyrically connected to army world. Second album *Operation Dance* was soon released after the single.

The hit machine started to lose its fuel. A new millennium was dawning, and new sounds were on the top of the charts. That's why Captain Jack took influences of the trendy trance music and a new single with new sound was released: *Dream A Dream*. Liza was replaced with Philippine-born Maria Lucia Lozanes. Still this new song wasn't as big a success as the previous hits. I still think that the third album, *The Captain's Revenge*, is probably the bands best with its rich melodies. The first three albums are without a doubt Captain Jack's golden age.

After these three albums, the project started to release pretty basic dance pop albums, until the death of Franky. After a few years, a new captain was in command, Bruce Lacy. The first new album with the new chosen captain, pronounced in its name that *Captain Jack Is Back*. But this wasn't a homecoming, because the album was almost a pure r'n'b / hip hop album, which didn't offer anything to the old fans. Outdated American flaccid sound didn't just fit into the style of the old energetic Captain Jack project. I think that I share this sentiment with many fans because the next album, *Back To The Dance floor*, was as the name said, back to dance beats. There were also new remixes of the old hits, accompanied by a couple of new songs.

Since then the project has steadily released new songs and remakes of the old classics.

In The Spotlight

▶️II

Udo Niebergall producer

Published with permission of Udo Niebergall

You are best known as a man behind the Captain Jack project. What other eurodance projects have you been involved with?

My focus is on Captain Jack. I did many dance productions in the 90's like Peter Schilling - *Major Tom '94*, M – *Razzia*, T'N'T Partyzone - *Vamos a la Playa*: that went into the charts. But I didn't work together with other eurodance acts in that time.

A friend of mine is HP from Scooter, I met him in the late 80's. We worked together for the same label, called Westside (Frankfurt). HP was frontman of the independent band Celebrate The Nun. My buddy from the 90's was Mark 'OH. I booked him to my Techno Club Palazzo in Bingen-Germany, and he did some remixes for Captain Jack. We spent time together on holiday.

How did Captain Jack begin? Was it your idea?

Yes, Captain Jack is my baby. I was snowboarding in Austria with my friends from Wiesbaden, my hometown. We had so much fun at the ski lodge and we sang funny shit.

One of those songs was "*Heyo Captain Jack*". This melody was burned into my brain. Back home in the studio I started producing. First I invited all my snowboard friends for the vocal recording, and it sounded terrible! When I realized the potential of the song I called my professional studio singers. My team and I finished the production and I was very happy with the result.

We offered the song to all major labels in Germany. EMI Electrola took it and made it a worldwide hit. I'm very thankful to Ully Jonas and Marco Quirini (Akropolis & EMI).

The original Captain was Franky Gee. How did you feel when you had to replace him? Was it a tough decision?

I have to clarify that: Captain Jack is a trademark. Same as James Bond. The "original" is the person who is currently on stage. And that is Bruce Lacy.

You speak of his predecessor. That was the great Franky Gee, yes! Franky was one of my best friends in the late 80's. He was a DJ in Wiesbaden (my hometown) and Rüsselsheim (my city of birth). We both started producing music in my living room with a computer, drum machine and synthesizer - long time before Captain Jack.

During the Captain Jack hype from 1995- 2005 we spent almost every weekend together, on tour, in the studio, private,...

I witnessed his death on Majorca, triggered by a stroke. It was terrible to see Franky, this energy pack, in coma - and we couldn't help him. I stopped all activities for Captain Jack. A continuation was out of the question for me.

But many fans wrote letters, emails. They asked me to continue the project that had given them so much joy in the past. In 2006 I started a singer contest. The winner was Bruce Lacy.

And the story continues....

How did you find Liza da Costa to sing for Captain Jack?

Liza is from Wiesbaden. It was luck to find a good singer in my hometown. I picked her up for a studio job. Some weeks later she was part of Captain Jack. Originally Lisa is a jazz singer and we always had to slow her down in the studio. But she has an excellent eurodance voice. I'm glad to have found her. Our females always take an important part in the Captain Jack Project.

How would you define what is eurodance?

Eurodance is powerful up-tempo dance music, made on computers, synths and samplers, male rap and female hook lines, catchy melodies.

As a music producer, how do you feel dance music (industry) has changed compared to the 90's?

OMG! It changed completely! Artists and labels have to do all the work and promotion. No big help from the record industry. Songs go on and off the charts. Everything is extremely short-lived. Today a Top 10 hit on Spotify, tomorrow a nobody. Of course, there are exceptions and new ways to succeed: YouTube, Soundcloud, Instagram,...

Captain Jack project started eventually move away from fast eurodance. Was it a change based on eurodance's declining popularity?

Good question! 150 bpm and more was good in the 90's. But the radio stations didn't like fast eurodance beats anymore. We started producing dance-latin-pop-songs (*Soldier Soldier, Get Up, Give it up, Say Captain Say Wot...*) for the summer season and we used special advertising channels to continue our success: Summer TV Music Shows, DJ Promotion on holiday resorts, Bravo & Ballermann Hit Compilations, Radio Open Air Festivals,....

In December we did the same for winter and ski season. That worked well and we have repeatedly met the same eurodance artists on TV for Apres Ski Hits, etc. (Rednex, Mr.President, Vengaboys,...).

How do you feel kids (millennials) see eurodance music? Do they really think it's cool or do they laugh at it?

Both. They love the music too, for sure! And they can laugh about the clothes of the 90's, ha-ha! There are so many 90's festivals in Europe, it's currently the hottest music in the world. Las Vegas, Wembley Stadium U.K., Schalke Arena Germany (Die 90er Live on tour), you won't believe what's going on now. All big 90's eurodance artists are fully booked

- all year round!

What's the thing that has kept Captain Jack project going all these years?

Captain Jack is unique. A black man in a white uniform with a big red cap. And a huge army full of sexy girls. That's a trademark, not only an artist. Since 1995 I have been in the studio working on new Captain Jack songs. Every 1-2 years we bring out new singles with professional videos and promotion. Have a look at *In The Army Now 2017*, more than 10 million views on two YouTube channels in a few months. In March 2018 we won the Akadamia Music Award LA for the best cover version.

We always try to be one step ahead.

WE LOVE THE 90's and we want to keep the 90s alive!

Heyo Captain Jack!

▶ Masterboy

Masterboy today: from left Enrico Zabler, Trixi Delgado and Tommy Schlech. Published with permission of Masterboy.

Maybe the most known eurodance act, Masterboy, started in 1989, when Enrico Zabler met DJ Tommy Schleh at a nightclub in London. They decided to make music together under the name Masterboy. The name came from the fact that they were two boys and their mix table was called Master.

Debut single *Dance To The Beat* was first meant for the opening of a club called The Kinki and only to be sold there. At first they hired singer Mendy Lee and rapper David Atterberry as frontmen to perform their song. To their surprise, the popularity of the song reached far beyond the club. Tommy and Enrico released another song (because there seemed to be demand for more of their music) *Shake It Up And Dance* (1991), which had the characteristic Tommy's raps (with thick accent). The song is one of the first songs that had shades of eurodance although at that time it still relied heavily on house music. The song started to climb the charts, so they started to plan their first album with David and Mendy. Album called *The Masterboy Family* was born, which contained house and hip house. In my opinion, one of their main influencers at that time was Technotronic.

The next year they started to develop Masterboy's sound forward. They hired a Swiss Beatrice Obrecht (aka Trixi Delgado) as the main singer. First single with Trixi, *Fall In Trance*, conquered the dance charts all over Europe like in England, France and Germany. An album, *Feelin Allright* (1993), soon followed. Although eurodance was rolling in the charts at that time, this second album was still more house than eurodance. Although the last song on the album, *Everybody Needs Somebody* (also released as a single), gave some foretaste of things to come…. Also, this album featured their iconic mascot in the cover, a joker face.

In 1994 the band realized their full eurodance potential. New songs like *Feel The Feat Of The Night* and *Is This The Love* would lift them to euro elite. *Feel The Heat Of The Night* is probably their biggest hit to date, it conquered charts all over Europe and one of its accomplishments is French single chart number two. It sold gold in Germany (over 300 000 copies). Masterboy had definitely found their own distinctive sound. Trixi sung the simple but catchy refrains while Tommy rapped, and all this was laced with an energetic melody and a heavy bass. Europe was on its knees.

Following the energetic hit, third album called *Different Dreams* came out, which was a total eurodance fantasy. The album and its singles created a bit of hysteria in France and Brazil. In France they received gold status and in addition to that they became the most popular foreign band with 2 Unlimited. In Brazil, their singles reached number one and in festivals they drew people in great numbers.

The band didn't let go of their energy: in 1995 came a new song *Generation Of Love*, which is also known for its futuristic music video, filmed in London. They had once again a success in their hands. A new album carrying the same name was released with the same hectic beats. But this time there were a couple of slower euro reggaes like *Land Of Dreaming*, which was released as a single too. The song performed in the charts very well too, although its style was different.

The next year meant changes for Masterboy: Trixi left the band because of family reasons so Tommy and Enrico had to find a new female singer. Linda Rocco was the chosen one. *Show Me Colours* with Linda had the typical Masterboy sound but the album *Colours,* contained lots of other sounds than eurodance too. Another euro reggae single was released, *Mister Feeling.* Mr President's reggae *Coco Jamboo* had been a huge hit, so this influenced other artists to release same kind of songs. *Colours* has been (so far) been their last album.

As the 90's was ending, so ended also Masterboy's typical sound. THP Orchestra cover *Dancin' Forever* was a quite awkward effort to cash-in with the trendy disco sound. In the next single, Linda was replaced with Annabell Krischak (aka Annabell K) to sing *Porque Te Vas* (once again cover)*, which had euro sound but with a lighter touch. The next ones were also of a different breed; *I Like To Like It* was more euro trance and *Ride Like The Wind* featured male vocals.

In the background Tommy had his own hard trance project Klubbingman, which scored a number of hits. With this trance sound he updated also Masterboy in 2002 with the song *I Need A Lover Tonight,* where Trixi was back again on the vocals. The song was a perfect Masterboy song: great refrain, Trixi's powerful voice and a bass that just won't quit!

Unfortunately, they didn't continue with this sound long, only *Feel The Heat Of The Night* update was done with the same style. Masterboy went on a hiatus, but nowadays they are touring again with Trixi. This reunion brought us a new a song, *Are You Ready (We Love The 90's).*

Masterboy's comeback single was released on CD, which was exceptional in 2018.

MASTERBOY AND OTHERS

Masterboy extended their sound also to other projects under the name Masterboy Beat Production. In addition to Enrico and Tommy, the production team had Lucas Cordalis, who used the alias Luke Skywalker. Their Cardenia project released mainly old italo disco covers like *Living On Video* (which featured Trixi on the vocals).

Cardenia's cover art.

The French Indra Kulassar had already done her share of dance music, mainly house and hip house. But she wanted some credibility in eurodance, so she turned to the hottest euro producers like Axel Breitung and Rico Novarini (Enrico Zabler's alias). *Party Going On* and *Take Me High* were her songs made by Enrico.

Ice MC also wanted his part of the Midas touch, although reluctantly (see chapter on Ice MC). The men produced single hits for him like *Music For Money* and *Give Me The Light*, but they did also a couple of album songs for the *Dreadatour* album.

Love Message collective gathered together biggest names in Germany's dance music in 1996. It had a good cause because they collected money for AIDS research. The song *Love Message* was produced by Masterboy and featured vocals from them, E-Rotic, U96, Fun Factory, Worlds Apart, Mr. President and Scooter (This song is the **only** genuine eurodance song where Scooter is involved). The message of the song was to promote safe sex and for some projects like E-Rotic, this was right on the nose. Also, a CD collection with the same name was released which contained songs by the previously mentioned artists. In 2005 Tommy revisited the song under his moniker Klubbingman and remade it into a hard trance song once again using Trixi on the vocals.

Lovemessage collective promoted safe sex.

Including the artists mentioned previously, the Masterboy has done singular songs for World Apart and X-pression and in addition to this they have been busy in the remix department, they have mixed for instance Captain Hollywood and Ann Lee. They have often used aliases and founded new projects through these pseudonyms, many though short-lived.

In The Spotlight

▶II

Enrico Zabler producer

You are one of the biggest names in eurodance. What made you turn to eurodance after house/hip house in the beginning of the 90's? Was it natural evolution or because of the popularity of the then new genre?

This question is relatively easy to answer, I'm Enrico the musician in the band and Tommy the DJ. At the beginning I worked with Thorsten Fenslau (Culture Beat), who didn't do eurodance at that time (1989-90). We just wanted to add more chorus to the song structure so that the feeling of this time would come across better in the songs ...

You have produced lots of songs for many other artists. Is it harder to make songs for someone else than your own project?

Personally, I don't find it difficult. You have to get involved with the artist, know where his vocal strengths lie "vocal range", etc. But it is very important that the artist also stands to the production, then it will also work.

What is the story behind your band name and the Joker face, your logo?

During our first joint production, *Dance to the Beat,* we sat at the mixdown and thought about a band name. At the mixer there is always a master fader, we thought master and since we were two guys... so the name was born, Masterboy. The joker came a bit later, we sat down with a graphic artist from Hamburg Richard Goutte (a French man) who made almost all the covers for us, there were many designs made that you can still see on the album *Feeling Alright* ... and then we decided on the album *Different Dreams* on the current joker head ...

Why Trixi decided to come back to Masterboy?

When Tommy and I reactivated the Masterboy project, it was clear to us that Beatrice should be part of it again, because she is the best vocalist for our songs. You can only be successful if everything fits together. Masterboy and the voice of Trixi are one unit.

How would you define what is eurodance?

This is Zeitgeist for party a nice carefree time, no violence, peaceful celebrating together, an attitude towards life which has shaped the 90's and unfortunately is past (except on the 90's parties).

How does German eurodance differ from other countries eurodance? Are there certain characteristics?

In the English speaking Eurodance, no matter if produced in Germany or in other countries, there is no big difference for me, this is rather the touch of the producers who give the whole thing a little difference.

Germany was maybe the biggest country in eurodance in the 90's. Why is that?

That's easy to explain: at that time a lot of musicians and DJ's got together to produce tracks, which was still very unusual at that time...but started in Germany...the next reason was that it was relatively easy to find good artists who came from the American crew, there were so many rappers and singers in our area (Heidelberg, Kaiserslautern, Frankfurt, Darmstadt) with an exceptionally good quality. But Masterboy is the only exception, all members are from Germany...

What artists were essential for the birth of eurodance? And why?

You can't just answer that question like that. It was often the producer and songwriter team that was extremely important for success. It is very clear that one voice carries the song and if that was given you had a hit ... Productions like Snap!, Culture Beat, La Bouche are surely examples how different eurodance can be.

Who do you think were your biggest competition in the 90's?

For me there is no competition in music, there is only successful and not successful music !

Do you feel pressure to make a new album or are you just happy to perform in the 90's festivals?

There's certainly no pressure to make the new album. Certainly, a certain expectation of our fans and we will fulfill it. Also, we have a lot of fun at the concerts with our fans together and if you do what is fun there is no stress and you can go to the studio with all the new impressions...

Why do you think eurodance is once again so popular?

It was the most innovative music decade ...Eurodance reflects this decade perfectly, carefree life, no violence, party, freedom and much more ... which unfortunately is no longer the case today ...that's why this music brings back this time for a few hours...

In The Spotlight

▶︎‖

Linda Rocco singer

Photographer Carsten Peter, published with permission of Linda Rocco

What led you to sing in Dance 2 Trance's *Power of American Natives*? Do people still recognize your voice from that song?

I had been working for a long time already with Rolf Elmer (Jam el Mar) and one day he asked if I would be interested in singing on Dance 2 Trance's new song. They had already released *Power of American Natives* as an instrumental but didn't have much success with it. I then wrote the spoken verses, sang the hook, and the rest is history.

And yes, people know exactly who I am on this song. It is still played numerous times a day around the world!!

You sang in Paternoster's *On Earth As It Is In Heaven* and it has very religious lyrics, are you a religious person?

I'm not overly religious, but I do believe.

You replaced Trixi in Masterboy for a while, describe your experience in being in a big eurodance group, was it hard to step on other singers' shoes?

First of all, it was very exciting. But don't forget, I was already successful with my voice being on all the female parts of Milli Vanilli, plus numerous projects that were also successful. But I had never heard of the eurodance community before that, and I absolutely loved it!! I was not worried about fitting into someone else's shoes, I was just concentrated on not tripping in my own...

How was it like working with Tommy and Enrico?

I liked them both very much!! I feel very lucky that they found me.

You have released *Fly With Me* as a solo artist, was there supposed to be an album in some point?

Fly With Me was a one-song deal and we never planned an album.

You have sung for DMN Records, was it easy to convince you to come to their stable?

I approached them myself, they never had to ask, lol. We have a very good working arrangement.

What keeps eurodance alive in your opinion?

I believe that eurodance is kept alive by the fans and the community that surrounds it.

Eurodance is not just some music, it's a feeling and a state of mind.

Do you perform in 90's festivals?

I just did two shows with Masterboy and Beatrix, it was fantastic. But I have a vocal school with my husband George Liszt (Scream Factory) and we have our own band, so we are constantly busy, and I just wouldn't have the time to travel all over again.

Love seeing my fans though!!!!

Something else you want to share about eurodance era?

I feel blessed to have had the chance to meet such wonderful artists like my friend Franky from Captain Jack. Also, working and singing with the Backstreet Boys, N'Sync, and so many amazing others, is something I will never forget. And last but not least, the feeling of belonging to something bigger than yourself,

EURODANCE...

▶ Maxx

Maxx is one of the most popular and well-known eurodance projects from the 90's, but their success was short-lived. In the following, we will get to know the history of Maxx and also M.C. Sar & The Real McCoy with an extra-long interview with German producer Jürgen Wind and British Singer Linda Meek.

In The Spotlight
▶II

Jürgen Wind producer

Linda Meek singer

What's the story behind the creation of Maxx and what does the project name stand for?

Jürgen:

I founded Maxx together with music industry executive David Brunner in 1993 in Berlin, Germany under the record label Intercord/Blow Up. I'm the main producer of that project. The name 'Maxx' is actually an acronym which means Max-iumum X-tasy. The premise behind Maxx is Jamaican style rap (also known as ragamuffin rap) combined with female singing over high energy dance floor beats.

What exactly is the connection between Maxx and your other project M.C. Sar & The Real McCoy?

Jürgen:

Under my music production company Freshline Records, I wrote and produced both Maxx and M.C. Sar &The Real McCoy simultaneously between 1993 and 1995. Producer Frank "Quickmix" Hassas worked closely with me on both projects. I was the main driving force behind the music production for Maxx while Frank had more of a co-producer role. For M.C. Sar & The Real McCoy, we had a more equal share as the writers and producers. By 1995 Maxx had ended and M.C. Sar& The Real McCoy continued under the shortened band name Real McCoy. In 1996, Frank left Freshline Records and I was the main producer of Real McCoy up until 1998. M.C. Sar & The Real McCoy lasted longer than Maxx and received more attention and care than the Maxx project did.

M.C. Sar & Real McCoy was initially founded in 1989 as a hip house style dance project under ZYX records. When we left ZYX records in 1992 and joined Hansa Records (then owned by BMG), the project was changed from being a hip house style project to a eurodance and pop music project.

David Brunner was an A& R at Hansa/BMG and he worked with me to develop the single *Another Night* for M.C. Sar & The Real McCoy. I produced the music and co-wrote the chorus lyrics/hooks and melody with Frank. David held an executive producer role in the team and managed all the business by mapping out all the marketing, promotion, distribution, and sales strategies in Europe with BMG President André Selleneit.

When looking for a singer to sing the chorus vocals on *Another Night*, I came into contact with a producer duo known as the Berman Brothers (siblings Frank and Christian Berman). The brothers offered their session singer Karin Kasar as a potential candidate for singing the choruses on the new single. After hearing a demo of her voice, I selected her for the role. In exchange for her participation in the project, the brothers made a deal with me to be listed as co-producers on the record. The brothers also made a deal with me to make all the remixes for the single. A mix created by the brothers was selected to be the official single version of the song. Singer Patricia "Patsy" Petersen and rapper and Olaf "O-Jay" Jeglitza fronted M.C. Sar & The Real McCoy as a rapper/singer duo. Patricia mimed Karin's vocals for live performances and music videos.

Bruce Hammond Earlam, a songwriter/producer whom we often collaborated with, secretly helped Olaf by proofreading and correcting his rap lyrics for *Another Night* while also coaching him vocally. I made the decision to add digital effects to deepen Olaf's voice for the rap vocals after seeing how well deep voiced rap worked for Captain Hollywood's single *More and More*. Since Olaf was a team member, shareholder, and a co-founder of Freshline, he was also given fake producer credits on the record and on all future releases for the project. He was never really a music producer at Freshline.

After working hard for nearly a year with David and André to prepare the single for release, *Another Night* was finally released in Summer 1993. Unfortunately for us, the single was not a big success when released. It barely made the Top 100 in several European countries and managed to only reach No. 20 in Germany.

The mediocre performance of *Another Night* motivated us to start another dance project. We decided to start developing the Maxx project under Intercord. We worked closely with Bruce to develop the debut Maxx single *Get-a-way*. David once again handled all the marketing, promotion, distribution, and sales for the music and had an executive producer role in the team.

I produced the music with Frank, and we wrote the chorus hooks. Bruce wrote the ragamuffin rap lyrics for the single and was the vocal coach for Maxx rapper Boris Köhler. Due to his contractual restraints with EMI, Bruce had to write for the project in secret without actually being credited. Boris was therefore given all of Bruce's songwriting credits for promotional reasons.

Why didn't your team use their real names in the song credits for Maxx?

Jürgen:

David decided that we all should use aliases in the Maxx song credits in order to hide our real identities. Intercord and Hansa Records (BMG Berlin) were both competitors in Germany and all of Europe. If we had released *Get-a-way* as Freshline song production with our real names in the credits we would've created a lot of enemies.

Therefore, the name "The Movement" was used in place of Freshline for the Maxx producer credits.

For the individual credits, I was George Torpey, David was The Hitman, Frank was Dakota O'Neill, Boris was Gary Bokoe aka Gary B. and Olaf was Dawhite. Olaf was once again granted fake production and writer credits due to his close association with Freshline Records. In reality, he had no real involvement in the production or songwriting of Maxx and was never really a member of the band whatsoever.

Our strategy of hiding our identities worked because nobody could ever figure out who exactly wrote and produced Maxx at first.

However, looking back I regret it because, I would have received an Echo Award in Germany in 1996 due to the major commercial success of my song production with Maxx in Europe and Real McCoy worldwide.

What was the story behind the original singer behind *Get-a-way*?

Jürgen:

The story is simple. The chorus vocals heard in "Get-a-way" were sung by a session singer named Samira Besic. After recording vocals for the single, we did not hire her again to participate further in the Maxx project. She was not an experienced live performer nor was she suitable to be the front woman for Maxx.

When filming for the debut Maxx music video began in Sweden, Turkish dancer and model Alice Montana was brought in to actually star in Samira's place and to mime her vocals. Alice was married to Olaf at the time. She briefly served as a front woman for the project alongside Boris in promotional photos for Maxx. She was falsely credited in the European media as the singer of Maxx in the early stages. As a result, many of the Maxx fans even to this day think that Alice and Samira are the same person. It is not true. Alice was simply a temporary front woman and a lip-sync performer hired for the Maxx music video and the early promo photos. Using lip-sync performers for music videos and not real singers was a common thing in the '90s in Europe.

Get-a-way was an instant hit in Germany when released in October 1993 and was quickly climbing up the charts, but we had one major problem, we didn't have a real singer/live performer to tour with Boris as Maxx and to record vocals for the next planned single and album. Samira was no longer involved in the project at this point and Alice couldn't really sing. Bruce therefore volunteered to help us find a new singer.

When exactly did Linda join Maxx and sing vocals on the second Maxx single? What was her background?

Linda:

I joined Maxx around February 1994 thanks to Sheila Gott, my singing teacher and mentor. I am originally from England. When Bruce began calling around in Europe looking for a singer for Maxx.

He came into contact with Sheila. They both had mutual contacts in England. At the time I was living in Osnabruck, Germany as a military wife. During the day I worked as a secretary on a military base and at night I would travel around Germany to perform live gigs at German night clubs and pubs. I had actually built up a name for myself due to competing in various singing contests in Germany. Prior to that I had had extensive experience performing in night clubs and pubs in England and as a lead singer in different cover bands.

When Bruce first contacted me, I was actually being offered a record deal for a solo project from a different group of people. I chose to go with Maxx because I recognized the popularity of Get-a-way and the opportunity to be on a world stage was appealing to me. After sharing a demo tape and some audition photos, I was flown into Berlin, Germany to do an audition in front of David and Jürgen. I sang the chorus to No More (I Can't Stand It). Initially, David and Jürgen were thinking of maybe hiring a Turkish singer or someone else, but Bruce convinced them that they needed me to be the new singer and front woman of Maxx because I was attractive, had a great voice, could sing live and because he felt I had a similar look to Lisa Stansfield at the time.

After joining the act, I immediately began touring live as Maxx with Boris. I performed on Top of the Pops and all the major dance chart shows. We toured all over Europe. We later recorded the vocals for No More (I Can't stand it) and filmed the music video in Marseille, France and I recorded vocals for the Maxx album during the summertime.

Was it difficult to produce both Maxx and M.C. Sar & The Real McCoy at the same time in the 90's? Which project was more successful?

Jürgen:

Yes. Producing both projects was hard and time consuming. There were many sleepless nights and many hours in the studio. We were always working non-stop around the clock to meet release deadlines.

The truth is Maxx was more successful than M.C. Sar & The Real McCoy at first. Both *Get-a-way* and *No More* were initially bigger hits than the M.C. Sar hits *No More* reached the Top 5 spot in over 18 other countries and nearly reached gold status in Germany like *Get-a-way* but missed the mark. When *Another Night* was released in Canada and then the USA, Maxx was quickly overtaken by the new success of M.C. Sar & The Real McCoy.

Another Night had been released in Canada by BMG in March 1994. The single quickly reached the No. 1 on the dance charts for multiple weeks. Clive Davis of Arista records took notice of the success in Canada.

We then began producing the album Space Invaders, the second album of M.C. Sar & The Real McCoy and the debut Maxx album *To the Maxximum* at the same time during the Summer of 1994.

Bruce took on a bigger role in the songwriting for the Maxx album. He wrote most of Linda's song lyrics and all of Boris' rap lyrics while also doing essential percussion and drums for different album tracks.

To the Maxximum was officially released on June 22, 1994 and had reached No. 22 on the German charts. The album was also a major success in Scandinavia, reaching No. 10 in Sweden and No. 6 in Finland. *Space Invaders* peaked at No. 65 in German charts. While the Maxx album was a modest commercial success in many European countries, it still failed to meet the high expectations of matching the sales of *Get-a-way* and *No More*. The album had also failed in key territories like England where it peaked at No. 66.

Due to the success of *Another Night* in Canada, Clive Davis decided to release the record in the U.S. under the shortened band name (Real McCoy) in July. Thanks to the promotional campaigns by Arista, *Another Night* had reached Platinum status in the U.S. by November. The success of *Another Night* in the U.S. under Arista Records created new interest in M.C. Sar & The Real McCoy worldwide.

The song *You Can Get It* was then picked from the Maxx album to be the third single and was released in September 1994. The single reached No. 21 in England and No. 13 in Finland. While still commercially successful, the single did not reach the same level of success as *Get-a-way* and *No More (I Can't Stand it)*. We then released a Christmas themed dance track titled *Power of Love* exclusively on a Bravo Hits compilation music CD called Bravo Dance X-Mas in October 1994.

By late 1994, the commercial success of Maxx had begun to decline while the commercial success of M.C. Sar & The Real McCoy was quickly rising in the U.S. market. Maxx was still very popular, but some bad strategic decisions were made with Maxx at Intercord.

At this time there were creative differences and other internal conflicts happening within our team regarding the Maxx. We were also having major difficulties dealing with bad behavior from rapper Boris.

What happened with the last two Maxx singles? Why did Maxx end and Real McCoy continue?

Jürgen:

In 1995, the Maxx album track *I Can Make You Feel Like* was released as a single in limited territories and was not a success. The single only charted in England at No. 52. While David and I were now struggling with Maxx commercially, we were having new success with M.C. Sar & The Real McCoy (now marketed as Real McCoy) in the U.S. market. *The Space Invaders* album had been re-released in the U.S. and re-titled *Another Night* in March 1995 and new songs were recorded for the release. Thanks to the promotional efforts of Arista Records and the continuing popularity of the platinum single *Another Night* and the now Gold single *Run Away*, the Real McCoy album had achieved multi-platinum status in the United States.

After the commercial failure of the final Maxx single *Move Your Body*, David and I decided to stop Maxx permanently. The reasons were: the declining records sales, the internal team conflicts, and the ongoing behavior problems with the Maxx rapper (Boris Köhler.) behind the scenes. We felt it was a better business decision to just focus strictly on Real McCoy since we were having bigger success with that project. As a result, Maxx disappeared for 20 years. Looking back on it now, I regret it. We should've found a way to continue Maxx. We made a bad decision.

When exactly did Maxx return to doing live shows again? When did Linda officially return to Maxx?

Jürgen:

At the beginning of 2014, I allowed Boris to do Maxx gigs again since many other '90s artists were beginning to tour again successfully. The resurgence of eurodance and '90s nostalgia was starting to pick up again around this time. He first appeared as Maxx in Finland at a nightclub called Club Onniteekki with an unknown singer not associated with Maxx. Many fans thought this girl that performed with Boris was the new singer of Maxx since this was his first appearance as Maxx since 1995, but this girl was merely an unknown work for hire singer. Boris later did shows in other countries using different singers, but I quickly became annoyed with Boris's poor performance and behavioral problems and poor work ethic while on tour. Rather than allow for more bad Maxx shows, I just chose to pull the plug. He currently is not legally allowed to use the name Maxx to do live shows nor is he allowed to use my Maxx song productions in any way for live performances.

In 2015, Linda reconnected with me through her business associate in America. I had not talked to her in over 20 years. We later decided to launch an official new Maxx website which was intended announce Linda's re-introduction to Maxx. The website also announced our intention to tour as Maxx without Boris. We quickly recruited a new team of rappers to perform in Boris' place. Linda needed a team because she couldn't just rely on only one rapper only to do all the live shows and club gigs over multiple countries on multiple dates.

Since 2016, she has been doing live concerts and club shows all over Europe using different rappers for different shows. I'm proud of her. She looks great and she has a great team of rappers working with her on stage. Some of the Maxx fans have also gotten confused and think that there is one new Maxx rapper. It is not true.

There is just too much false information written online about Linda, the history of Maxx and the current status of the group. Thankfully, the English language Wikipedia article on Maxx has correct information, but the German language Wikipedia article on Maxx currently has a lot of false information in it. It is quite amusing to read. I wish someone would correct it. The fans who post false information online are not professional music journalists. They are just passionate fans. The truth about Maxx is that Linda has always had a team of male performers working with her on stage since her return to Maxx. She uses them interchangeably depending on the country, the venue. the time of the year. Her team is always growing and changing. The men who perform with her on stage are all temporary work-for-hire performers who have not had professional recording careers like Linda. She has simply hired them to wear a stage costume of her choice and to perform the ragamuffin rap of the Maxx hits on stage. They are NOT Maxx band members and never will be. Linda Meek is the singer and face of Maxx right now. I, Jürgen Wind (George Torpey), am the producer. I am also the co-founder of the project along with David Brunner (The Hitman). I run Maxx from behind the scenes and I make the decisions. This is the truth about the current status of Maxx. The fans must understand this as well as these websites

that present false or inaccurate information about Maxx. Her shows have been going well so far.

Maxx was one of the biggest eurodance projects in the '90s with just one album and a few singles. Do you wish there would have been a second album?

Linda:

Yes. It would've been nice to have continued. If I remember correctly, a lot of people and fans were surprised when we stopped suddenly without explanation.

Jürgen:

Yes. Maxx should've continued. But the project literally died before it even got off the ground. Maxx failed to reach its full potential.

83

How would you define eurodance?

Jürgen:

In my opinion eurodance is danceable pop music with direct influences from the italo pop genre.

Some of the same instruments and sounds heard in italo pop can also be heard in the typical eurodance song. I also hear influences from other 1980's tunes originally produced in Europe.

Some people also feel there are some influences from techno music and other genres found in eurodance, but I mainly hear italo pop influences. The most recognizable format for a eurodance song is a female singing the chorus hook and a male performing the rap, but there are many eurodance songs that only feature one main vocalist.

The first true eurodance songs that defined the genre were *More and More* by Captain Hollywood Project, *Somebody Dance with Me* by DJ Bobo, *It's My Life* by Dr. Alban, *What is Love* by Haddaway and *Rhythm is a Dancer* by Snap! The commercial success of these hits influenced existing artists and bands to follow the trend while also inspiring the creation of new eurodance acts throughout Europe.

When producing *Another Night,* we were definitely inspired by *More and More* by Captain Hollywood Project. Like I said earlier, I chose to digitally enhance Olaf's voice to be deeper for the raps after noticing how well it worked for Captain Hollywood Project. *Another Night* was also inspired by many other musical influences as well.

M.C. Sar & The Real McCoy (later just Real McCoy) was always meant to have a softer mainstream pop sound. The remixes for the singles had a eurodance sound. The Maxx hits were the opposite and were meant to have a much harder sound and were strictly eurodance.

Do you think that German eurodance has different characteristics than other countries eurodance? And if yes, what are these characteristics?

Jürgen:

German eurodance was definitely different, usually cheaply and poorly produced with fake lip- sync artists fronting the acts. Different producers wanted to cash in on the new eurodance rave happening that started around 1992 and the result was a lot of bad music was released in the '90s.

German eurodance at that time developed a bad reputation as a result. Only a handful of groups in Germany were truly good and produced good songs that became hits, many were horrible.

At Freshline Records, we tried to be a bit different, we had always tried to comply with the international standard by making our song productions as high quality as possible. Our success with Real McCoy was also almost exclusively outside Germany. Our success with Maxx, though short-lived, was in Germany and throughout Europe.

Linda, have you sung in other eurodance projects besides Maxx?

Linda:

After Maxx ended in 1995, I joined with a different team of producers. I attempted to go solo as Linda M; in 1997 with the single *Rhythm of Love* which was a direct cover of an album track by singer Nina Gerhard from her 1995 *Dare* album. Legendary 90s songwriter Nosie Katzmann co- wrote the lyrics to the original version of the song recorded by Gerhard. My version was produced by German producer Gena Wernik (aka Gena B. Good).

Unfortunately, my version didn't receive a music video or an adequate marketing budget in Europe and was simply given to DJs in Europe as a cover/remix single. As a result, it was not a success and managed to only sell 3,000 copies. After that. I pretty much left the music business.

Was there a lot of competition in the 90s between German Eurodance projects? And if so, who was your biggest competitor? and why?

Jürgen:

I saw no competition with other producers, we just focused on ourselves and did our own thing.

The German market became less important to us, especially when we started having success in America with Real McCoy. As a result, the others were no competition. Envy and jealousy are foreign to me, it's just not my thing. The only competition that actually existed was within the BMG Berlin in relation to Real McCoy.

There was always some debate about who received more budget and resources – Dieter Bohlen, Frank Farian, or my team (Freshline Records). We were always given less, and we therefore had to try to find other ways to become successful. We were successful internationally, but in Germany not so much. As a result, we were always in a situation where we were not a big priority BMG Berlin. We did not have this problem with Intercord when dealing with Maxx. All the strategic decisions for Maxx were made between David Brunner and myself and therefore everything went great up until 1995.

Are you going to release more songs?

Linda:

We don't have any firm plans to do new music, but we have discussed some different possibilities.

We are definitely interested in maybe doing something new and different, but we aren't sure right now. We are mainly focused on live touring.

You did a couple of music videos with Maxx. Do you think that videos were important in making you famous?

Linda:

Yes. The exposure I received from the Maxx music videos *No More* and *You Can Get It* got me recognized in a big way. Performing on all the major dance chart shows on television also gave me major exposure as well. Even today people still ask me "hey are you that girl with the short hair from that Maxx music videos?"

How do you remember the 90´s eurodance era? Good or bad?

Linda:

Well to be honest I wasn't a fan of eurodance at first. My singing background is rooted soul,funk and r'n'b music. I have had a lot of extensive vocal training and a long history with singing lead in cover bands in England. Eurodance at first seemed very cheesy and not really as cool. I often joked with my mentor and called eurodance "euro-cheese" because the sound didn't appeal to me at first.

But when I joined Maxx, I was very impressed with the quality of Jürgen's

music production. When I began working with the team more, my point of view changed. I had fun touring around Europe and performing in front of massive crowds of Maxx fans. It was fun.

But to be honest, I didn't always get along well with Boris and the two German dancers that we toured with. I think they saw me as an outsider because I was British, and they were German.

Maxx released one new single after the album, Move your body, and it was more house than eurodance. Why this change of direction?

Jürgen:

Yes. You are correct about the drastic change. The truth is that Intercord forced me to produce this song in this style. I was very much against it and I didn't want to produce it. *Move Your Body* is very similar to the hit *I Like To Move It* which was a major world hit at the time.

Intercord wanted to try to cash in on that sound. So, our usual sound and formula was abandoned for this track. The song was a success in Finland and Austria, but we had limitations with distribution in Europe, so the song was not really a big success like Intercord wanted.

All the pictures in the Maxx chapter published with permission of the artist.

▶ *M.C. Sar & The Real McCoy*

>>Also look Maxx chapter

M.C. Sar & The Real McCoy, which personified mainly to Olaf Jeglitza, started in the same way as many other euro band: with hip house. The first commercial release from the band was a Technotronic cover *Pump Up The Jam.* The song was a hit in Germany as was the next single, *It's On You.*

The success gained in Germany wasn't nothing compared to the mega hits from the second album, *Space Invaders. Another Night* single combined pop and eurodance, which attracted the attention of many people. Also, the songs like *Runaway* and *Automatic Lover* (which borrowed the melody from Bronski Beat's *Smalltown boy*) helped the band break into the charts in the US. *Space Invaders* album was modified for US markets and retitled as *Another Night.* It sold multiple platinum according to Real McCoy's official Facebook page.

During the band's biggest success, singer Patricia Petersen was hired to accompany Olaf and later another singer Vanessa Mason joined these two. Later, after the band broke up, it was revealed that the women didn't sing all the songs in studio, Patricia's vocals were performed by Karin Kasar.

The bands last album *One More Time* was just a pale interpretation of the old dance band. The songs were light house songs or downtempo. Petersen was replaced with Lisa Cork. In this last album, Lisa and Vanessa got to finally sing in the studio. As was expected, this last album didn't fare so well in the US. Soon after this, the band broke up.

In 2009 Olaf decided to assemble the band again. Nowadays the original singer Karin is touring alongside Olaf. The band has sold over 20 million records and is therefore one of the most sold eurodance bands.

▶ *Fun Factory*

Like many other euro band, also Fun Factory's story begins before eurodance era in 1990. Producer Rainer Kesselbaur's idea started as a studio project with an instrumental *Fun Factory's theme*. It circulated as a vinyl through a small record company, but it didn't create a lot of buzz. Two years later Rainer released the song on CD, with four different mixes.

Kesselbaur noticed that the poppy eurodance sound had started to be the sound of now, so he decided to build a band around his previous project. The line-up was a multinational effort which reflected the boundary-crossing eurodance sound. The leading lady Marie-Anett Mey was French, rapper Rodney Hardison (aka Rod D.) American, Toni Cottura (rap, backing vocals, dancer) Italian and dancer Stephan Browarczyk was German. Balca Tözün, who was the unofficial member, was the real voice behind the female vocals while Marie-Anett lip-synced live and on videos.

First Fun Factory single with vocals was *Groove Me*. It gained huge popularity in Israel, like the next Fun Factory songs. Biggest fame was just around the corner: *Close To You*, *Take Your Chance* and *Pain* took the charts by storm followed by an album *Nonstop! – The Album*. It was, as the title says, a dance orgy mixed together, only the slow r'n'b songs like *Hey Little Girl* slowed down the motion.

Immediately on the second album, *Fun-Tastic* (1995), the band changed its style from serious eurodance to happy euro reggae like *Celebration*. Also, the single release *Do Wah Diddy* (a cover of the old 60's The Exciters hit) was a poor effort to cash-in with the house sound á la Reel 2 Real. Although the album had a couple of good eurodance songs in it, it was far away from the hectic beats of the first album.

1997 meant big chances for the band, because all the four members quit. Three new members were chosen for the new generation: Alfonso Walser and Tiger One (aka T-Roc) as rappers and Anett Möller for vocals. This new version of Fun Factory managed to get some success in Asia, especially in Japan where two of their albums were released, *Next Generation* and *ABC Of Music*. Both the albums were stylistically all over the place, even trance pop, so it was no wonder that the band vanished from the music scene in 2003. In these albums, female vocals were mainly sung by the 1980's italo disco star , Lian Ross, using an alias.

However, after a few years, Rekardo Heilig (who owned the band name) decided to power up the project once again, this time with four new faces. Even a new album was planned, but only a couple of new songs emerged like *On Top Of The World*.

It was quite a surprise when part of the original line-up, Toni, Stephan, and the previously unofficial member Balca, returned to the band with a new song *Let's Get Crunk*. It was trendy electro house, but the dullness of this new song was soon compensated: new LP *Back To The Factory*, which gave us in addition to new songs also remakes of their old hits. It was positive to hear that the songs where updated to just slightly so they would hold the same 90's magic.

▶ *DJ Company*

DJ Company is one of those few euro bands who prospered also in the US. Four of DJ Company's songs charted there.

January Ordu was the main vocalist, while raps were performed by various men. Production-wise big eurodance names like Jam El Mar, Louis Lasky and Stefan Benz were involved.

Rhythm Of Love (1995) is the projects biggest hit. In its publication year it was especially popular also in Canada. Other singles still weren't as big as this. Their first album was released in the same year.

It was 1997 when *Rhythm Of Love* conquered USA. Raps were deleted and more female vocals were added. Also, an expensive looking music video gathered more success for the song. Their first album was released again but it was modified to answer the American taste, for example Alphaville cover *Forever Young* was added.

However, the band relied mostly on eurodance and in 1997 it was a dying genre. The project disappeared completely soon after.

In The Spotlight

▶❚❚

Stefan Benz *producer*

Published with permission of Stefan Benz.

You've been involved in many dance projects over the years. Do you have a favorite project?

Actually no. Being involved in writing and producing music was all it took to make me happy - No matter which artist, project, or collaboration, I just loved doing what I did at that time!

How did you ended up producing dance/eurodance ?

Well, I've always been into music. I learned playing drums at the age of eleven, played in high school bands and the school orchestra. One day my dad brought me a Casio Synthesizer from one of his business trips to Japan. I was totally fascinated by this more or less 'toy'. I spent many nights pressing chords, writing lyrics, and imagining how all of that could sound as finished music productions. At the age of nineteen I went to a bank and got myself a massive loan to buy everything you needed to write and produce electronic music. That same year while studying marketing I got to know Ulli Brenner who was a DJ in one of the most famous clubs in Frankfurt Germany - The Dorian Gray. Because the people knew we both were into music, someone from business school introduced us to his cousin Rolf Ellmer (aka Jam El Mar) who was a successful classical guitar player at that time. But Rolf also had a well-equipped studio in the cellar of his parents' house!! He had a PPG Waveterm 2.3 Synthesizer and lots of other cool stuff that was nearly unaffordable at that time. We started hanging out in his studio and Ulli and I introduced Rolf to our passion: dance music! Ulli had some contacts to the music industry. While Rolf and I started writing and producing tracks, Ulli did the business part and we actually started to get releases on EMI/Cool Groove. Another year later I got a job as an A&R Manager at CBS, founded a label called Dance Pool and became its label manager. Right after that Rolf and I founded Allstar Music Productions right into the eurodance era...

Do you think that German eurodance is different compared to other countries eurodance?

Yes, I do. For electronically produced music Germany provided an 'identity' for those involved. R&b was American, pop was English but synthetic music had its roots in Germany (Kraftwerk :-) etc...) - at least that's how I saw it. We didn't 'want to be like', no, we just did our own thing and felt we had every right to do so.

B.G. The Prince of Rap's third album *Get The Groove On* was a bit lighter than the previous eurodance album. Why is that? Was it because changing trends?

Yes, I think it was because of changing trends. Having a major deal can sometimes be a burden. You're expected to write and produce hits. Sometimes it leads to leaving your original path and the pressure takes too much influence on your work.

Was there a lot of competition in the 90's between dance projects, especially in Germany?

Personally, I never had that feeling. The cake was big enough for all of us !

Why DJ Company's album was changed a bit mellower when released in the US ?

Crave (Mariah Careys label) wanted it that way. Craves A&R Manager Michael Ellis said that we needed a ballad (he gave us a Dianne Warren copyright *Wishing On The Same Star* for that) and he wanted us to do a cover of Alphaville's *Forever Young* to be released as a second single. We trusted on his opinion and did what he said.

Do you think that DJ Company should have had longer lasting success?

For sure! Unfortunately, the lead singer January Ordu decided to leave the project due to health issues. At that time, she was living in New York, good friends with Mariah and the Asia tour was planned and scheduled. Approximately two or three weeks before the tour she called us and said she would go back to Germany and no longer be part of DJ Company. Actually, we never saw her again since that call. Of course, that was the death of DJ Company. Sad!

What are your opinions about today's dance music, like EDM? Do you see it as an offspring of 90's eurodance/dance music?

All music done today is influenced by music done to date. Therefore yes, partially for sure. But there are lots of other influences too! It depends on the track (the writers, the artists and the producers involved) - no rules, no schemes - the music universe always leaves its traces...

Are you involved in dance music nowadays?

Yes, I'm still into music. New stuff coming in the near future! Just two months ago one of my old hard trance tracks (Busted - Tricky Tricky) was covered and sampled by W&W, Timmy Trumpet and Will Sparks! Check it out! Finest EDM of today:)

▶ *Mr. President*

Before Mr. President was personified as the trio we all came to know as one of the greatest successes in the 90's, bands producer Kai Matthiessen used the name to release a tribute song for Marilyn Monroe called *MM (1993)*, which even sampled the famous birthday song, which Marilyn sang for John F. Kennedy.

Mr. President's saga starts in 1991, when DJ's Matthiessen and Jens Neumann founded a band called Satellite One. American George Jones (aka Sir Prophet) and Daniela Haak (aka Lady Danii) were part of this band and were soon joined by Judith Hinkelmann (aka T-Seven).

For some time, the band toured on clubs, but they didn't get much success so the producers Matthiessen and Neumann decided to change the name to Mr. President and release the previously mentioned single *MM.* The song gained some underground success, which enabled them to release their first eurodance song, *Up'n'Away*. The song gained gold status in Germany, although it didn't break into Top 10. As the song gained more popularity, Sir Prophet started to behave badly. He was replaced by a new rapper, British Delroy Rennalls (LayZee). Sir Prophet's raps were replaced with Delroy's in the debut album. Now the trio were formed to its best-known line-up.

The first rappers (Sir Prophet, in the middle) bad behaviour was too much, so he got kicked out of the band after this single

Up'n'Away the album saw the light of day in 1995. Another energetic song, *4 On The Floor*, was also released as a single. The whole album is almost 100 percent eurodance album, of course done with a pop mentality. The highlights of this LP are *I Would Die For You*, *I Believe* and *Never Leave Me*. It had a happy vibe, which was going to be one of the characteristics of Mr. President.

The next chapter in the saga would be one for the history books: the producers decided to have a go with a totally different sound. *Coco Jamboo* was a euro reggae which borrowed a little something from Ace Of Base and Loft. It proved out to be quite a summer hit and it took the world by storm. British single chart Top 10 and USA Billboard position 21 were some of its accomplishments.

Gaining the success of the masses did (naturally) influence the band's sound. The previous eurodance tone was replaced with even more poppy sound (although their albums still featured euro songs). Still it was a good thing that the second album, *We See The Same Sun*, didn't contain just a bunch of *Coco Jamboo* copies. There were still hard dance tracks like *Don't You Ever Stop*.

In their homeland, Mr. President didn't seem to be so popular: the album didn't get higher than position 16 in the Germany's album chart. But all over Europe it was a success: even their debut album was re-released with bonus tracks.

Coco Jamboo had been such a home run, so they had to release new material fast, so that the audience didn't mistake them to be a one-hit wonder. Third album was Night Club (1997), in which the band lightened their sound even more. A bit artificial single Jojo Action gained some top positions in Europe. Anyhow, also this album had some interesting tracks, like Take Me To The Limit, in which they tried to bring out their sexy side. The track Happy People though was too much like Coco Jamboo.

During the Nightclub promo tour Lady Danii took a little time-out from Mr. President, in order to try out her own solo career with Reset (not the Norwegian dance act) but was soon back in the ranks of Mr. President. Around the same time the band was faced with a scandal: Stern magazine alleged that the members of Mr. President weren't the real voices behind the songs. Matthiessen and Neumann answered this accusation in an interview with German Viva channel that the singers were indeed Lady Danii, T-Seven and LayZee, but their voices had been electronically altered in the studio. However later it became clear that T-Seven's vocals and LayZee's singing vocals were sung by backing vocalists.

All in all, their popularity was waning. Their next album came in the verge of new millennium: Space Gate (1999). This was a more interesting album, because the sound was more club than the previous ones, although this one had quite a boring euro reggae Simbaleo.

The band sealed the 90's with a collection A Kind Of... Best! (2000), which collected all their hits and a reloaded Up'n'Away 2K -version. Around this time T-Seven left the band for solo career.

The band accomplished something that many 90's band hasn't: to continue their recording career to a new decade. In the beginning of 2000's they showed up again to the music scene (Myra Beckmann was hired to replace T-Seven). Love, Sex & Sunshine single offered light summer vibes and Japan-only album Forever & One Day (2003) gave the listeners a little bit of everything, even trance sounds.

Since 2008 Delroy aka LayZee has toured as Mr. President performing their biggest hits. Nowadays he is accompanied by Hungarian Erika Kovacs. In addition to this Delroy has released solo singles like Summertime.

In The Spotlight

▶II

Delroy Rennalls aka LayZee singer

Published in the permission of Delroy Rennalls

How did you become a part of Mr. President?

As the original rapper left the band or was basically thrown out. The producer and manager who I had known for some years before asked if I could fill in until they found a replacement.

Had you sung dance music before Mr. President?

I was part of a dance project before that was called Fresh & Fly with my brother, part owner of Peppermint Jam, SPV and writer of hits such as *Horny* and *Sex Bomb* by Mousse T and many other world class hits. We released three songs at the time, but decided to do different things after a while, which worked out well for all of us.

How was it like working with Kai Matthiesen?

What can I say? Kai was much like any other producer I ever worked with. He had his vision.

So, there is not much to say there.

Coco Jamboo was a massive hit. Do you ever get tired of performing it?

This and really all the songs I perform, I never get sick or tired of. They are a part of me because a part of them came out of me. So, there is no real way I can get tired of them.

Mr. President's recording career lasted about 10 years, what are your feelings about this?

Yes! We managed to do five albums and a best of. Which was not bad for a band that everyone said would never make it. Then go on to win two Echo awards and numerous other dance awards all over the world.

Why did the band eventually break up in the 2000's?

My main reason was that I was fed up a lot of things around me. Both private and public life. So, I had to make a change for myself because no one else was interested in making that change for me.

Mr. President has mainly a very happy sound, do you think that you should have done more darker songs?

We have enough darkness in the world. Why fill it with more. Happy songs are harder to write as darker songs.

Do you think that eurodance is still alive today? What do you consider as eurodance?

Well first we need to establish what eurodance really is. Here the definition: This genre of music is heavily influenced by the use of rich melodic vocals, either exclusively by itself or inclusively with rapped verses. This, combined with cutting-edge synthesizer, strong bass rhythm and melodic hooks, establishes the core foundation of eurodance music.

Eurodance production continues to evolve with a more modernized style. Is it really alive I would say no. It's more of a revival. Reliving a time in history were Europe was faced with a massive cultural change due to the opening of borders resulting from the fall of the so-called Iron Curtain. Parts of Europe lived this change in different ways. Many Eastern European countries embraced it with open arms while, many just saw it as a sign of the times. I notice the way people take to the music while on tour. West Europe are more with the entertain me attitude while Eastern Europe are more pleased to join our party.

Is Mr. President still active? If so, who are the members beside you?

Actually, LayZee is active, as a member of Mr. President. Which was one of the changes I made to get back more control over my artist abilities. I had a few singers working with me since 2006 when I started my own project based on the successes we had. But since the last five years I have been working with one singer that absolutely understands what my project is about and has just as much energy on the stage as myself. Who is very down to earth and doesn't put herself in front the main artist.

She is a singer I was introduced in Hungary as one of my singer could not bother to turn up. Erika has been with me for over five years and I hope we can continue until...Well, let's see what happens. That chapter has not been written yet.

▶ Haddaway

"What is love, baby don't hurt me...". There are not many people in this Earth who have avoided hearing this song, which summarizes the whole 1990's. It has had a tremendous impact on dance music and an inspiration to many bands, eurodance or other.

Trinidad-born Nestor Haddaway (b.1965) was nine years old when he moved to Washington D.C. where he was exposed to music of Louis Armstrong, which inspired him to start playing the trumpet at the age of 14. He started a band called Chances there. In 1989 this future eurodance star moved to Germany, where he worked in bars.

He also started a band in Germany, called Elegato, with the keyboard player Alex Trime (who played on Haddaway's songs). But it was meeting the producer duo Dee Dee Halligan and Junior Torello (aka Tony Hendrik and Karin Hartmann) that changed his life completely. They were in charge of Coconut Records and escorted Nestor into solo career.

The first solo effort *What Is Love* (1992) hurled him straight away to stardom. The song was originally meant to be a ballad but done in the language of dance music it came fully alive. It is probably the most successful eurodance song ever, for example in Germany it sold almost million units, charting number two in the charts. According to Haddaway's official Facebook page, the international sale was 2,6 million copies in the beginning of 1994.

The songs popularity has inspired countless of bands and it has had a huge meaning to the development and success of eurodance sound. Nowadays it's one of most known and wished-for songs, and no wonder: the refrain and melody are easy to remember. Production-wise it has something timeless and that's why the song will never grow old.

Although the next single *Life* wasn't as near as big of a success as *What Is Love*, it also managed to sell 1,5 copies worldwide by 1994. Also, the ballad *I Miss You* and the rocking *Rock My Heart* from the LP *The Album* sold well. In my opinion the album wasn't as great as the hits, but it still sold a couple of million units. Album doesn't satisfy the dance music enthusiast because there are too many fillers like *Stir It Up* and too many ballads. This makes the album unstable. Having said that, there's one of the best remixes of the 90's in the end, *Life* (Mission Control remix).

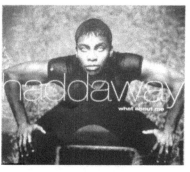

The Drive (1995) was the name of the next album and it created hits like the underrated *Fly Away* and *Catch A Fire*. The success of those songs was still nothing compared to the mega hits of the debut LP. However, *The Drive* is a much better album than the hastily composed first album. It has more dance songs and a song that should have definitely been released as a single, *Waiting For A Better World*. Although *The Drive* has its share of ballads, they are much more balanced compared to the big picture. The American songwriter Desmond Child contributed in two songs.

What About Me (1997) offered more soulful Haddaway, but the single *Who Do You Love* reminded us of his hit sound. The album *Let's Do It Now*, despite its beautiful cover, meant slow receding from the womb of eurodance. In addition to aforementioned songs and the single *You're Taking My Heart,* the album didn't contain anything interesting.

In 1998 Haddaway started to get new attention for a surprising reason. Saturday Night Live legends Will Ferrell and Steve Kattan starred in a film called *A Night At The Roxbury*. In the movie, the social butterfly brothers starred by those two are dreaming of owning a club. Their favorite song is *What Is Love,* which is played several times in the movie.

On the other hand, Haddaway didn't get much attention when it came to his new music. *Let's Do It Now* didn't sell well. The next LP *My Face* (2001) didn't get anyone's attention although it had some dance songs like *Deep*. Mainly the album had your basic pop, soul and r'n'b. The next album *Love Makes* was probably his more organic, where there wasn't even a trace of the old eurodance legend.

A faint glimmer of hope was visible in the next one, *Pop Splits* (2005), which had been divided into four parts and one part was called *Party Trax*. During that time, Haddaway was in two different TV shows in Germany and in England, which featured old and forgotten artists. With this exposure, Haddaway got a moderate hit in Germany with a song raised from *Pop Splits, Spaceman*.

Because soul and other genres outside dance music didn't seem to interest people, he contacted another eurodance legend, Dr.Alban. Together they created *I Love The 90's* (2008). The song was a dance song alright, but it didn't remind 90's at all. The next year, when the German DJ Klaas remixed old 90's hit (Guru Josh: *Infinity),* he also remixed *What Is Love*. The new version was called Klaas vs Haddaway *What Is Love 2K9* and it fared quite well, although the version itself was really awful with its disturbing electro sound.

You Gave Me Love (2010) single was a minor comeback to Haddaway's old sound. It was produced by a man behind his mega hit, Tony Hendrik. It was nothing new, but food for the nostalgic. Two years later Nestor collaborated with another 90's dance man, The Mad Stuntman (Reel 2 Real) with the song *Up And Up,* which was a Top 20 dance hit in US. After that Haddaway has featured on other people's songs, lastly with Wolfram (*My Love Is For Real*). His latest new song is from this year, *I Wanna Be For You.*

▶ E-Rotic / S.E.X. Appeal /

In addition to E-Type, E-Rotic is the only other eurodance band who didn't ditch eurodance sound when it started to fade. The singer Liane Hegemann aka Lyane Leigh (b.1969) was acquaintance of producer David Brandes, when they formed a band together. Accompanied was also another producer, Felix J. Gauder. There was definitely something sexy missing in the eurodance scene at that time, so E-Rotic with an openly sexual image was formed.   Lyane was joined by rapper Richard Michael Smith aka Raz-Ma-Taz.

The first single *Max Don't Have Sex With Your Ex* (1994) was immediately a big success all over Europe with its nasty lyrics. It also introduced us a first character from the E-Rotic cast, Max. The next single, *Fred Come To Bed*, continued the same story: "*Fred, come to bed cause my Max had sex with his sexy ex*". Phonesex-promoting *Sex On The Phone* sealed their success. The characters continued to appear in their songs in the future and they were also in cartoon form in CD covers and music videos.

Album *Sex Affairs* collected the hit singles and offered what the singles promised: great sexy and melodic eurodance with Lyane moaning on the side. Album tracks like *Sex Me* and *Big Max* were really catchy and could have been also released as singles. In my opinion, *Sex Affairs* is one of the best eurodance albums ever, it flourished especially in Germany and in Finland.

Willy Use A Billy...Boy, which was a taster from a forthcoming album, introduced us a condom figure who promoted safe sex humoristically. In *Fritz Love My Tits* singles video, Fritz slided between giant breasts. Surprisingly, euro reggae *Help Me Dr.Dick*, rose to be one of the biggest hits of E-Rotic. New album *The Power Of Sex,* gave us an even more impressive collection of sex tracks, with a Shiva-like figure in the cover.

During the second album, Lyane and Richard had some quarrels with their manager. Because of this, Lyane and Richard left the band. They both didn't want to give up fame earned with the sexy eurodance sound, so they started together a new saucy band, S.E.X. Appeal (later more about this band). E-Rotic was given a new line-up, a model Jeanette Christensen, and a rapper Terence D'arby. Because of contractual reasons, Lyane was still forced to provide all the female vocals for E-Rotic until 1999.

Third LP *Sexual Madness* (1997) was a little break from the sexual sound. Although it had its share of horny songs, like the single *Turn Me On*, emotional side of love was more visible. The album had also two reworks of old Brandes-produced songs: *Sexual Madness* was a version of Beat Control's *Dancing Madness* and *Gotta Get It Groovin'* had belonged first to a project called IQ-Check (where Lyane had previously sung). In both cases E-Rotic's versions are far better.

Total break from sex happened with the theme album *Thank You For The Music*, which nobody could have anticipated. E-Rotic covered old Abba songs giving them a bit more flavor. This was also the first time, when real people were featured on the cover (previously only cartoon characters). Although there has been an abundance of Abba covers, in my opinion E-Rotic managed to update them quite well.

In 1998 the project wrapped up their biggest hits into a collection called *Greatest Tits*, which also contained a couple of great new songs and a megamix called *Die Geilste Single Der Welt* (The Horniest Single In The World). You might have thought that their time was over, but that was not the case...

The next album was released in two versions: with the name *Kiss Me* in Japan and in Europe with the title *Mambo No Sex.* The difference was the album's title song: Japan got a great eurodance song with *Kiss Me,* but Europe had to settle for a poor Lou Bega copy with *Mambo No Sex.* Otherwise the album was a return to the horny euro sound with songs like *Oh Nick Please Not So Quick* and *Don't Talk Dirty To Me.*

In 2000 Lydia Pockaj started to provide E-Rotic's female vocals. She was already familiar from another Brandes project called Missing Heart. Jeanette still continued as the leading lady. In the same year Jeanette was faced with a challenge: E-Rotic tried out to be a representative for Eurovision song contest in Germany and Jeanette had to sing live according to Eurovision rules. They made it through the preliminaries, but they didn't get the chance to represent their home country. It was a pity, *Queen Of Light* was a really good dance song. A new album *Gimme*

Gimme Gimme was released again in the same year containing the new Eurovision song. Eurodance sound was still aboard, although other styles were present too.

New millennium meant focusing more strongly on Asian market. While the couple previous albums had featured Jeanette on the cover, the new *Sex Generation* gave us once again wacky cartoon characters. Songs like *Billy Jive (With Willy's Wife)* were familiar stories of these fantasy characters. During this LP, the leading lady changed to Das Modul singer Yasemin Baisal, at least for a minute.

The same year as *Sex Generation* (2001), another album called *Sexual Healing* surfaced with the same familiar sound. This was released a little more extensively than the previous one, which was only released in Japan and Germany. The next long play *Cocktail E-Rotic* came two years later, now once again focusing more on love than sex.

For the time being, last E-Rotic album has been *Total Recall*, which had remade versions of E-Rotic's old hits, mainly in hard trance style. It didn't have anything that would have surpassed the appeal of the originals. The German version of this was a mixed bag: it had also some songs from the previous *Cocktail E-Rotic*.

After that they laid low: Lydia left and Brandes focused on other projects, one of which was Shanadoo, Japanese girlband, who covered old E-Rotic songs with new lyrics.

E-Rotic came back in 2015 with the original singer, Lyane. On gigs, Lyane is accompanied by the rapper Stephen Appleton. Instead of empty promises, E-Rotic really provided new material: *Video Starlet* has a fairly familiar E-Rotic sound with dirty vocals, and *Mr. Mister* continued with the same vibe. Apparently a new album is on the works.

▶▶ S.E.X. Appeal / Lyane Leigh

First song from the ex-E-Rotic guys, Lyanne and Richard, was *Voulez Vous Coucher Avec Moi*. It is a really classy eurodance song and one of the best songs of the 90's. It didn't have typical humor associated with E-Rotic, instead it succeeds being a really sensual and respectable euro song. After this first single, humor was clearly evident in the single *Sex Is A Thrill With The Pill*, which sounded straight out of E-Rotic's catalogue.

The first album from them appeared not until 1999. Equipped with a horrible cover, it had sexy songs but something else also, like a Kim Wilde cover *Kids In America*.

Soon Lyane was left by herself on the project. It formed into a hard trance project in the popular style of Cascada. Although the band had sexy lyrics, the rugged hard trance sounds took your mind from anything sensual. Last album from S.E.X.Appeal has been *Russian Roulette*, which is mainly electro house.

In addition to previously mentioned bands, Lyane has sang background vocals e.g. to Bad Boys Blue and Fancy. She has also a solo career as a schlager singer.

DAVID BRANDES aka DAVID BRÄNDLE

David Brandes recycled his own productions. Especially with E-Rotic he used songs made for his smaller projects and remade them with E-Rotic's unique sound. It has also been revealed that he has been the voice behind the rap parts.

Alongside E-Rotic he had a couple of other eurodance projects. Project called Heart Attack lasted a few singles like *Move Me Stranger* and *Get Me Going* which sounded very E-Rotic. Act called The Lovers lasted only for one single, *Love Me To The Limit,* but it showed that David could do another kind of euro too.

Brandes' Missing Heart project intertwined with E-Rotic. Lyane Leigh sang the 90's songs *Wild Angels* and *Charlene*. Around the new millennium Brandes reloaded the project with a new singer Lydia (who sang for E-Rotic too). One album, *Mystery,* was released which also contained E-Rotic song, *Queen Of Light.* The album was released only in Japan, and it's quite expensive nowadays if you manage to get a hold of it. But I could not recommend it enough, it is a joy for lovers of eurodance and trance pop.

David's career wasn't without scandals. In 2005 he admitted that he had manipulated the German single charts by buying vast amounts of Garcia and Shanadoo singles (both Brandes' projects) in order to get them to rise higher in the charts. After this the singles were deleted from the charts.

In The Spotlight

▶❚❚

Lyane Leigh singer

Published with permission of Lyane Leigh.

How would you define eurodance music?

Happy music with simple but melodious hooklines for fun, dancing and singing along. Enjoyment of life.

E-Rotic is one of the long-standing eurodance acts out there. What is the key to its long success?

Catchy hooklines combined with sensual voices and funny sexy lyrics and we perform a lot all around the world and do produce and release also new songs.

What led you to sing eurodance?

I was also singing pop music before my time with E-Rotic and eurodance was THE music style in the 90's so it naturally led to eurodance for me.

Was it pressuring to produce more hits in the 90's? Eurodance was very hit-oriented.

That you should ask the producer David Brandes since that time I was the lead singer but not producer or writer.

Did you have feedback from your lyrics? They were quite dirty ;-)

Only good feedback, those lyrics about sex are all in a funny way and should not be taken to serious.

You also have a group called S.E.X. Appeal. What made you to start this band?

I was leaving E-Rotic by that time and wanted to start something similar so people would recognize the songs from my time being with E-Rotic.

Playback was very typical way to perform live among eurodance acts How did you feel about it?

It was in the 90's, there also were some fake acts never singing in the studio, I think people want to hear more live nowadays.

How do you see the eurodance era in the 90's compared to musical landscape of today? Do you remember it with love or hate?

I remember it with love since that was my main time as an artist, today everything is very scattered and undefinable

▶▶ The Free

One of the producers of E-Rotic, Felix J.Gauder, had another successful band with The Free. He started it with Olaf Roberto Bossi in 1994. It was mainly based on eurodance sound, but it had also more soulful dimensions. American singer Charles Simmons was chosen as the frontman. In the beginning their female singer was Iris Trevisan but was soon changed to Ayla J (Alida Johnson) because of health reasons.

Born Crazy single gave us very similar sound than with E-Rotic and *Lover On The Line* continued with more of the same. The latter one could very well be relative of E-Rotic's *Sex On The Phone,* the topic was the same but in The Free's version the vocals weren't so dirty. Cooing with your lover on the telephone was a big hit for The Free, which guaranteed them plenty of gigs in Germany. Also, the next song, really fast *Dance The Night Away*, was a success.

The next single release was quite a surprise. It wasn't another club banger but a cover of old Tears For Fears song, *Shout,* which was done in a more soul/house manner. Charles sang it alone. This proved out to be their biggest hit, the lighter touch appealed larger audience.

It was time to release the LP *Crazy Worlds* (1996). Although the album had slower songs than the hectic eurodance songs, it is one of the best albums in its genre, because the hard remixes in the end balance the whole album. Another single from it, *Loveletter from Space*, was a hit like *Shout* and is probably their best known song.

Although they enjoyed some success, eventually the band just vanished. In 1999 they planned for a single called *Fly,* but it was only released as a promo. After this their contract with record company Dance Pool expired, and it naturally wasn't renewed.

In an interview for the Eurokdj site in 2003, Simmons told that the performers and producers had other projects, so The Free wouldn't probably reunite anytime soon. After The Free, Simmons has featured with other artists and in 2001 he updated their biggest hit *Loveletter From Space* with a project called Relounge. Ten years later he took part in the German version of The Voice TV show.

In The Spotlight

▶II

Charles Simmons *singer, producer*

Published with the permission of Charles Simmons.

How did you get involved with dance music? How were you chosen for The Free?

I first met Felix Gauder in 1993. He was just getting started in the music business and we worked together with some other producers in our hometown, Stuttgart. We had a small project called NOW and released our first single in 1993. After that project, I recorded some demos for him and later on, he asked me if I would like to be part of a project he was working on. That project was The Free.

The Free was Felix J.Gauder's Project. Did you ever feel that you were left on the shadow by other Felix's projects like E-Rotic who had huge success?

I wouldn't say that I felt left out because of the success of E-Rotic or Das Modul. They were unique and dealt with a subject that everybody loves: sex. It was a formula that worked, and I was very happy for him and his success.

The Free had also more soulful songs like *Love Letter From Space*. Did you feel more comfortable singing those than full-on eurodance songs?

I felt very comfortable singing the songs, especially because I was allowed to sing 😊 Don't forget: in the beginning, I was the rapper for The Free. Our first three single releases in Germany were all in the typical "male rapper + female singer" format. Our song *Shout!* was the first time I got to sing in the project.

What other dance projects you were involved with and in what capacity?

After The Free, I did some studio work for a few other dance acts, mostly background vocals. I then became a very active live singer, performing in many different cover bands. I started producing r & b and house music and eventually started my own label in 2005.

Are you still in music business?

I am still active as a musician and producer, but not in the music business. I've been a vocal coach and teacher since 2008 and have worked with a lot of successful international pop stars, the most famous one currently is Alice Merton (hit song *No Roots*). She is one of my students. I was also on the German version of The Voice in 2011-2012. I'm also a fitness trainer and the creator of VOXXBODY, the world's first workout to combine fitness and singing.

Is The Free ever going to make a comeback?

The Free was a fun project and I was proud to be a part of it. However, there are no plans for a revival of the group.

▶ *Lian Ross*

published with permission of Team 33 Music.

Josephine Hiebel (aka Lian Ross, b.1962) is a woman behind many dance projects although the larger audience doesn't recognize her name. With the alias Lian Ross she got rather big hits in the 1980's with italo disco songs like *Fantasy* and *Say You'll Never*.

In the 1990's she was involved in a eurodance band called Tears'N'Joy. Luis Rodriquez (who is Lian's husband and has produced her music since the 80's) was behind the band. The band released a couple singles like the Dolly Parton cover *I Will Always Love You* before releasing the album *Enjoy*.

Enjoy is regrettably one of the most overlooked euro albums. Despite its boring cover art, it's an explosion of melodic eurodance from start to finish. Made with more durable sounds than many other contemporaries, it's a must-have for euro fans who want to dive more deeper into the sound. The little attention it had was probably due to the fact that it was only released in Spain.

Under Lian Ross alias, she released a full-fledged eurodance song called *Keep This Feeling* (1994). It was a really great release, and that's why it's a shame that she didn't release any more pure blooded euro songs. She has continued her career through the decades playing around with various dance music genres. Ross released her first solo albums not until 2013. Lately she has returned to italo disco sound.

In addition to the previously mentioned projects she has been the lead singer for 2 Eivissa and sang for Fun Factory's two albums. She has also had pseudonyms, through which she has featured in numerous projects.

▶ Loft

Published with the permission of Courtney Williams.

Loft, who was founded by Jamaican brothers Richard and Courtney Williams, used various female vocalists in their songs. For example, eurodance legends like Lori Glori and Christiane Eiben gave their contribution to Loft songs.

Because the brothers' ethnic background, first release was summery euro reggae *Summer* Summer, but only the second single *Hold On* built up to be a moderate hit. Nosie Katzmann (of Culture Beat's *Mr. Vain* fame) had given them his golden touch with *Hold On*. Fast, but also a ragga-influenced song, was sung by Kim Sanders. It wasn't that popular in the 90's but in retrospect, the song has been lifted in the canon of eurodance music.

Debut album *Wake The World* (1994) was released in a totally green CD cover. According to Eurokdj, Gina Mohammed sang the female vocals in this LP. The next album *Future World* (1995) had yellow CD cover and it took a more extensive step toward eurodance, having less reggae sounds than the previous one. It reminded a bit like the sound of DJ Bobo and Captain Hollywood Project. This was because of the fact that the producers were partially same as with those artists, like Axel Breitung. Singles released from this LP, like *Don't Stop Me Now* (Germany single chart position 61), didn't raise much attention. Also, the main singer had changed to Sandra Steinborn.

But Loft's story was far from over. They released sunny latino euro called *Mallorca*, which was a perfect summer song. *Long John Silver* single on the other hand was a naive bubblegum reggae. After these singles they went on a hiatus...

..which lasted for a couple of years. But when the 90's acts like Snap! and Culture Beat started to update their biggest hits in the beginning of the millennium, also Loft decided to remake their first single with new vocals. *Summer Summer (Recall)* was a moderate success so they released a brand new song *Still No 1*, which was reggae once again. Other songs followed: *Gigolo*, which was a fairly faster reggae and *Love Can't Be Wrong,* a bit boring ballad. According to Eurokdj, they had planned to release a new album around that time, but nothing came out.

109

In The Spotlight

▶️ II

Courtney Williams *singer*

Published with the permission of Courtney Williams.

How Loft was born? And what does the band name stand for?

Loft was a put together by a German Producer named Michael Eisler from DMP Dance Music Productions with myself Courtney and late brother Richard Williams in 1993.The concept came together when we were invited to do a track for a well-known German song writer Nosie Katzmann. The song (*Summer Summer*) went straight into the Media Control Top 100 Charts and it was in Top 10 of the best songs of that year 1993. From there began the story of Loft.

Live Our Father's Teachings is the meaning of LOFT. Simply stated means we all should learn from our ancestors and try to live this life from what we have learned from them. May it be good or bad we should apply the best of ourselves to make this world a better place for the generations that come after us.

Loft used a lot of different female vocalists, why is that?

Yes, we used different females for different reasons. Firstly I must say that I have no problems with all the singers of the Loft project but after the first album was done and we toured Europe, Gina Mohammed (the first singer of the project) decided to leave the group and go to the United States with her boyfriend who she became pregnant from and got married and started her family life. With this situation we had no choice but to wish her all the best with her decision and gave her our blessings.

So that's how the change of females started. The show had to go on, so Sandra Steinborn was brought into the project by our then management. After the second album was completed we went on tour and the internal problems came up between Sandra and the manager. And then Sue was brought in later by the same manager, she was the producer's girlfriend. She sang with Loft songs as *Still no.1* and *We Pray*. After that experience we had a totally different opinion of where Loft was heading. Especially that she was being the main voice on all his productions was not ok with us. So, it was at this point that my brother and I decided to show them who was Loft in case they had forgotten. So, we smartly got out of the management contract.

Loft remained in the shadows until 2016 when a promoter from Lima, Peru linked me and wanted Loft to do a show in Lima. He literally begged me to do the show because after my late brother passed on four years ago I had never thought of ever doing a Loft gig again. But with encouragement from friends and family I put the group back together with Richards son as his replacement and Gina Mohammed and did the show in Lima which was a new starting point for the new Loft. Thanks to Gonzalo Terry I should mention.

You released two albums; how do they differ from each other? Do you think that the then current eurodance sound changed in a year?

Very good question! If one listens to the both albums there is definitely a difference. The first album was a completely different sound with quality and sound, but the second album was with a different studio Cyborg which at the time had a brand new digital mix board Euphnonics, which made the *Future World* album. The first single *Don't Stop Me Now,* which only featured the then new singer Sandra, which was a very unwise move on the Cyborg team. They brought a new singer in the project and then the Loft sound was gone. So, they made new sound with techno and with some euro reggae and eurodance songs, that's what you hear on the *Future World*. So, the difference between the two albums is obviously two different set of producers and studios.

At this point the industry was rapidly changing so the music scene was taking a new form. Creative new music was being published by the companies so the eurodance scene was slowly fading away. So, there was a need to also ride the waves and change with the changes which one would notice with the songs after the *Future World* album. So for sure the music did not only change in a year but it kept on changing and was basically replaced with German songs, from r'n'b, hip hop, ballads, rock was all changed to German songs with other cultures music and melodies being sung in German text and it was the new direction of the German music groups.

It's just a few years now that eurodance is being requested and music of the artists and groups of the 90's are now being booked to bring back the great sound and songs of that era.

You had euro reggae songs also, do you like reggae more than eurodance?

I love all types of music but being Jamaican it's natural to love reggae music especially that Bob Marley's music has been so influential all over the world. Time Magazine named him the greatest song writer of the last millennium. With that said I also lived in Germany for many years and eurodance was invented while I was living there so of course I love eurodance too.

Actually, *Summer Summer* was the first combination of eurodance and reggae fusion which worked perfectly for the time it was made.

Mallorca is a very cool summer track, what inspired you to make that song?

Mallorca was fun. Making the song and video the inspiration came up because of Ballamann Mallorca where Germans actually own that town. It's a party place where people from all over Europe spend their vacation having a great time just being free from the everyday life of work work work.

Actually, we were in Mexico with 20 other groups from Europe and while on tour *Mallorca* hit no.1 there , that was great vibes for Loft back then. Believe it or not it was not shown in Germany.

But the song was really about Mallorca itself which is a very beautiful island similar to Jamaica with a Spanish culture. I loved it there.

Your sound changed drastically around the millennium (no more eurodance), why is that?

Yes, it did, but as I stated earlier that the industry was changing so at that point eurodance was on the decline so doing the euro reggae was natural to us just as *Summer Summer* was. That was the main reason eurodance had faded out. You can do the research to see for yourself. Our euro reggae tracks were never really pushed by the Germans even though Loft's first hit was a eurodance reggae.

Now Loft only does shows from our past hits but as far as a new Loft single is concerned it has to be backed by the right engines and crew before I go into any productions. Until then look out for us on tour.

Much Love and Respect Maximum.

On behalf of my late brother Richard Williams RIP, Gina Mohammed, Sandra Steinborn, Sue and myself we would like to thank all who had made this possible and to all our fans all over the world, we love you all.

▶ *Intermission*

Legendary foursome production crew DMP was responsible for the awesome sounds of Intermission. The team consisted for example from Nosie Katzmann and Thorsten Adler. They got their name from the words *Dance Music Production*. Often they cooperated with a duo Cyborg (Marc Kamradt ja Frank Schlingloff). Their mutual respect and coordination were so natural that later they joined to become a super production team Cyborg DMP GmbH.

So German Intermission's sound was on capable hands. First, fairly rough, single was *Honesty* (1993), which was sung by Nina Gerhard. It had some success but the next song, *Piece Of My Heart,* would turn out to be eurodance classic. It borrowed the melody from synth-pop band Real Life's *Send Me An Angel* –hit but adds another layer to it with Valerie Scott's greatly vocalized refrain. It struck into euro people's heart and it got its 15 minutes of fame, it was 12 weeks in Germanys single chart Top 20. The next single, *Six Days* (feat. Lori Glori) fared also quite well.

Their only album *Piece Of My Heart* was put out in 1995, but the single *Give Peace A Chance* released in the same year, was overshadowed by the previous hits. *Planet Love* (sung by Raquel Gomez) single took the project into a happier hardcore direction. Captain Hollywood Project had triumphed with that sound, so Intermission tried to take a page out of their book. The cheerful *All Together Now* and *Miracle Of Love* singles gave more of the same..

The last new song from them has been *Blow Your Mind (with DJ M.A.R.S.S)* which was far away from eurodance being more progressive house and trance. The project fell asleep, only to be awoken briefly in 2003 when trance duo Grey & Frost updated their biggest hit *Piece Of My Heart* into a modern hard trance sound.

In The Spotlight

▶❚❚

Lori Glori singer

Published with the permission of Lori Glori.

You are an American singer; how did you end up in Europe to sing dance music?

I came to Europe in 1983 with a group called Bill Summers and Summers Heat. We had top ten hits in America and a Gold Album *Call It What You Want*. We toured England and Germany for six months. When it was time to get on the plane back to America, at the Frankfurt Airport I turned around and never went back, making Europe my home forever.

Intermission is maybe your best known project. How did you become the singer of that band?

I had one of the first dance hits called *My Body And Soul* produced by Frank Farian after the Milli Vanilli scandal which didn't do so good cause music world was very disappointed at the time with Frank , but the song got me recognition in the eurodance scene and I was approached by the DMP production team for Intermission to be the face and voice of the project.

You've sang in other projects too, what kind of memories do you have for example working with DJ Bobo or Turbo B. (Centory)?

Yes, my voice was on many hit projects all at one time and the memories are not happy ones because I was deceived. I had no idea they would use my voice and not let me perform. But I don't think about it anymore. I have forgiven and moved on; my day will come.

What kind of music do you like to sing the most?

I love inspirational music. That's what I call my new music

Eurodance is a worldwide phenomenon, what makes it popular, in your opinion?

Eurodance was music that made you happy and free.

In many eurodance projects it was common to use different people in videos and in publicity than the ones who sang the songs, what do you think of that?

I think it's a very sad thing if you're not in agreement with it.

Do you have favorite eurodance acts, and if so, who?

I loved Culture Beat because of Tania Evans' unique voice and the songs were great.

114

What the future has in store for you?

Have a new single coming in February (2020). My book is now in English to be released in May and a film documentary in the making and teaching vocal lessons to children as well as cooking my soul food cuisine.

▶ *Odyssey*

While 90's Europe was a cornucopia of eurodance, many acts fell into oblivion. Odyssey was one of those acts. It shared a name with a 1970's disco group which had some hits. Odyssey lacked a one standout hit that would have been engraved in dance music's history books.

According to Discogs, the project was a family effort with Martin, Giorgio, Suna and Gabi Koppehele while Lisa Cash sang the vocals. *Let Yourself Go* raised some interest and the public was given more music: . *Talk To Me,* very traditionally named *Move Your Body* and *Riding On A Train,* which represents the best material from this group.

The album *Love Train* (1994) collected all the single releases, but it was only released in Germany. This is a shame because it's one of the purest eurodance albums out there.

Odyssey didn't become discouraged by the meager distribution of their LP, instead they decided to put out new songs like *Face To Face* and *Boom Boom Free Your Mind*. You might have guessed that their story ended there, but that was not the case: in 1999 they released a second album *Boom Boom,* also in Germany. Although eurodance wasn't popular anymore at that time, their second effort is surprisingly euro although it has traces of trance. Also, the female singer had been changed to Suna. After this they disappeared from the scene.

▶ *Future Beat / Megatronic*

Peter Ballweg-produced Future Beat falls into the same category as Odyssey: a band who made decent eurodance but failed to achieve that big mega hit.

Future Beat stayed quite faceless from beginning to end, even the CD covers were decorated with scifi-like, abstract design. Despite the anonymity they used at least four different rappers in their songs like Ian Carma, who featured on the first release, *It's My Party* (1993). It was a cover from a Lesley Gore's sugary pop hit from 1963. Future Beat's version was far from basic pop, incorporating heavy trance sounds.

After the cover it was time to release original material like *Faith The Night* and *Destiny*. They received some attention and moderate chart positions. The songs were collected on the LP *Destiny*, which is maybe the best and purest eurodance albums. It has a kind of a cult status; Its CD version value is something between 50 to 100 euros.

After a couple of years silence, they put out *Dancin Factory*, which was a fairly light piano/euro house, in the vain of Alex Party. In the same year 1996 they released a more euro song, *100% Pure Love*, which used the same kind of flute sound as was used in the Dance 2 Trance classic *The Power Of American Natives*.

Another Ballweg's project was Megatronic, who got some success with a song Power *Of Dancing* (1994). This song was also put on the Future Beat's album under the name Future Beat feat. Megatronic. Ballweg released new versions of the hit in 1997 and 2000. I prefer the *Into The Fire* single, especially because it was sung by eurodance queen Kristina Safrany. Megatronic's short saga ended in 1998 with the odd freestyle song *Electric Operator*.

▶ *General Base*

German DJ Thomas Kukula (b.1959) felt that just playing music wasn't enough for him, so he set up a dance project in the beginning of the 90's called General Base, through which he could exercise his creativity more extensively. He had started his career in small clubs in Düsseldorf. The first singles from General Base were instrumentals like *Mein Gott, Es Ist Voller Sterne,* but they already had a distinctive eurodance sound.

Breakthrough happened when Thomas managed to get disco queen Claudja Barry to sing on the *Poison* (1993) single. She had had a string of disco and hi-NRG hits in the 70's and in the 80's. While a rising artist Thomas got credit, also Claudja was re-introduced to a new generation. *Poison* gathered fame in Europe, Israel and even some parts in the US.

In the same year, Thomas released the projects only album, *First.* After this release he ganged up with rapper Michael Kassner and few female singers and the result was their biggest hit to date, *Base Of Love*, although the biggest success was in their home country. With this hit, the album was re-released containing *Base Of Love* .

Published with permission of Thomas Kukula.

General Base released a few additional singles in the 90's but Thomas started to concentrate more on his Red 5 project, as the general music trends changed. Red 5 had several more club-oriented hits like   *I Love You...Stop,* which conquered charts all over Europe. In addition to this he had other dance projects like THK, which was progressive house and trance.

Later Kukula updated *Base Of Love* in 2003 into a natural trance form and *Poison* in 2011 with typical EDM style.

Published with permission of Thomas Kukula.

117

In The Spotlight

▶II

Thomas Kukula *producer*

How General Base started?

The first General Base (GB)track was *Mein Gott, Es Ist Voller Sterne* which translates: *my god, it's full of stars*. It was a great success. That was the same time I wrote Candy Beat, *Saxy*. Candy Beat was wanted by two companies. EMI was the first - Rough Trade 2nd. So Rough Trade got *Mein Gott...* and EMI got *Saxy*. That was the beginning of GB. General Base was musically more my style, so I invested more energy in it. With the song *Poison* (Vocals by Claudja Barry) GB started with vocal trance/(euro-)dance. After that I casted (with help from Woody van Eyden) the right people for General Base, with Sarah, MIC + dancers and wrote *Base Of Love, I See You...*

Which songs were your biggest hits and why do you think those were the songs that rose to fame?

GB: *Poison* and *Base Of Love*, RED 5: *Da Beat Goes* & *I Love You...Stop, Lift Me Up*

I think with these songs I was at the right place at the right time. I was a DJ ; I saw what the people liked and so I produced songs what I liked myself. It was a mix of what I and the crowd liked.

Tell me a little bit about your creative work with *Base Of Love?*

In fact, I worked a long time on *Base Of Love*. It was ready and I gave it to the record company - and a few weeks later I called Rough Trade and decided that I must change the song. They said OK and I worked again a few weeks on it. After that I was satisfied.

1997 seems to be last year for General Base with the song *On & On*, was it because declining popularity of eurodance?

Ending GB was not the aim. I produced *Da Beat Goes* and heard that the style did not fit into General Base. That's how RED5 came into being. With RED5 *Da Beat Goes*, pizzicato-house was born.

How would you say General Base's and Red 5's sounds differ from each other?

I see GB more a dance/trance/eurodance - project. RED5 was more housy/dance and more progressive with pizzicato sounds.

As a music producer, how you see the dance music sounds have changed in the last 25 years? What are your feelings about EDM?

There were many decades of dance music. End of 80's = acid & house, early 90's = techno with harder/aggressive sounds, after that came eurodance, Pizzicato house and happy hardcore. I like EDM, but the deeper house of that genre.

Anything else you want to add?

The first GB song had help from Ramon Zenker & Jens Lissat (Interactive) - I was very grateful for that, which also inspired me to help newcomers: in the early 90's a young guy gave me a demo tape with an interesting song on it. So, we produced this song together in my old studio. Now he is one of the most successful DJ's in Europe: ATB!

▶ *Activate*

In 1995, published with the permission of Thomas Detert.

Activate enticed people to dance, even with its name. Four producers and musicians founded the band in 1993: Thomas Detert, Mike Griesheimer, Manfred Poppe and

119

Nicole Wetzel. Thomas and Mike were the bands rappers while the female vocalists changed.

Nicole, who was one of the four, vocalized the first single, *Let The Rhythm Take Control*, after which he left the band due to personal reasons. Also Manfred left in the beginning to start his own project, X-Fade, which released only one single. Nicole was replaced with Rachelle Rack.

Let The Rhythm Take Control and the follow-up, *Beat Of The Drum,* had succeeded satisfactorily, that the record company greenlighted the album, *Visions* (1994). Rachelle re-sung the first single for the album replacing Nicole's vocals.

The first chart hit came with *Save Me*. With this song they were accepted into the company of other euro royals like Masterboy. They even toured with them.

After the recording of their album, the band faced loss once again: Rachelle returned to USA, and she was replaced with Nanni Zagar. The choice was great because she is still with the band.

After eurodance hysteria had calmed down, Thomas and Mike decided to set up a music production company. Activate was forgotten and they established a devilish progressive house project, 666, which enjoyed massive success all over Europe with hits like *Alarma*. Activate's songs were recycled with 666: *Alarma* had been on Activate's album and it was remade to fit satanic needs with 666. Also, the project covered Activate's *Let The Rhythm Take Control,* with a title *Rhythm Takes Control*. Later in the 2000's, the guys also started an electro house project, Vinylshakerz.

While Thomas and Mike were busy with 666, Activate's old record company Dance Street decided to release under Activate's name a new song called *Fall In Love With You*, without asking for permission of the original members. It should never have been published, because the songs euro reggae sound doesn't do justice to Activate.

New Activate songs resurfaced in 2012, when a digital EP *Lost & Found* was released. It contained previously unreleased songs and a rare 1996 version of the debut single. Also 90's nostalgia had started to raise its head and so Activate was reactivated. New song *Spotlight* was a throwback of the great 90's eurodance days. Nowadays Mike and Nanni tour as Activate in 90's festivals.

Mike Griesheimer and Nanni Zagar are Activate, published with permission of Thomas Detert

In The Spotlight

Thomas Detert producer

published with the permission of Thomas Detert

How did Activate start?

I already had a little studio due to the fact that I was working in the games industry. Then I met Mike and we decided to do a track together, which was *Let The Rhythm Take Control.*

What other dance projects you have been involved with?

Production wise are: DEEN, Eddy .N and IN-Motion

What led you to produce eurodance?

It was the Sound of that time, and on top of it we loved the music.

How would you define eurodance?

Well, that's a tough question, but eurodance always gave me a good feeling. Very positive vibe so to speak.

Has the band gained more success because of 90's being so popular again?

No unfortunately not more success, but the interest in the group has grown a bit again, but nothing to write home about to be honest.

Is it easier to make eurodance than other dance music? Or harder?

I found it always easier than other genres.

You released *Spotlight* in 2016 and its pure eurodance heaven. Was it a hard decision to make 90's sound or to make EDM which is so popular also?

No, for us it was no question at all. We always said, that if we do a new track for Activate one day, it will be as authentic as possible. Kind of a big thank you to the fans of our music if you like.

How do you see 90's eurodance compared todays EDM?

EDM is just a new dance genre, I like some of the tunes, but it has not a fan base like eurodance had or still has. Cannot really compare both, both have their pros and cons.

Is Activate going to make more songs?

You never know ;-)

▶ *Sqeezer*

Despite its happy and positive attitude, Sqeezer faced some misfortune. A model Jim Reeves founded this very colorful and cheesy band in 1995. Sqeezer has had a long line of changing members, but Reeves was always a member. Also, it has been a kind of open secret that Alexandra Prince has been the real voice behind their songs.

In 1995 *Scandy Randy* was released, which offered bubblegum vocals with a definite eurodance vibe. Everybody seemed to fancy *Blue Jeans*, because it fared quite well, for example in Spanish single chart. Also, *Sweet Kisses* was a big hit there. The fame was sealed with a provocatively named *Drop Your Pants* (1996).

Sqeezer decorated their eurodance with a 50's imagery, ideology and sounds and samples of that era. In the same manner as Pharao had its Egypt, in Sqeezer's videos people strolled on the beach in dated swimsuits and everything was cute and sweet and wholesome, although a bit sarcastically.

The first tragedy that the band faced, was that one of the band members, Marc Theven, committed suicide. They were supposed to go on a tour in Spain, but it had to be canceled. In addition to that, they were shaken by the fact that Marc left a letter, in which he blamed the other members for his suicide.

Still Sqeezer managed to collect their ranks and released a single *Tamagotchi* (1997), which became the official song of that virtual toy. The Danish bubblegum band Daze had a song with the same name (and around the same time), but they were forced to rename their song into *The Cyber Pet Song*.

Sqeezer's style faced a drastic change on the second album. Singles like *Wake Up!* predicted a completely different style, which was closer to hip hop than dance music. *Streetlife* (1998) album had maybe street credibility (at least if you asked members of the band) but the fans quickly turned their backs to them.. Sqeezer still released in the beginning of the 2000's a few singles like *Hot Ski Teeny,* which was an official theme song for a winter event Apres Ski-Hits 2004.

Second tragedy befell them in 2016 when two Polish young men tortured the 47 year old founding member Jim Reeves so that he died from his wounds. The motive was homophobic.

Nevertheless, the tragedies, the band sold over million records and it is hard to find a band who is genuinely happy, and whose positivity isn't superimposed.

LET THE BEAT GO ON - SWEDEN

In addition to Germany, Sweden was one of the most important production countries of eurodance. Compared to Germany, the Swedish made their euro with a lot more care: they used better singers and the frontmen didn't look so cheap compared to German counterparts. Even in the short-lived projects, the members were clearly visible in record covers and videos. Ever since Abba, the Swedish have mastered the art of writing catchy pop songs and this is also clearly visible in eurodance. Even the producer legend Max Martin, did eurodance in the 90's, (E-Type, Herbie).

▶ *Pandora*

Published with permission of Anneli Magnusson.

Beautiful blond singer, Anneli Magnusson (b.1970) was from a small district, near Västerås. Three guys, (Henrik Andersson, Martin Ankelius and Peka P. and Hit Vision) from Anneli's hometown was looking for a singer for their dance project. They were searching a voice with attitude. They turned to local music high school, where they were advised to talk to Anneli. Demo recordings led to first single, *Trust Me* (1993). Anneli was given an artist name, Pandora.

The song became an instant hit with its hard euro sound and strong refrain. It went immediately into Top 5 in Sweden and it sold so well that it became the most sold single in Sweden that year. In other Nordic countries (and in Israel) the song was a hit. Fairly quickly the debut album *One Of A Kind* was released, and it was a fierce collection of hard eurodance. Couple of other singles like the more cheerful *Come On And Do It* and a ballad *Something's Gone* were released from the album.

Anneli in Come On And Do It music video shoot.
Published with the permission of Peter Johansson.

The next album, *Tell The World* (1995), was still mainly eurodance, but it had more lighter shades of pop. The first single from it carried the albums name and was euro reggae in the vain of Ace Of Base. The next single *Don't You Know*, has turned out to be one of the biggest classics of euro, alongside the debut *Trust Me*. It was accompanied by a colorful music video with drag queens and such. The next single *The Naked Sun* was an oriental hit and it was Pandora's fifth Top 5 single in Finland. Her big success in Finland was evident, even the second album got a deluxe edition in Finland, added with *One Of Us* EP.

In the beginning of her career, Pandora was on everybody's lips, but not always in a positive sense. After *Tell The World* album a certain newspaper wrote about her with a headline album "talentless and tacky blond". According to them, Pandora was just another dull eurodisco artist, who nobody could remember the next day. They couldn't have been more wrong..

Changes (1996) was, like its name, a change to a lighter side. Like any other eurodance artist, Pandora had noticed that she couldn't keep on doing the same sound if she were to have a longer music career. *A Little Bit* single from *Chances* was a bit dry euro reggae and the really light house song *Smile'n'Shine* was even

125

released in the UK. Only song worth mentioning from this album, was a melancholic Latino song *The Sands Of Time*.

Fortunately, the next LP *This Could Be Heaven* (1997) was a step for the better, in my opinion. Although it had only one thoroughbred eurodance song (*Shout It Out*), it had generally a happier tone compared to *Changes*. New albums sound had taken influences from euro house, euro reggae and hi-NRG.

Especially during the second album, Anneli had started to become a celebrity in Japan. For example. *Tell The World* was famous ZIP FM –radio stations most popular song for six months. While her popularity in other parts of the world diminished in the 90's, she was still a big thing in Japan. This happened with many other eurodance bands too: when the artist vanished from the charts for Europeans, it meant that he/she was focusing on Asian market (for example Solid Base and Look Twice). In Pandora's case, she released a bunch of albums in Japan. She also got to record the official theme song, *Spirit To Win*, for Nagano Winter Olympics in 1998.

After the turn of the millennium, she was reintroduced to Scandinavians with the pop album *Won't Look Back* (2002). It was a soulmate of *Changes* but with an even more acoustic sound. It had also some songs previously released on Japan-only albums. Still this wasn't such a big hit album.

Anneli tried another approach in order to remind the public who she is. She took part in Swedish Melodifestivalen (Swedish Eurovision Song Contest tryouts) with a song *You* (2003) but couldn't even make it to the finals. In the wake of this, new LP *9 Lives* ,was released, but it was more of the same poppy sound. She still didn't give up: next year she took part again with *Runaway,* but this either didn't make it to the finals.

Pandora's connections to Eurovision Song Contest didn't end there. In 2007 she claimed that the British contestant Scooch's *Flying The Flag* was plagiarized from her song *No Regrets*. BBC responded by stating that the Scooch's song writers weren't even aware of Pandora's song, so her songs have not been copied.

Popstar Kylie Minogue loaned Pandoras song *On A Night Like This*. Pandora was angry for a reason. Kylie had gotten the song from the same songwriter. Anneli said that the song hadn't appeared in an album in its publication year 1999, but she had performed it live.

Pandora's career wasn't without misfortunes outside the music world. She was sentenced in 2003 of a tax fraud. She had let her then husband to manage her company and economy and the man had done several accounting violations in her name. She was sentenced a hundred hours of community service, but the verdict was revoked in 2016. The marriage ended in divorce.

In terms of music, there was light at the end of the tunnel. 2007 gave birth to a musical project called United DJ's VS Pandora, which gave new life to many Pandora classics by remixing them to a new generation. Among the best, was Vasco & Millboy's remix of *Trust Me*. Pandora seems to like it also, because she performs that version in live gigs. Collection of these reinterpretations was released with the under the album title *Celebration*. While it didn't have much success in Sweden (album chart position 38), demand for Pandora's live performances increased.

I believe that after this album, Pandora realized that the public wanted dance music from her. For the time being, a pure dance album *Head Up High* (2011) has been her latest LP, it had many interesting songs in different styles, like electro house *You Believed* and synth-pop *You Woke My Heart* ft. the Finnish JS16.

Anneli has become a mainstay in many 90's music festivals. After her adversities and musical misses, she has embraced her status as a Nordic dance queen. She has also found love with Finnish former ice hockey player, Mikko Peltonen.

In The Spotlight

▶️II

Peter Johansson producer

Published with the permission of Peter Johansson.

Tell me a little about your musical background, how did you end up in producing dance music?

I started playing the drums at the age of 12 or 13, heavily inspired by (and a huge fan of) British bands such as Iron Maiden, Saxon and Motörhead. I was a long-haired metal-head at the time and played in a band called Headline in the mid-eighties. We weren't very successful, and I later turned to playing the piano to be able to create. Having known Henrik for quite some time we decided to invest in some equipment and we then – with great help from my father- built our first own studio in the garage of my parent's house. So, you could really say that Pandora from the beginning was a true garage band!

What was/is your role in Pandora?

In the late 80's my friend Henrik Andersson and I were producing dance pop tunes using very rudimentary equipment such as a couple of synths, a sampler and a drum machine – all being controlled via a classic Atari 1040ST. We needed someone to sing our songs and we tried out a lot of different local singers from Västerås, where we were based at the time, but none of them had what we were looking for. I eventually asked my piano teacher if he knew someone and he immediately responded he knew one girl that had that special voice. The girl in question was of course Anneli Pandora Magnusson and we started working together around 1988. We later teamed up with Martin Ankelius and then started working on what would later be "Pandora" in 1993 when our debut single *Trust Me* was released. It was a huge success and actually became the biggest selling Swedish single that year. So to answer your question, my role in this constellation has always been a combination of a songwriter and a producer.

Pandora's sound was full-on eurodance at the beginning but started to change soon to a more pop sound. Why is that?

You are absolutely right. The first two albums were both pure eurodance with some additions of reggae-pop and that changed a bit with the third album. I mean, even the name of the third album was *Changes* so something was definitely happening. We basically wanted to develop Pandora to be more melodic and have greater variation to the songs. If I remember correctly we only had one track featuring rap for instance. The album overall is a lot more melancholic than its two predecessors. Unfortunately, it didn't do so well in Sweden, but it sold gold in Finland and platinum in Japan, so we didn't complain. Worth mentioning is that three of the songs on the *Changes* album have been covered by other artists, *Smile'n'shine* by Irish boy band NV, *Sands Of Time* by Finnish singer Maarit Peltoniemi and *Why* by Russian singer Larisa Chernikova.

Have you produced other eurodance projects? If you have could you tell a little about them?

Yes, I have – but none of them being close to the success of Pandora, so let's just leave it there. I have officially declared myself retired from the music industry since 1998 but I have done some writing after that primarily for metal bands such as Swedish industry metal band PAIN and Swedish melodic death metal band The Unguided. Actually, an old Pandora song which I wrote (and never got recorded) was transformed into a metal song and released by the band Sunset Force in 2015. Have a listen to the song *Let's Go Get Crazee* and imagine what it would have sounded with Pandora singing!

Peter, Ken (Pandora's first rapper), Henrik and Martin in the studio in 1993. Published with the permission of Peter Johansson.

Pandora is very popular in Japan, why do you think that many eurodance artists have had big success there?

This is a topic that has been discussed many times over the years and I believe the common opinion is that Swedish music has a melancholic touch to it which appeals to Japanese people.

Your feelings about the 90's dance music? How would you compare it to today's dance music?

I simply love 90's dance music! I grew up in that era, I had the privilege of contributing to the scene and I had a truly great time in my life. Compared to today's dance music? Back in the days dance music was accused of sounding "too programmed" or "too sterile" but compared to today's dance music I must say there was a lot more variation to the music than today. I mean, in the early 90's we used a lot of different hardware. We ended up having tons of synthesizers and samplers. We spent an enormous amount of time sampling loops and sounds from different sources combining them with preset sounds from commercial synths creating something unique – in my opinion. We also recorded the music to old-school tape in a real studio. Today, you produce music on a laptop using software synths, which gives you a somewhat flat and sterile sound for sure – also in my opinion. I am aware I am now generalizing a bit and I'm not saying this is bad, it is just my observation how technology has been a key driver in how dance music is being produced today.

What do you think is eurodance's legacy to today's music?

Dance music still exists, and today's EDM scene is simply eurodance evolved. I am really happy that we now, 25+ years later, have huge festivals such as We Love The 90's. This is proof that we all made a huge impact in the early nineties and I am really proud to have played a (small) part of that.

Anything else you want to share?

Well, a lot of crazy things happened during this period in time – both good and bad, but I think it's better to keep that for Pandora's biography which I know she has in the works :)

▶ *Basic Element*

Basic Element today: Peter in the middle.
Published with the permission of Peter Thelenius

If I had to choose the best eurodance band, for me it would be Basic Element. Bands fiery sound and raw expression have appealed to me from the very start.

The original line-up consisted of rapper Peter Thelenius (aka Petrus, b. 1973), singer Zetma Prenbo and keyboardist Cesar Zamini. Peter and Cesar were friends from Malmö, who wanted to earn some money and pop stardom was one way to achieve that. According to Eurokdj they met Zetma at a job center and recruited her to their band. Zetma sang and EMI released their first single, *Move Me* (1993), but it didn't raise much interest.

But the next single, *The Promise Man* (1994), was one of the most played songs on the radio in Sweden and was number one in almost every dance chart in Scandinavia. The album *Basic Injection* gave a 100 percent pure eurodance album, one of the best euro albums ever. No ballads, no euro reggae, just pure euro heaven. It's also very rare to find an album with no fillers and this had catchy dance songs from top to bottom. In addition to singles like *Touch,* there was also great album tracks like *Lights N Fire*. In Sweden it sold 35 000 units.

When Zetma got pregnant, B.E. had to find a new female singer (later Zetma sang with another Swedish euro band Magic Motion). Peter and Cesar also met the new singer in an everyday environment, at the supermarket. Fiercely looking Ethiopian Saunet Sparell (b.1971) gave an even better voice to bands fast rhythm.

Basic Element's sound changed to even faster. Saunet's image was much bolder and more aggressive than Zetma's. The first single with Saunet, *The Ride,* gave us a glimpse of what she was made of. In the video she has kidnapped the guys and is transporting them to somewhere on a speedboat. The other singles released from the new LP *The Ultimate Ride* (1995), were the same aggressive style. *The Fiddle, This Must Be A Dream* and *Queen Of Love* have all left their marks on euro fans hearts. Especially it's hard to forget *The Fiddle* with lyrics like these: *"The Fiddle will play loud and clear, rip up all your underwear, hypnotized like a mad man's eye, you can't run away"*.

Saunet commemorates her time in the band:
"My biggest gift from this time is the memories that people still stop me in the streets to tell me. To have had an impact on people's life is truly a blessing".
Published with the permission of Saunet Sparell

The Ultimate Ride is truly an amazing journey. Listener doesn't get any mercy in this ultimate dance party, until the end with the hip hop *Who's That Boy.* The crew had obviously been inspired by The Prodigy because the song, *The Cross,* sounds like an offspring of *Voodoo People.* The album is pure eurodance joy and I would definitely say it's one of best albums of this genre.

According to Eurokdj, around the second album there was some conflicts between the members which as a result led to Cesar leaving the band. Peter won the rights to the band's name and continued in B.E. with Saunet and the producer Stefan Andersson. Departure of Cesar meant a total stylistic change. Cesar tried to lift-off his own solo career with an alias Cezar, but managed to produce only one single, *I Want To (Oh-Ah)*.

For many Basic Element fans, the new single *The Shame* (1996) was probably quite a shock. They had given up their natural sound and even eurodance. *The Shame* was a 70's disco pastiche. Also, Petrus' previous hairstyle (spikes with dyed silver) had changed to dreadlocks. The third album *Star Tracks* was also a big disappointment, because it had only one good dance song, *Rule Your World*. Otherwise it was disco, ballads and drum'n' bass. You can easily say that this album is the least favorite among B.E. fans, because the change of sound was so massive.

After the poor performance of *Star Tracks,* Petrus probably felt that it was time to try a solo career. He released Roxette cover *Listen To Your Heart* and *China In Your Hand*, which was an old T'Pau song. Petrus 'own style was from dance music, it was hip hop, although with a Scandinavian flavor. *Trust Then Pain* LP (1997) followed, it also contained the hip hop song, which had been on the second B.E. album. His solo career didn't last farther than this.

Basic Element was in shambles, because Saunet left the band after the flop album.

After the dark Saunet, it was time to bring in a blond girl, Marie Fredriksson (not the Roxette singer). Petrus heard accidentally Marie singing in the studio and realized that her voice reminded Saunet's voice. Petrus asked Marie to join and Marie agreed.

With the new singer, band was once again renewed. Previous ultralight style gave way to harder beats (once again), this time the sound had shades of trance and progressive house. *Rok The World* and *Love 4 Real* singles were fairly familiar Basic Element and the album *The Earthquake* (1998) told even with its name that the hard B.E. had come back! Although the it's a really good dance album, it still doesn't reach on the same level of the first two albums. Although the content was good, the success wasn't great.

After their fourth album they decided to go on a break. The band entered the new 2000's era with a remake of *This Must Be A Dream* in 2005. This new version gave a glimpse of what kind of sound they would do next...

Petrus decided that it was time for a proper comeback because the remake broke into Swedish single chart Top 10. *Raise The Gain* (2006) was the first new song of the millennium. The style had changed to pop house in the vain of Eric Prydz (*Call On Me*), but there was lot more melodic opulence compared to said Prydz song. It was sung by Uganda-born DJ and singer Charlie King. The next single *I'll Never Let You Know* also gave Peter the change to sing, instead of rapping. *To You* brought back Charlie. The music video was quite fun: Petrus dresses as a woman in front of a mirror.

Basic Elements re-emergence was received well, so soon followed an album, *The Empire Strikes Back (2007)*, which was released in Sweden and Finland. I have to say, that I had some doubts regarding the B.E's new house sound but they really showed on the album that it was the same aggressively melodic band, although updated into the 2000's. They continued with the same sound on to the next LP *The Truth*. For the last few years, they have done separate songs, lastly with Dr. Alban, *Good To You* (2016).

Basic Element has achieved something that many can't: with the renewed sound and line-up they have found new fans but also kept the old ones. They are a good example of that euro projects had to renew themselves in order to stay interesting for a bigger audience.

In The Spotlight

Peter Thelenius singer

Who are the current members in Basic Element?

Peter & Linda Thelenius + Jonas Wesslander.

Basic Element was and is one of the big names in eurodance. How do you think you have survived through the decades when other eurodance acts have vanished?

By being ahead all the time. We are the only act from the 90's (that we know of), who made new big international hits after the millennium.

You're the only original member of B.E. Do you miss "the good old days" or are you glad that B.E. has changed over the years?

I miss Cesar sometimes, but mostly because we are friends. I'm very happy with the constellation right now. Jonas is one of my closer friends, and my wife is my wife....can't dream of any better team!

The Ultimate Ride **was an aggressive album. Did it come naturally, or did you decide "Let's do a kick-ass hard party album!?"**

We wanted to make our music a bit harder after *Basic Injection*, but for those who listen to all our albums, we change our directions a lot. We like to do what's on our minds at the moment, and not stick with one music style!

Star Tracks **was a change in another direction, why? Was it because eurodance's popularity was diminishing?**

Actually, we were just tired of using the same sound, and wanted to develop a bit with live musicians etc. It was a good idea, because it opened up Japan for us:-)

Earthquake **was once again a hard dance album. Was it something that you wanted to correct something because of the previous "softer" album?**

I refer you to fourth question :-)

Do you think that Swedish eurodance has characteristics that eurodance of other countries doesn't have?

Yes, it's a bit different sound. I don't want to go into it more than so!

How would you define eurodance?

Great melodies, high energy, up-cheering, and club friendly!

What artists and producers have been essential in eurodance, in your opinion?

Denniz Pop who opened up the International market with Leila K, E-Type etc. but also of course our own producers Tomas Kollder and Stefan Andersson.

You made a big comeback in 2000's with a softer house sound. What kind of feedback you received from the old fans?

When we released *Touch You Right Now* for instance a whole new world opened up for us when it was placed no 1 in Russia, Netherlands among many, so I guess we recruited "new" Basic fans + got to keep the old ones. We haven't got much negative feedback. It was worse when we release *Startracks*:-)

134

Is there a new album in sight?

Maybe not an album, but maybe a new single... let's see:-)

▶ *Dr. Alban*

Published with the permission of photographer Alexander Avram

One of the artists who had a strong ethnic vibe in their euro dance, was Dr. Alban (aka Alban Nwaba, b. 1957). He actually is a doctor: at the age of 23 he started to study to be a dentist. He had to pay his studies somehow, so he started working as a DJ in a famous club called Alphabet Street in Stockholm. He soon became popular, because he had the habit on singing on top of the songs he played. When he finished his studies, he started his own practice but kept the DJing as a sideline.

In 1990 he met the producer guru Denniz Pop from Swemix record company. With him Dr. Alban made his first single *Hello Africa ft. Leila K*, which was successful immediately. Even in the beginning, Alban wanted his lyrics to be something other than trivial rhyming. *Hello Africa* was a tribute to his homeland and the next song *No Coke* was a stop sign for drugs. LP *Hello Africa -The Album* sold about million copies worldwide. In this first phase, Alban's music was mainly hip hop and reggae, but the hit single from the next album would mark him forever to eurodance genre...

It's My Life (1992), despite its lightness, is one of the first eurodance songs out there. It rose into worldwide success because it was played on a Tampax commercial and it eventually led into 1,6 million sales all over the world and number one position for example in Germany, Netherlands, and number two in England. The next, more housier single *Sing Hallelujah* is also one of the most recognizable Alban songs. The LP, *One Love (The Album),* sales were commendable, 1,7 million copies. It was a clearer step into the arena of dance music, but the most danceable albums were still to come.

Look Who's Talking (1994) (female vocal by Nana Hedin) was the most purest eurodance single from the doctor so far and the third album (which carried the same name) gave us once again big hits like *Let The Beat Go On* and a perfect euro reggae song *Away From Home*. It was the most euro album yet from the doctor, one of the reasons being that it was published in the "deepest" euro time in 1994. The LP balanced between eurodance and reggae.

Alban wasn't going to leave the music world anytime soon, so he released new material next year. *This Time I'm Free* was surprisingly different, with its breakbeat sound it would stand out from the other euro efforts at that time. It was produced by Ari Lehtonen, who would later revisit the song with his La Cream project. Although the single was awesome, the album *Born In Africa* was a flop in my opinion: majority of the songs are ethnic reggae with a couple of dance songs. Ethnicity had been brought to the front stage. Having said that, there were some diamonds like *I Feel The Music*, which foreshadowed the next albums sound.

I Believe (1997) album was a return to good old dance music. Singles like *Mr. DJ* and *Long Time Ago* were typical Alban songs but updated to incorporate more progressive house and trance. Although this album had its share of reggae, even those songs were done more vigorously and electronically. The next LP, *Prescription* , was far away from dance music and was mainly basic pop. Luckily, the last album (so far), *Back To Basics* (2008) was once again made for the dance floors.

In the 90's Alban founded his own label, Dr. Records, through which he released his own material and other artists like La Cream, Amadin and Drömhus. He has also diligently featured on other artists songs. With Sash! he sang the irritatingly happy *Colour The World* and with the euro trancer DJ Aligator he covered the old Reel 2 Real hit *I Like To Move It*. Alban has done also duets with other euro dance artists like Haddaway (*I Love The 90's,* although the song wasn't eurodance or 90's sound) and a song with Basic Element *(Good To You)*.

Because of his African roots, Alban has managed to carve out instantly recognizable style. His fairly long hit streak is also noteworthy, because euro artists usually don't get so many hits during their career. Nowadays he is also one of the most active artists, when it comes to new songs.

▶ E-Type

E-Type live in Finland, Lahti in 2014. Published with permission of photographer Antti Mäkijärvi

Stockholmer Martin Eriksson has one of the weirdest eurodance artist background: he started his music career as a drummer in a heavy metal bands like Maninnya Blade and Hexenhaus. First step into pop world was when he encountered the rap duo Stakka Bo, with whom he recorded a couple of songs. Because of this cooperation, he got a job as a VJ in Swedish TV station.

First solo single *I'm Falling* (1993) flopped. Success was however just around the corner, when he met the masters of the legendary studio Cheiron: Denniz Pop, Max Martin and Amadin. Energetic single *Set The World On Fire* achieved gold status in Sweden and in Israel got to Top 10. Similar catchy songs like *This Is The Way* and Jonas Berggren-(Ace Of Base)penned *Russian Lullaby* dug their claws into eurodance people's hearts. *This Is The Way* even managed to break into British and US club charts. The album *Made In Sweden* followed, with 100 000 copies sold and album chart longevity of 26 weeks. Martin was rewarded with three different awards in 1995 Swedish Dance Music Awards.

Despite his appearance, E-Type made dance music, not heavy metal.

The next LP, *The Explorer* (1996), was a big mistake. It had only a couple dance songs like the single release *Back In The Loop*. Everything else was ballads, hip hop, or reggae. Fans were not happy, because it sold only one fifth of what the debut album had.

Luckily, E-Type realized his mistake. *Angels Crying* (1998) was a big comeback to eurodance and it has formed to be one of the biggest hits of E-Type. It was accompanied by a great music video: A homage to 80's slasher horror genre, where also the bands dancer Dee also got to show her assets. The third albums name *Last Man Standing* probably meant that Martin was the last artist making eurodance during that era, because by 1998 the genre had died, and the artists had moved on to make other genres.

Last Man Standing was a big hit: it went to number one in Sweden and in Finland. It sold over three million copies worldwide and is therefore his most successful album. Sales were increased due to other hit singles like *Here I Go Again* and the stylish euro reggae *Princess Of Egypt*.

The new decade came. E-Type recorded a football theme *Campione* and dueted with the German happy hardcore lady, Blümchen (*Es Ist Nie Vorbei*). *Life* (2001) gave us once again pure eurodance and it seemed like it was a question of honor for E-Type to continue being the last advocate for the dead and buried genre. He proclaimed himself as eurodance king on an album *Euro IV Ever*. This LP is Martins best, after the first album, and it has absolutely fantastic eurodance songs. There were also some shades of trance music.

Martin's career just kept going on: completely new single *Paradise* was familiar E-Type, fast eurodance. As was expected, a new album followed the new single. *Loud Pipes Save Lives* (2004), was like *Euro IV Ever* part 2. More of the same, but enjoyable. There was even trance pop , *Dans La Fantasie* was done in the vain of Kate Ryan.

Every Swedish pop artist has to try Melodifestivalen (Swedish Eurovision preliminaries), thought Martin. So, he participated the contest with a rock band The Poodles and a song *Line Of Fire* but didn't get to represent his country.

E-Type as a king of his own euro country.

Typical E-Type songs appeared as singles in 2007 to inform that the king was going to release a new album. Hastily done *Eurotopia* (2008) had been abridged into nine songs. While most of them were your typical euro, corners had been cut. Even the euros were quite boring, and the last song was an awful attempt to duplicate Benny Benassi's tek-house sound.

British record company AATW got interested about E-Type quite late in 2008. They released a couple of his songs in England, like *True Believer.*

During the last few years, E-Type hasn't been busy making new material. Two new songs have materialized in the 2010's. *Back 2 Life*, wasn't eurodance anymore although it was written by his previous producer Max Martin. There's nothing positive to say about this boring dance song. Also *Ride Like The Lightning* from last year is more of the same.

E-Type's sound has affected in surprising directions. For instance, Swedish metal band Amaranthe has admitted that they liked eurodance bands like 2 Unlimited, Basic Element and E-Type in the 90's. It is evident that Amaranthe's music is heavily influenced by E-Type, their melodies and refrains are like straight out of E-Type's biggest hits.

THE WOMAN BEHIND THE MAN – NANA HEDIN

Photographer: Ove Lundkvist, published with permission of Nana Hedin.

Martin shouldn't get all the glory from the E-Type hits. Nana Hedin (b.1968) has sung about in half of his songs, the most remarkable part, the refrain.

In addition to E-Type, Nana's part in Swedish dance music has been great. She has sung the euro classics like *Let The Beat Go On* (Dr. Alban) and *Wake Up* (Flexx), featured on Stakka Bo's songs and been a background singer for example Britney Spears, Celine Dion and Ace Of Base. She has done some solo songs under the name Nana D'Aquini. In 2005 she was in Melodifestivalen with the song *Whenever You Go.*

In live performances and videos, sexy dancer Dilnarin Demirpag (aka Dee) lip-synced to Nana's vocals. For example, in *Angels Crying* video she is imposingly singing the refrain. On the other hand, Nana was in some E-Type videos like *Life*.

In 2009, tragedy struck Nana: she got tongue cancer. After the radiation therapy she had to learn how to talk again but her singing ability remained. Because of radiotherapy, her jawbone has become brittle, so she needs a new jaw. She has started collecting donations for her expensive treatments. Her old bandmate Martin has donated money for her.

For her vast achievements in the field of dance music, she got recognition in 2018. She was given a Denniz Pop Award for her work in the sidelines and to Cheiron record company. The award is given to those who bring notable fame to Swedish music tradition and who continue the legacy began by Denniz Pop.

▶ *Melodie MC*

Kent Lövgren (b.1970) aka Melodie MC achieved European stardom from a little district called Sundvall. He met his future producer, Erik Svensson (aka Statikk), already during their time at school, and whom with he started the production group Sidelake Productions between the 80's and the 90's.

Sidelake consisted of enthusiastic and youthful music fans, who had their musical roots in hip hop and British underground scene. Gradually they started to make some good tunes in the studio but selling them forward turned out to be problematic. Sidelake business guru Anders Melin noticed a good opportunity at the Gilberts Dance Music Awards. There the best Swedish DJ's received so called "goodie bag", which contained new music. Anders managed to slip in Kent's alias Melodie MC's 12" single *Feel Your Body Moving* into these bags. In addition to this, he also managed to book Kent as a performer to this event. The gig went great and a week later the DJ's voted the song into Swedish Dance Chart Top 5.

The record companies who had previously declined to sign Melodie MC to their label, started to phone with great enthusiasm. Kent and Erik made their first contract with Sonet Music, which released *Feel Your Body Moving* immediately. The song continued to rise on Swedish dance charts and also the commercial radios started to play the song. After the second single, *Take Me Away,* Sonet changed their CEO. Because the new person in charge wanted the company to focus more on rock music, Melodie MC and Statikk changed the company to Virgin Records. The new label released *Dum Da Dum* (1993) which was a breakthrough hit: Virgin got so excited about it, that they released the song all over the world. Soon the album *Northland Wonderland* followed.

After the successful first phase, it was time to plan the next move. Second album brought more depth into Melodie MC's music with a more euro edge. As the first one, *The Return* (1995) was done with a joint effort with many artists and producers. For example, Charlie King, St. James and Mayomi sang the lead vocals and songs were produced by the likes of Rohan Heath of Urban Cookie Collective and etc. The biggest hits from this were probably *Give It Up! (For The Melody)* and *Anyone Out There.* The LP had been backed full of catchy hit material.

The next long play lightened the sound. Disco diva Jocelyn Brown (b. 1950) was brought in to sing just a couple of songs, but because the chemistry between the artists was so great, they decided to record seven songs with Jocelyn. The result was *The Ultimate Experience* (1997), house music mixed with Melodie MC's own sound. Great singles like *Real Man* and *Embrace The Power* were released from it.

In 1998 Kent decided to leave the music scene because of schisms between him and Statikk and Virgin Records. Statikk continued producing other artists like the house project Eric S. Kent continued studying and finally set up his own advertising agency in Sundvall. He also holds lectures about marketing and branding, and he has a brokerage firm with this brother.

But in 2019 it was time for a comeback. Friends Kent and Erik met once again and started to revive the Melodie MC project. The first step was to get to perform in 90'festivals but also to make new music for a new generation and to old fans too.

In The Spotlight

▶II

Kent Lövgren *singer*

Statikk and Melodie MC, published with the permission of Kent Lövgren.

You are a very skillful rapper. How you ended up in dance music industry? Would you have liked to do more hip hop-influenced music?

As you probably already know I came from the hip hop culture, so rap had been a part of my life since the early 1980's. In the beginning I actually did hip hop songs but not with Statikk.

With Statikk, and especially after Tom Droid became a part of Sidelake Production, everything changed for me. Up until then I was like every other hip hop head, hip hop music was my life and I did not even once consider doing anything but hip hop.

But Statikk and Tom Droid opened up my ears to dance and club music and from that moment dance music was my way forward.

Important though to understand is that I still kept writing hip hop rap lyrics, the only thing that changed was the music we did to that rap.

This was made to Melodie MC to stand out from the rest of the dance acts I believe. Hip hop rap to dance beats.

Why do you think Sweden mastered the eurodance sound so fantastically? Do you think that there are certain characteristics in Swedish eurodance that other countries eurodance doesn't have?

First of all, I have to explain that I hated the term "euro" and "eurodance" since I first heard of the term.

When we started off in the late 80's, early 90's the term did not exist. What we did was dance music or club music. It was not until later the term "euro" came along.

I have never identified mine and Statikk's music as "euro", we have always done dance music or club music.

To me "euro" is everything that came from 1993/94 and forward mostly acts that all sounded the same and, excuse me for saying so, with quite poor rap.

To answer your question then.

Yes, I do believe we have a certain Swedish characteristic way of doing dance music. With that said you have to realize that the where a lot of different dance acts that came out of the 90's with everything from early Rob'n'Raz/Leila K, Ace of Base, Alban, E-Type, me to more hard stuff like Antiloop etc.

What we all have in common is the fact is that we all had a studio to go to. Some of us had our own like us (Sidelake Studio), while others could rent studio time quite easily.

This is what made up the foundation of the "Swedish music wonder" I believe.

The Ultimate Experience album is quite a drastic change compared to the first two albums; the sound is more house. Why is that?

With our first album *Northland Wonderland* we still had a foot in late 80's-early 90's underground dance and club vibe, with its roots in both early Chicago house and underground club music from the UK.

Moving in to the second album *The Return* we did take on some of the euro influences that was around at the time, so with the third album *The Ultimate Experience* we just tried to take back some of our original club roots but in a new way.

The fact that we did get big voice and soul diva Jocelyn Brown to sing on the album made that choice even easier.

How was it like working with the fabulous Jocelyn Brown?

Humbling is the word that comes to mind.

I remember sitting like a little schoolboy in front of her listening to stories about when she performed at the original Woodstock and how she had a party with Janis Joplin.

She also told us about her time in New York before she moved to London. She used to work as a studio singer and it was during that time she for example recorded the *"I got the Power"* for DJ 45 King, later used by Snap! that she never even got paid for.

She came to Sundsvall to record only one song but ended up having such a good time with us, so she ended up doing seven songs instead.

Youve been on a long break. Are you planning to do new music?

At the moment we are only focusing on joining the 90's circus again. Both me and Statikk now have other business projects (not music related) so if that is going to happen both of us need to find time to do so.

Why do you think eurodance is once again so popular?

It's not "eurodance" per say that's popular again. It's the fact that people always crave nostalgy. You see this within both hard rock and 80's music. This is no different.

After 25+ years, how do you see your time in the spotlight in the 90's?

I had a blast, but also, at the same time, left with no regrets. My time the music industry had both its ups and downs.

Loved creating music and sharing it with others but did not like the dirty backside to the music industry, which I still believe is around.

I remember saying that "the porn business probably has more morals and ethics then the music industry".

I have missed the music part, but not the business part.

What do you think of the dance music scene like EDM today?

I like some of it but not all. I think some of the acts/DJ's lost the house/dance/club music DNA that is the core of all dance music.

The have mixed it up so much with other types of music, to such a degree, that you no longer could call it dance music.

Some stay true to the roots, but now you see so many new acts popping up that don't even know the dance music history and therefore lost their way but still call what they do "dance music".

► **Flexx**

Flexx's previous line-up with Kajsa, picture in the right: Laila, rappers Chris and Malwern.
published with permission of Johan Lagerlöf.

Flexx was one of those fabulous eurodance bands who came in the wake of Basic Element's success. Despite their short career, they left a lasting impact with their fast and catchy singles and awesome album.

In The Spotlight

►ΙΙ

Johan Lagerlöf producer

How did Flexx was born?

"The birth of the Stockholm Euro wave"

The true story (not record company version) was that Johan & Janne (Bass Nation) were in the studio recording a song with a new band called Cool James & Black Teacher and songwriter Per Aronsson. When the rap part was recorded, Cool James thought that it wasn't right for them with the "euro sound" even if everybody enjoyed the song. Therefore, James proposed that his friend Malwern could try to rap on it. At the same time a group called Navigators were visiting the studio and they had a friend Chris, who they said also could try to write a rap for the song. Therefore, Chris and Malwern wrote one rap each. When the rap was recorded everybody felt that now the chorus could be adapted to fit the new rap. A new chorus was written by Johan & Janne and recorded with Nana Hedin who was in the studio singing on demos for another new artist, E-Type.

So, now a first song was created, but the group was still to be defined. A video team that recently recorded a video for Culture Beat - *Mr Vain* was in the same studio recording a new video for Army Of Lovers. They agreed to record a low budget video

145

for *Wake Up* at the same time. We remembered a girl from the *Mr Vain* video and asked them if she could join the video and band as well. That girl was Kajsa Mellgren.

So, the band now consisted of Chris, Malwern & Kajsa. Johan & Janne were also co-band owners, producers, and songwriters.

The first song *Wake Up* was released. It almost instantly was Top 5 in the Swedish charts and become the first euro success and a hit for the label Stockholm Records.

This was the start of a bigger euro wave in Stockholm.

After the success, Cool James & Black Teacher decided to go "euro sound" as well and recorded *Dr Feelgood* written by Pat "Rednex" Reiniz. *Dr Feelgood* fast became a no 1 hit and Cool James & Black Teacher started to tour with Flexx.

Flexx released four more Top 20 songs in Sweden. Johan & Janne continued to work with Cool James & Black Teacher and Pat Reiniz and later with E-Type, Blümchen, Drömhus, La Cream, Markoolio and others.

E-Type later worked with Nana Hedin on his first euro track *Set The World On Fire* and then on many euro hits thereafter.

Reiniz founded Rednex and released *Cotton Eye Joe* six months later which became one of the most sold singles in history.

All this was part of the Stockholm euro wave.

Cool James, Chris, Rob&Raz, Johan & Janne, Navigators, parts of Swedish House Mafia and many others are all from the suburbs around Solna in Stockholm.

What was your role in the band?

Founder, songwriter, producer, instruments.

In what countries you were popular?

Mainly Scandinavia.

How would you define eurodance?

A 90's dance phenomenon inspired by 80's synth songs, 90's house and rap that was a mix of pure energy, keyboard riffs and melodic choruses. Early songs and artists that defined the sound are Snap!, U96, KLF, 2 Unlimited.

Who came up the idea of the movie influenced song *The Good The Bad and The Ugly*? And why?

There was a sound on a synth called TX81Z that reminded very much of a whistle, Janne came up with the theme and Johan the chorus.

Why did you eventually disband?

We moved on to create music in other genres. Euro was cool in the beginning but as with all popular genres they become more and more cheesy as they stop to develop. Eventually a new trend appears. Same as for disco.

You released a couple of new songs after the album. Were they successful?

The Euro genre eventually faded so the interest from all parties faded as well. Chris started to do his thing, Malwern his thing and Johan & Janne produced and wrote music for other artists. Kajsa started to work in television.

Was there talk about a second album?

Actually, no. We all were busy with other stuff.

How do you see your time in Flexx after 20 plus years?

I think we all moved on and forgot about it, but now there seems to be a revival again. Flexx is going to perform again for the first time this summer (2019) at a big 90's festival in Stockholm.

Are you in music business now? And if so, what kind of music you are doing?

Chris and Malwern are songwriters, Johan works at Spotify, Janne has a design company and Kajsa works with casting for television.

In your opinion, what made eurodance so popular?

It was all culturally relevant at the time and the club experience was very strong. A lot of energy, the melodies were strong, and the sound was new. Also, it was part of the youth culture at the time. It was relevant in all parts of Europe, also the eastern parts, that just had opened the borders and a "new" Europe was formed. Therefore, euro music was related to the political situation and liberation for the youth there as well, even if that part is forgotten now.

▶ Cool James & Black Teacher

>>Check also Johan Lagerlöf's interview

When euro was THE sound, duo Jamie Dandu (aka Cool James) and José Masena (aka Black Teacher) tried to achieve success with it. Bands first songs didn't raise any interest and neither the first LP *Undercover Lovers*, songs were mainly hip house and hip hop.

People woke up to *Dr. Feelgood*, which was a big jump into to the euro arena, it became 21st bestselling single in Sweden in 1994. Also, the singles with the same style, *Godfather* and *Rhythm Of The Tribe* continued their success and gained a lot of radio play. While the singles were good, the album *Zooming You* was compiled around the hit singles and result was messy, and far away from a decent euro album.

The following singles like *Free* did not chart anymore and according to Eurokdj they called it a day because of financial reasons. Cool James embarked on a solo career but stayed far away from eurodance. He continued with rap music in his home country in Tanzania, until he died in a car accident in 2002.

▶ Look Twice

Published with the permission of Look Twice

Håkan Lidbo-produced project from Malmö, consisted in the beginning of Grazy G (Imre Öze) and Wincent (Patrik Wincent). First songs were mainly house and hip hop, but they grabbed the heart of eurodance with a cover of Michael Zager Band's disco classic, *Let's All Chant*. Look Twice named their version *Move That Body* (1994). Officially the refrain is sung by Gladys, but the voice really sounds like Basic Elements first singer Zetma Prenbo, I would bet my money on her. The song is exceptional, because the male raps speed up the song better than the monotonously done refrain.

It was a hit because of its recognizability. Similar single, *Mr.Dance & Mr. Groove*, was released, which also was not so fluid because of its forced refrain. Debut album *Twice As Nice* (1994) is a mix of eurodance songs and hip hop.

Then they put out two of the biggest eurodance diamonds, in my opinion: *Feel The Night* and *Go Away*. The songs are energetic and beautifully done with a hard edge and they are unforgivable eurodance.

Their second LP, *Happy Hour,* was released in Japan and in Taizan, where these previously mentioned awesome songs were placed among the songs from the first album and some new efforts.

But it's easy to fall from the heights, as it was in this case: the band abandoned their euro sound after *Happy Hour* and moved on to make funk / hip hop. The album *Celebrate* was full of this non-euro. The last LP so far, *3 Is A Crowd* (2001), was more of the same, although there were some house influences. Apparently they were successful in Japan with this sound because the last album was released only there.

According to Eurokdj, Imre performed under Look Twice's name with different singers in 2008, although the rights to that name belonged to Wincent. Nowadays the band is touring with Wincent as the frontman. The last new songs have not sounded euro at all, *Fire* ja *Keep On Moving* (which were published in the 2010's) were monotonic electro house.

▶ Solid Base

Solid Base before and now, published with the permission of Remixed Records

Solid Base, who got its name from a synthesizer, consisted of Isabelle Heitman (b. 1972) from Norway and rapper Thomas Nordin (aka. Theo T.) (b.1971). When Theo T. met the producers Johan Eriksson and Thomas Eliasson, they started to develop a band together. First single (with Isabelle) was *Together*, but success started to show up with the next catchy singles like *You Never Know* and *Mirror Mirror*, which were perfectly light to suit the needs of a casual pop listener.

The debut album *Finally* (1996) sold well all over Europe. It balanced between harder eurodance and lighter dance-pop, plus it had great album tracks like *Stars In The Night* and *How Can We Survive*, albums sound was well developed. Second LP, *The Take Off*, showed the non-believers that you couldn't make a one-hit-wonder out of this band. It mainly continued with the same style but added more euro reggae, like the single *Sunny Holiday*, which would be a major part of the band's sound in the future.

At the dawn of a new millennium, they continued with more of the same, by releasing a new album, *Express* (1999). While it was definitely familiar Solid Base, it had also new shades like the fantastic *Fantasy,* which emulated the trance duo Antiloop, and the cheerful euro house, *Sha La Long*. Euro reggae had its big share of the LP too.

I Like It single meant a new era for the band. Although it was a dance song, however the new album *In Action* mainly consisted of happy euro reggae. It felt that the album had been done solely for the Asian market, where that sound was popular. And so far, it has been their last one. They wrapped up their career with a collection *Greatest Hits*, after which they left the scene.

However, in 2014 Solid Base came alive with a new singer, Camilla Alvestad. For a while Solid Base and Camilla's own Norwegian euro band Reset made joint gigs under the title Reset Vs. Solid Base. With Camilla on board, Solid Base released a couple new songs, but they couldn't capture the allure of the 90's songs. Nowadays Theo T. is touring with a totally new singer, Jenny Redenkvist.

In their homeland, Sweden, Solid Base didn't enjoy big success but in Norway and Sweden they were loved really much, but also elsewhere in Europe. They had their share of critique from the Swedish and Norwegian media, but that didn't bother them. They received many gold and platinum records for their efforts.

In The Spotlight

▶II

Isabelle Holender (born Heitman) singer

Isabelle is nowadays focused on family, published with permission of Isabelle Holender.

How you got in the music business and what led you to become a lead singer in Solid Base? The first single *Dance To The Beat* didn't take off so great, was that a disappointment?

I got into the music business by being asked to come to the studio to sing for the producer Pat Reiniz (who did *Cotton Eye Joe*) His brother had heard me sing at a talent show and asked me to come sing. My first studio job, was back-ground vocal for a group called Cool James and Black Teacher, *Dr. Feelgood*. Shortly after that, I was talking to a colleague of mine at the video store where I used to work. He was a DJ who worked for Remixed Records, and he knew of a band called Solid Base, and they were looking for a new vocalist. They had released one single already, and that was *Dance To The Beat*. So, I never sang on that song. I went in to audition for that job, an got it.

I have been singing all my life, and I knew I wanted to become a singer. So finally, my dreams came true. Before that, I attended Theatre School at Södra Latin in Stockholm, and before that, I attended Stage school in Gothenburg.

So, no, I was not disappointed, because it wasn't my song.

Did you know anything about eurodance when you started to sing that genre?

Well, I knew a few hit songs that were out, but eurodance was not what I usually sang. Pop, r'n'b and musicals was my kind of music. I LOVED Whitney Houston above all when it came to singing. She was my absolute Queen. Other favorites were George Michael, Mariah Carey, Christina Aguilera, Queen and Michael Jackson.

Mirror, Mirror and _You Never Know_ were massive hits, why do you think that they were the biggest hits from your first album?

Mirror, Mirror and _You Never Know_ were the first two songs that I wrote the melody and lyrics for. Why they became such hits, who knows? But we're happy they did.

I wrote other songs after that, that didn't become hits, so it wasn't just because I wrote them (Not the music).

They are very repetitive and have catchy melodies. I think that helps a lot.

You are familiar not just from your eurodance songs but euro reggae like _Sunny Holiday_, too. Why did you make so much euro reggae, was that something you felt was natural to your band?

We wanted to do lots of different euro pop songs. We didn't want every song to sound the same, that would be boring for the audience and us as well. We felt that happy euro songs with some reggae inspiration, felt warm and sunny. Like u want to party and have a good time. Since _Sunny Holiday_ turned out to be a hit in Japan, we wanted to do more of those kinds of songs.

You were big in Japan, why do you think that many eurodance bands have enjoyed lots of success there?

I think when you have had previous success somewhere, it is much easier to feed the next song to the public.

I would also say that Japanese pop is quite light and fun, so with the catchy melodies. So maybe that is a reason they already like that kind of music.

Why did Solid Base retire in the early 2000's?

Our popularity started to decline, and I had had enough. I wanted to do other things, so I left the group

If you had the chance, would you do something differently regarding your music career?

No, I wouldn't do anything different. I think we did a good job with what we had to work with. It was an amazing ride, and I feel truly blessed to have been able to be a part of it. There aren't many people that get to experience the things we got to experience. It was some of the lowest and highest points in my life, and I am proud to have been a part of it. I'm so happy I got to live that life.

What do you think about Solid Base making a comeback without you?

I think it is great that Solid Base is still going. To be honest, it was a strange feeling at first, because I felt that Solid Base was Totte and I. But then I asked myself, did I want to go on tour with Solid Base right now? No! I can't do Solid Base now; I have three kids that need me here. So, the next question was would I rather have Solid Base dead and buried, or would I like someone to continue to play our songs so more people can hear and love our music? Yes!! So even if it stings a little to see someone else singing my songs, it's better than nothing happening at all.

The record company tried to get together a tour with me, but it just couldn't be done. It would be too costly, and inconvenient.

Are you currently in music business?

No, I'm am not in the music business. I was very happy and content with my nine years. It was blood, sweat and tears. I was the one who decided to leave the group, and I have never regretted it.

I am now working from home with my husband's business and taking care of our three kids. I am thinking of starting my own business in the future, but first I am going to do a little college studying.

▶ West Inc

Published with the permission of Mimmi Siegel

A certain Swedish radio show in the 90's compared West Inc to 2 Unlimited. It's not a far stretch, because they have the same aggressiveness in their songs like 2 Unlimited.

The band only got to start properly when they hired Mimmi Siegel as their singer. First song with Mimmi was *Rhythm Takes You Higher* (1994). Same explosive energy was given in *I'm Gonna Get You (Anyway)*. *Mr Livingstone* in the other hand could have been a mega hit when bubblegum genre became popular in the end of the 90's.

Eventually Mimmi left the band and she was replaced with another singer, Marina. With the updated line-up, they released a couple of singles, but didn't even get minimal success.

The men from West Inc, Henrik Westman ja Stefan Persson, later founded a bubblegum band called Dominoo.

154

In The Spotlight

▶❙❙

Mimmi Siegel singer

Published with permission of Mimmi Siegel.

How West Inc was born and what's the story behind the name?

I was not part of the group from the start. I think they were called West Coast to start and did totally different music, like west coast soft rock. Then they added a girl singer and did the first single *Set Your Body Free.* But she left and they found me via some record company contacts. I was experienced as a performer and singer with many years on stage already, so it was a lift up. I had been doing rock, pop etc. on tour as well as a singing waitress at Golden Hits in Stockholm. They changed the name before I came along, West Coast did not fit the new music style so someone thought West Inc would fit better.

How would you define eurodance?

It's a rhythmic pulse with hypnotizing sounds along with it, great vocals usually. Fun upbeat party music I would say.

Was there any talk about an album? You released several singles.

Yes, we did talk about an album a long time, the record company held us on a tight leash I felt, they didn't want to give us too much. They said to us to do singles to see if any one of them would take off, then they would have possibly let us do an album. We had songs enough for an album for sure. It was sad, I would have loved to do an album.

You had very different songs- was it because you were pressured to produce hits?

Well in a way yes. Actually, the songs came out different when we made them. I was not part of the base line; I came in when they had rhythm and some sort of hook in place. I then usually just stood in the studio for a while singing ad lipping, improvising until we had something good catchy to go on. Then build it from there. I wrote the singing parts the melodies and lyrics and Horpe wrote the "rap" parts. The sounds beats etc. was Persson and the other two.

Did you have other eurodance acts from which you took influences?

I am sure the boys did, but for me I wanted to be and felt unique. I made my own outfits and sang with a rock voice often so I didn't follow any others just myself. But the boys i think listened too much to others (Ace of Base for sure!) that's one of the reasons we didn't take off, the songs were not original or made from love, but made from "let's make a hit" or "should sound like" etc.

Do you think that eurodance has influenced modern dance music?

Absolutely. We made a sound that has been developed now.

Why did West Inc eventually vanish from the music world?

I for one quit in 1997-98 as I was tired of the music, the lip-syncing, "only" singing small parts of the songs, just that it didn't feel genuine. I wanted to do real music and went into the studio and made pop and jazz after that. West Inc did continue after that with other singers, not sure how well they did though, didn't really follow them. I think if we had had just one bigger hit we would have had a better chance. The songs were good definitely but they didn't take off enough, just enough to let us make one more and one more.

U GOT 2 LET THE MUSIC – ITALY

▶ *Cappella / Anticappella / Clubhouse / 49ers*

Italian eurodance was very dominant in the 90's dance music charts. Gianfranco Bortolotti is probably the most famous and most prolific producer of that era. Media Records, which he managed, is responsible for many 90's dance classics.

When Bortolotti was young, he started doing DJ gigs in order to earn extra money for his studies. DJ Pierre introduced him into the secrets of club life and when Pierre's own career started to get better, Bortolotti was his partner. Gianfranco managed to get some money, so he invested on a home studio and set up Media Records label. His headquarters was in Brescia, North Italy, where he founded a hit factory in the vain of SAW, which spewed out dozens of hits.

As eurodance consisted of several different styles that were mixed together, also Bortolotti's sound got its ingredients from many genre. In the beginning of his career in the 80's he started with italo disco but started to become interested about house, which was not so well-known genre at the time in Europe.

▶▶ *Cappella – Bortolotti's flagship*

Bortolotti decided to make house music with the project he had set up, called Cappella. Under this alias he released the first song, *Bauhaus* (1987), which was a mix between hip house and house. Steadily he started to produce house-oriented songs like *Helyom Halib* (1988) and *Get Out Of My Case* (1989). In 1989 Cappella's first album, *Helyom Halib*, was released. The LP's title song climbed into British single chart number 11. These previously mentioned songs were typical of that time, puzzles compiled of several different samples. Although all the album's vocals were samples, model Ettore Foresti was hired to dance and lip-sync the songs in music videos. During this time, there weren't many people in Bortolotti's production team and the assistant producer was Pieradis Rossini (interview later on).

157

Take Me Away sampled Loleatta Holloway.

In 1991 new material was released, (single *Everybody)* and Bortolotti's production team got some new members. Legendary disco divas, Loleatta Holloway's vocals from her own disco classic *Love Sensation* were sampled and the result was *Take Me Away,* in which you can see the first signs of the eurodance Cappella: diva-like vocals and a clear catchy melody. But the first real eurodance from Cappella was *U Got 2 Know*, where the speed and energy had been enhanced to the maximum. The easy refrain was been lifted from DJ Ralphi Rosario's house classic, *You Used To Hold Me.*

Kelly and Rodney's epic pose.

The first real mega hit and a true eurodance classic was just around the corner: *U Got 2 Let The Music.* It contained a speeded-up melody of Alphaville's *Sounds Like A Melody* and the refrain was once again taken from a US house song: J.M. Silk *Let The Music Take Control.* The result was mind-blowing: *U Got 2 Let The Music* was an enormous hit in Europe and even charted in the US. Top 10 was reached in many countries.

U got 2 Let The Music is Bortolotti's production at its best: it rises above from just being a sample song and really owns its different parts by fusing them to a dance floor smasher. You can't talk about this song without mentioning the fantastic music video where they use Egyptian mythology in the settings and costumes. It's also a debut for two new British leading figures, Kelly Overett and Rodney Bishop. It's quite funny on the video how Kelly is lip-syncing to the refrain, which actually is sampled from male vocals.

Move On Baby was the next single and it became a hit because of the same infectious energy. Using the same mythology on the video as in *U Got 2 Let The Music,* they went into British number one.

Second Cappella album was a different breed than first one. *U Got 2 Know* (1994) stroke gold because it was being released during the hottest eurodance era. It was a success with several other hit singles released from it: *U & Me, Move It Up* and *Don't Be Proud.* After *Don't Be Proud,* Kelly left Cappella. According to rumors, they wanted to replace her with a woman who could really sing. If you see their live performances of that era, you can see that Kelly has probably been recruited to Cappella because of her dancing skills. After Cappella, Kelly released a euro house single *Follow Your Heart* under her own name. You can definitely hear that she isn't a singer and doesn't sound anything like the vocals heard on Cappella album.

Kelly and Rodney probably didn't have many vocals on the album, maybe none at all. It was typical for this genre to use different singers than the frontmen, so *U Got 2 Know* album had various singers. For example, soul and jazz singer Jackie Rawe has revealed in an interview that she lent her voice to *Move It Up.* Some of the raps were performed by Dutch MC Fixx It (Ricardo Overman), in *U & Me* and *Move On Baby.*

Rodney was fired when Kelly left and two new members were hired: British Patrick Osborne (from Worlds Apart boyband and later a stripper) and Allison Jordan, who won a talent competition in 1992 and released two solo singles, *Boy From New York City* and *Heart & Soul.* With these new leaders, Cappella released a new song in Italy, but it was so bad, that the local radio stations didn't want to play it. Patrick (who in 1995 released one Bortolotti-produced eurodance single, *Love Me*) was fired soon after, and he only managed to do a few live performances with Allison. Rodney was called back and so Cappella was reborn.

Allison and Rodney, from War In Heaven albums leaflet.

With the help of Rodney and Allison, a completely new single *Tell Me The Way* (1995) was released and it was a worthy successor to the line of hits this project had already given to the world of dance music. It was a success in the charts especially in Italy, but also in other countries. It was a typical combination of explosive energy and quality production flavored with a couple of samples and diva vocals. Very similar *I Need Your Love* followed, after which their third album *War In Heaven* saw the light of day in 1995. This is clearly Cappella's most cohesive LP. It has a perfect length of 10 songs, and they all are dance songs. One of the best songs is *Turn It Up & Down*, which was remixed in single form to contain more trance sounds.

Finland probably had a special part in Cappella's heart because an exclusive single *Do You Run Away Now* CD single was released only there. The song loans the melody from   Duran Duran's *Save A Prayer*. Nowadays the CD is quite rare collector's item and will not come cheap.

In 1997 new singles from the upcoming album were released, *Be My Baby* and *U Tore My World Apart*. Although they had the almost same energy as the previous ones, something was missing. They were good but not good enough, in my opinion, they tried to repeat the formula of the hits too much. So, it's no wonder that their last album so far, *Cappella,* was only released in Japan. It's a mix of their typical fast style, but there are some excruciating downtempo pop songs too. They probably tried to please the Asian market with this decision. They clearly wanted to make this a more traditional dance pop album with almost fully sung vocals and the songs were not collected from samples like their previous songs. Although Allison may have sung at least some vocals on *War In Heaven*, on *Cappella* her voice was replaced with a voice of a Scottish session singer, who recorded only two additional songs for Media Records. Also, Rodney was just a face on the cover because his raps are performed by someone else.

Although their fame had declined over the years, after this fourth LP in 1998 a new song *U R The Power Of Love* was released with a mix from Mauro Picotto. In the same year they tried to raise interest by releasing *U Got 2 Let The Music* in remixed from, this time in Australia.

Because Cappella didn't get any more hits, Bortolotti dropped out of the project in 1999, but returned five years later to produce a new song, *Angel,* which was so far been the last new song from Cappella. Stylistically it was far from the band's energy, nearest comparison is Gigi D'Agostino. In 2004 *U Got 2 Let The Music* was remixed with hard trance sound. In 2013, when the euro nostalgia conquered people's hearts, Cappella joined the 90's tour circuit. This time two new youngish people were introduced as the frontmen of Cappella: English couple, Lis and Marcus Birks. This line-up tours as Cappella nowadays, but no new completely material has been released.

Bortolotti wasn't of course solely responsible for Cappella. He was the main producer, whose big production team consisted many musicians and DJ's, for example Steven Zucchini, Diego Leoni, Mauro Picotto, Tiziano Pagani, Massimo Castrezzati and Gianpiero Viani. Picotto is most well-known because of his solo career as a trance DJ. This team and several other auteurs were part of Bortolotti's ever-changing projects.

Cappella was a familiar name also in the remix department. The team remixed a lot other artists, even some surprising names like Jimmy Somerville, Erasure, Kim Wilde, Pet Shop Boys and Masterboy.

There has been a lot of speculation about the real voices on Cappella records, and the truth is that most vocals that were not direct samples were performed by various different session singers. Jackie Rawe is one who has admitted having sung the vocals on *Move It Up*, others are just guesses. The identities of these session singers are irrelevant because they were not official part of the group, they were only hired to provide their vocals to the songs. To correct some of the false claims; Zeeteah Massiah is not the lead vocalist on *War In Heaven* album, Beverley Skeete doesn't sing lead vocals on any Cappella record and Tiziano Pagani is not the actual rapper on *Cappella* album.

Ultimately Cappella was a project that released four albums, four different eras lead by Ettore Foresti, Kelly Overett, Rodney Bishop and Allison Jordan. They were the performers and the heart of this project.

▶▶ *Anticappella*

Bortolotti decided that every force has an anti-force, even Cappella. So Anticappella was born. First and strangely mathematically named *2√231* (1991) was an instrumental and a hit. After that project gave birth to songs like *Everyday* and *I Wanna Love You*. Their biggest hit is without a doubt *Move Your Body* (1994),in which rapped the previously mentioned MC Fixx It (also in Twenty 4 Seven during their hip house era) and refrain was sung by Beverley Skeete, who also performed vocals for Clock and Clubzone. The song was a success in many European countries.

Sometimes the cover art was very plain.

The next, *Express Your Freedom,* should have been a bigger hit after the previous mega hit, but it didn't go well: it visited only a few dance charts in Scandinavia, UK and Italy. It's a real shame, because the song is much better than *Move Your Body* in my opinion.

In 1997-98 the project released several new songs, that foreshadowed an album, but nothing came out. Still there's an unofficial promo version of the album on the circuit, which contains all the songs they released.

In The Spotlight

▶II

Bruno Guerrini producer

Published with permission of Bruno Guerrini.

What was your role in the Cappella, Anticappella and Clubhouse bands? Would you have liked to have been more involved in these projects?

As arranger musician of Media Records, record company in which I worked for four years, I participated in the realization of some songs by these artists as composer, arranger, and studio technician (or sound engineer), indifferently.

To create a song, Media Records used the help of several professionals who worked simultaneously in team on the same project with the final supervision of Gianfranco Bortolotti (owner and partner of Media Records).

Have you worked a lot with Gianfranco Bortolotti? What was it like working with him?

Working with Gianfranco was never easy, as all creative people had a very 'whimsical' character but knew how to gratify their artists and technicians and used specific and far-sighted production and promotion criteria that had given surprising results, bringing style Media Records tops the charts all over the world.

You did several remixes, what was the most difficult to do and why?

Yes, I made many remixes of famous artists also under the pseudonym of Doubles, I don't remember any particular difficulties, but the ones with which I had the greatest satisfaction were those that I made in my studio in Milan, outside of Media Records.

I had the pleasure of working with many Italian singers (including Vasco Rossi and Domenico Modugno) and many international singers, in particular I like to remember the RMX of a song by Gloria Gaynor with which I stayed for three consecutive weeks at the NOVE number of the Bilboard's SALE Chart ranking. (titled *Mighty High*).

How do you think the sound of eurodance evolved in the 90's?

In dance music, but more generally in life, one must have the courage to renew oneself!

Over the years I have collaborated with several record companies for which I have composed songs for artists such as Systematic, Bob Sinclar, Daddy Yankee, El Cubano, Ann Lee, Regina, Bob Marley and others, but every time they tried to do something artistically beautiful and not necessarily linked to the fashion of the moment.

Even today, in fact, listening to those songs I don't find them particularly dated, and some I use them in some DJ sets that call me to attend (dance house music genre).

There is an evolution of music and it is simply a reshuffle of the present past and innovative technologies mixed together. Today anyone at home can equip themselves with technologies that allow him to create a musical production, it is necessary to understand if these technologies are usable by everyone.

The secret is to love all music, from classical to jazz, from dance to trance ....

You have been involved in many euro projects that have only released one or two singles, do you have a favorite among these projects?

Honestly not. Each production has its why.

Who is your greatest musical idol and why?

I have never had an idol to inspire me, I like many artists and I listen to all kinds of music.

What is the state of eurodance today? Do you see it in today's music?

The eurodance has never died, it has turned cyclically .... today you have to create a 'true' artist, who has all the qualities to be credible (especially in a live) and propose more pop songs with catchy melodies and strong ideas. Unfortunately, the image is also very important, but promotion is fundamental.

With the advent of the network and digital music, physical support is over and digital promotion is all.

Club House

Club House is maybe the oldest Bortolotti project, because it got started in the beginning of the 80's, when Bortolotti made medley-style covers by fusing together hit songs and samples. Gradually Club House started to make their own songs like *Deep In My Heart* (1990). A step toward euro happened with a song *Take Your Time*, which was song by US-born Carl Fanini. Carl's handsome voice united with electric beat turned out to be a great combination so the name of the project was changed into Club House feat. Carl.

Housier *Light My Fire* turned out to be a hit and managed to get into many dance collections in the 90's. Club House hardened the grip with *Living In The Sunshine* (1994), which was thoroughbred eurodance. *Nowhere Land* single increased the pace and so an album carrying the same name was released. It still wasn't released in many countries but gladly ZYX Records re-released an enhanced version of the album as a 2CD edition in 2016, with a remixes and songs from the beginning of the 90's thrown as a bonus.

After the album Club House continued with a cover of Sting classic *Don't Stand So Close To Me* (1996). Projects style started to gradually change more into your basic house, as in other Bortolotti projects. In the end of the millennium a perfectly boring house with a different male vocalist was launched. It was so bad, that it was released only on vinyl. Surprisingly in 2006 Club House was resurrected with the awful cover of Coldplay song, *Speed Of Sound*.

Fanini was a vocalist in couple of other dance projects like East Side Beat ja Base Of Dreams. He had such big success with Club House that they tried to launch a solo career for him with the name Carl. He has also sang in the 2010's for DJ's like Nari & Milani and Provenzano.

In The Spotlight

►II

Carl Fanini singer

Carl Fanini then and now, published with permission of Carl Fanini.

How did you become a member of East Side Beat and Club House?

In 1990 I met DJ Cinols with whom I started writing songs- we sent a few demos and fortunately signed with Media Rec in the same year: *Divin In The Beat* was our debut single and our project became East Side Beat named after his home studio East side studio as we live on the east coast of Italy- in 1993. I started featuring with Club House project led by Mauro Picotto and history repeated

How was it like working with Bortolotti?

In some ways I will always be grateful to the man as he gave me the opportunity to reach the top of the European charts several times also giving me the chance to work with an awesome team of producers that had taught me what being professional is all about.

Why did you leave Club House?

Unfortunately, my contract expired after five long years and in 1996. I think that his idea of letting DJ:s become the future artists & performers of the dance scene gave me no chance in staying with Media Rec.

How do you see your time in the eurodance era? Good or bad memories?

I have still incredible memories of the 90's and definitely think that in some ways I have lived a dream come true after so many hits, gigs ,tv shows and all that an artist could ever want.

Do you still work in dance music?

I still do work in the music biz : last year (2018) I released a Christmas album and am currently working on some new collabs.

అ

Bortolotti also produced many projects in the 90's that released only a couple of singles but then faded away. One of strongest characteristics of his productions was his ability to integrate different parts from various sources and make them work as one song, you could almost believe that samples weren't used. Downside here was that they didn't always remember to ask for permission to use the samples. In addition to borrowed pieces, Bortolotti used original singers, but he liked to keep the public in the dark about who was really singing.

It was also common, that different countries got different versions of the single releases. Sometimes a remix done by other Media Records project was chosen as the radio version. They tried to choose a more suited version to match the countries own preferences. Every single release had about 15 to 20 different mixes. Also singles in some countries had versions that weren't in more wide releases.

Media Records 90's productions are the cornerstone of eurodance, in my opinion. Their quality and brilliance are still looking for its equal in dance music genre. Some have tried to emulate Bortolotti`s unique sound like the Japanese Tetsua Komuro with his Eurogroove project. For example, *Dive Into Paradise* could easily have been one of Cappella's songs. Also, the masters from SAW, Stock and Waterman tried similar sound with Kuttin'Edge *I Believe In You.*

▶▶ **49ers** and **Sharada House Gang**

Fierce Ann-Marie in the cover of 49ers collection

Although Ann-Marie Smith featured on the song, she didn't get to be on cover.

Ann-Marie Smith was the woman who personified 49ers, which got its name from American football team. Although in the first song, *Die Walküre* (1988), Ann-Marie wasn't heard, because it was composed of several samples. The first album *49ers* (1990) was like a puzzle, but it had imaginative samples like in the song, *Touch Me*. Next year a remix album followed.

Smith was on the verge of breakthrough when Bortolotti was searching a singer for 49ers. After hearing Smith on a demo tape, Bortolotti knew that the band had found its voice.

With Smith as a frontwoman and a real singer, another album called *Playing With My Heart* came out, where Ann-Marie let her amazing vocal abilities shine in songs like *The Message* and *Move Your Feet*.

Ann-Marie had such a distinctive voice that other Media Records and Bortolotti projects wanted to use her. In 1992 Fargetta (aka DJ Mario Fargetta(used Smith in his *Music Is Moving* and in a John Miles cover called *Music.* Smith's vocals were also sampled in Clock's first single release.

In 1993 49ers sound switched into eurodance gear. *Keep Your Love* is a classic Bortolotti eurodance song. It's a cover of Ann-Marie's old band, New Life's hit. . So in 49ers she is kind of covering herself, because she also sang the original vocals with the band. I have to admit that the Media Records version is much saucier than the original.

Rockin My Body, *Hangin' Onto Love* and *Lovin' You* continued with the same hyper energic euro, but when the millennium was coming nearer and eurodance faded, their sound started to move more into house. Cover *Let The Sunshine In* (1998) was a pure house song. In the 2000's 49ers tried to get on top once again with a light *Escape My Heart*, but time had run past them. So far their last songs have been the boring EDM era songs like *Je Cherche Apres Titine* and *Shine On In Love.*

Ann-Marie was also out on loan to Sharada House Gang project, which got started in 1988. Like with Cappella and 49ers, their first efforts were house and hip house, but at the dawn of eurodance, they moved into more euro and harder material. *Let The Rhythm Move You* (1993) dipped its head into euro, but the next *Dancing Through The Night* (with Ann-Marie) took a giant leap into it. Zeeteah Massiah

167

performed *Keep It Up,* which gave us more of the same. Smith was called again to sing the single *You Are Deep In My Heart,* and now with a slightly more trance atmosphere. But eventually, like with 49ers, they changed more into house music with the last songs *Gipsy Boy* (although the single had a real cool euro remix done by Pagani) and *Real Love* in the end of the 90's.

In The Spotlight

▶II

Zeeteah Massiah singer

Published with permission of Zeeteah Massiah.

You started your solo career in the 80's, can you tell us about that more?

I started my music career In 1974, when I recorded my first single. It was a reggae version of the Jackson Five's song, *We Got A Good Thing Going*. Shortly after that I recorded a cover of Diana Ross's *I'm Still Waiting*, also in reggae.

In 1978, I was the lead singer in a band called Lady Love. It was my first ever tour. We toured Poland as the support band to Mungo Jerry. We were also the first Western band to perform behind the Iron Curtain (as it was known in those days).

The 80's was a very interesting time for me as I left my secure job to become a full-time singer. My dad thought I'd lost my marbles. I was 28 years old, married with a small child. I couldn't resist the strong calling for me to follow the dream I had had since I was five years old.

I had a residency in the Beachcomber Restaurant at The Mayfair Hotel, where I performed for four hours, six nights a week. I sang 40 songs each night. I knew every key and every lyric. It was the best training ever.

I went from there to the Empire Leicester Square, just a few hundred yards away – one of the top venues in London's West End at that time. I stayed there for six months before being offered the part of Chiffon in the hit musical Little Shop Of Horrors. It was my first taste of theatre and acting and I loved it. I was there for the last nine months of the run though I wished it would never end. The theatre family is very different from the pop family, and I really liked it. Perhaps it was that people in the theatre tended to form a stronger bond because of the length of time spent together.

After that, my journey took me back into the recording studio and to live performances as an additional vocalist with some of the biggest artists of the time. My second big tour was with Kim Wilde, supporting Michael Jackson on the European leg of his Bad Tour.

During the 80's I also sang with Jonathan Butler on Dutch TV; with Julia Fordham on the Comfort Of Strangers Tour; with Thrashing Doves on their album Trouble In The Home; with Barry Manilow on Keep Each Other Warm; with One Nation on What You See and My Commitment; with Climie Fisher on their UK tour; with the River Detectives on their single Sunday Night, Sunday Morning, and many others.

When it comes to dance music, you have sung in many productions like Cappella. Did you sing other songs than *Do You Runaway now*?

I don't remember singing this song *Do You Runaway Now*? It probably wasn't me who sung it.

I have so much stuff. Please check out my Discogs page. All the info you need about all my recordings is on there.

90's was very much in the style of different singers singing the songs in studio than the people who performed it live (lip-syncing). How did it feel when someone else took the credit, so to speak?

With regard to the lip-syncing thing, I found it surprising that people really did that. But anyway, by the time I found out about some of the tracks I'd been featured on being presented in this way, it was too late to do anything about it. The record companies had already got their person of choice to front the video and mime to my voice. They got away with a lot of stuff back then because we didn't know any better.

But on one occasion I was the one doing the lip-syncing: I was asked to front a track for a video by Carl Cox, *I Want You Forever*, which I did because I really liked the track. I think it was a sample. I tried to find out who did the original vocals but so far haven't been able to.

"Taking the credit": I don't think anyone could really take the credit away from me because those songs were obviously my voice and fortunately, Discogs has all the data should anyone be in doubt.

Have you met Bortolotti? If you have, what's your impression of him?

It was a long time ago when I recorded all of those songs in Italy. Honestly, I don't remember if I met Bortolotti or not.

You were a singer for Haddaway's *Rock My Heart*. How was it like working with Haddaway?

I did a Far East tour with Haddaway and found him, honestly, to be not such a nice person. I didn't complete the second tour because of his vile behavior. I met him again many years later when I lived in Germany and he was as nice as pie. Weird.

Are you involved with music nowadays?

Music is my great love and I'm still very active musically. I've had my own band since returning from Germany in 2012. We play a mixture of jazz, blues, reggae, rock, and ska, and perform regularly in some of London's top venues.

I've also been working with my husband, producer, and songwriter Paul Caplin. He has produced two of my recent studio albums, *Juice* and *Maybe Tomorrow*. We're getting ready to start our third. I'm very excited!

Best and worst memories of the 90's, could be music or non-music related?

The best times were touring with Tom Jones, Johnny Hallyday and Eichiki Yazawa. And touring with Michael Jackson, of course. My other best memory of the 90's was performing to millions of people, live on TV for the UK Eurovision Song Contest Finals. Those were amazing experiences.

Working with Haddaway and Mick Hucknall were the worst memories, sadly.

▶ *Fargetta / Mars Plastic*

Italian DJ and producer Mario Fargetta also got to experience the powers of Bortolotti's golden touch. Mario's career had started already when he was 16 working as a DJ and remixer, but the first single was with Media Records singer Ann-Marie, *Music*. You had to move people to the music, so the next one *Music Is Moving* cranked it up a notch. Also, *Your Love* was a fairly lighter euro song.

Singles came thin and people had to wait for an album until 1997. *You Got It* LP could have been massively better, if it had been released two years earlier. In 1997 other sounds than euro were more popular, and the album embodied that. It was mainly house music, with a faint sprinkle of euro. Mario continued recording career into the 2000's, using sometimes his whole name.

"FIND THE WAY"

Mars Plastic, which carried the same name as the eraser model, became most known from its many remixes made for Bortolotti's projects, but also known for its own original songs. It got started in 1992, so it was more steadily attached to euro than many other Bortolotti acts who started in the 80's.

Mars Plastics' career encompasses a few singles, last of them, *Can You Gimme More Time,* came out in digital form in 2009. I think that their best effort was the magically atmospheric *Find The Way*.

▶ *Space Master*

It's a pity that Space Master was overshadowed by Cappella, because they had at least as good dance songs like its more popular older brother. Their songs were a great combination of lethally good melodies and carefully placed samples and vocals. Space Masters father was Pieradis Rossini.

Published with permission of Pieradis Rossini.

In The Spotlight

▶❙❙

Pieradis Rossini producer

Published with permission of Pieradis Rossini.

What led you to produce eurodance?

I started early as a boy in various cover bands around Italy as a musician and singer, then while I was studying, I started as a sound engineer in the recording studio, from there I started producing dance music.

Tell me a little about the DJ Movement label, how was it born?

As soon as I left the M.Rec, I founded the DJM label that turned into a DJ MOVEMENT company, but immediately the first pieces climbed the international charts and without marketing or licensing or someone (big business men)offices but only with the fame and just with the hard work previously formed.

You were one of the men behind Cappella, tell me how their songs were made, they were brilliantly combined.

I consider Cappella, 49ers, Space Master and many others my sons, since in the studio I was the main composer and the user of the samples from the vinyls with the first Akay 900-950-1000-1100 samplers series, then each of us in the various teams did their job, maybe this is the real secret of every HIT.

Space Master was one of your projects, how was it born? And why didn't you release an album from Space Master?

Space Master was one of my groups created immediately after the Media Records era and I immediately made the number one in the dance charts of the whole world, for me it was the redemption that I was waiting for to show to myself first of all, that it always takes a good product to make successes , not just the arrogant people who sell them, without taking anything away from the sellers.

Italians produce eurodance with great melodies and wonderful singers. Why do you think Italians are so good?

Well, the music on my own after the absolute master J.S.Bach has always been melodically speaking the Italian music, perhaps inspired by Vivaldi maybe for the poetry of the country.

How was it like working with Bortolotti?

A nightmare, he was just interested on my work and nothing else, when I understood business well, I left it and created DJ MOVEMENT.

What kind of music are you doing nowadays?

I'm producer for rap customers, trap music, but also continuing with house music and techno with different artists everywhere.

What is the legacy of eurodance for today's dance music?

An unattainable goal because we already wrote the best years of the 80'90 dance music, now lack the imagination and the notes are always those, perhaps too many people think they are a true artists and there are too much people in the world that thinking that.

ROBYX HITFACTORY

Savage aka Roberto Zanetti (b.1956), who made a glorious career with his italo disco in the 80's, was also responsible for many eurodance hits. In 90's projects he wasn't the leading man, but a producer in the shadows who made music (using the alias Robyx) to for example Ice MC, Double You, Alexia, Netzwerk and DJ Bobo.

In The Spotlight

▶II

Roberto Zanetti aka **Savage** *producer and singer*

Published with the permission of Roberto Zanetti.

As a producer, you were a pioneer for eurodance music. In how many eurodance projects you were involved in the 90's?

Yes, I was one of the creators of eurodance. I was involved in many projects like Double You, Corona, ICE MC, Alexia, Netzwerk, DJ Bobo.

How would you define eurodance?

Eurodance is a musical style that mix a strong electronic beat with romantic/melodic vocals

How does making eurodance differ from making italo disco? Was it natural to transition from italo to eurodance?

Eurodance was an evolution of italo disco. In the beginning all recordings were done by real musicians over 24 tracks tape. That's why italo disco is simpler and vocals are more important than rhythm or effects. At the end of 80's dance music was entirely done by computers, and many musical softwares were created giving to musicians and producers the possibility to easily record more tracks, more effects, more beats.

I think that the evolution was because new powerful keyboards/instruments/drum machines were created.

What genres and artists were essential for the evolution of eurodance?

My first eurodance artists were Double You and ICE MC. ICE MC's *Take Away The Colour* was one of the first records with male rap and female singer that later was one of the most important style of eurodisco. Many groups copied me and my style, KWS over all was a poor copy of Double You.

Did you feel pressure to produce hit singles because of the popularity of Alexia and Ice Mc?

After a big hit you always are afraid to miss the way and to be no more able to write a hit. I really was under pressure but at the end I left music coming out...and it was OK.

Do you think that Italian eurodance have characteristics that eurodance from other countries doesn't have?

Italians were often more creative than main competitors (Germany and Sweden). We were strong in melodies while for example Germans were stronger in technology. The sound of German records was perfect compared to Italian. The Swedish were strong in organization, they created professional production teams, labels, and fantastic recording studios.

Why do you think that eurodance is once again so popular?

I think that is a natural evolution. People that now are 40/50 years old want to listen the songs of their youth. Doing that they promote the 90's songs to young boys that love the catchy melodies of that genre. Also, I think that new dance music has a lack of artists. All songs are by DJs while songs of the 90's had real artists.

How do you see the eurodance era in the 90's now? Do you remember it with love or hate? What would you change if you had the chance?

It was a nice era, dance music everywhere, the same songs that were played on discos and were on radio too. People were happy and made parties on every discotheque. I love that era and I have great memories of that. I think it was perfect, no need to change anything.

What kind of music you listen to now?

I'm fan of electronic pop music of the 80's, Depeche Mode, Yazoo, Human League, OMD, Tears for Fears, Erasure, Pet shop Boys, Communards, Alison Moyet, FYC.

▶ *Corona*

Zanetti's records company DWA (Dance World Attack) released Coronas aka Olga Maria Souza's first song *The Rhythm Of The Night* in the fall of 1993. Olga, who was a well-known mode, wasn't though the singer in this. Vocalist was Sicilian Giovanna Bersola aka Jenny B. Jenny didn't get any credit for singing this, not even after the song became a worldwide mega hit by breaking into Top Ten in 14 countries. It was also one of the few euro songs that managed to break into US Billboard Top 20. Vibe.com has listed the song as one of the most significant dance songs of the 90's.

Olga smiled a lot on the record covers.

The next single, *Baby Baby*, featured another vocalist, Sandy Chambers. *Baby Baby*'s success really didn't pale in comparison with the first hit, a few of its accomplishments rising to number one in Italy and number six in Finland.

Sandys voice fitted well with Corona project, so that she got to continue, so she got to continue singing more songs like *Try Me Out* and *I Don't Wanna Be A Star,* which earned more fame to Corona. The latter one was also made into a 70's disco version. The first album called *The Rhythm Of The Night* (1995) featured the hits plus other dance songs with the same sound. Corona had strong producer power behind her: for example, Francesco Bontempi (Lee Marrow) and the Spagnas, Ivana and Giorgio, were familiar names from italo disco scene. Lee Marrow recycled his own accomplishments when making this album.

The Rhythm Of The Night is a great accomplishment. If you forget the fact, that the frontlady Olga doesn't sing any of these songs in the studio, is a real enjoyable example of Robyx's trademark sound and the quality of Italian eurodance. The entirety is perfected by the remixes in the end, in one of them another Robyx star features Corona, Ice MC.

The contract with DWA ended in 1997 and so ended the bigger success. *The Power Of Love* was a weak attempt to change Coronas style. The refrain is unbelievably boring and although Sandy sings well (as usual), the songs seems very distant. Nevertheless, another long play was released, *Walking On Music*. It's a slightly confused mix of dance, 80's, funk and there's even a SAW pastiche, *I Belong To You (80's).*

Corona was apparently still a big thing in Brazil, because they got an exclusive release of Coronas third album *And Me U* (2000), while the artist name in this publication was Corona X. During this album Olga started to sing for herself. New singles came up during the 2000's, but another album had to be waited until 2010, *Y Generation*. *Angel* single released from this tried to remind people of Corona's biggest hits. Actually, *Y Generation* is one of the best efforts of old eurodance artists.

Olgas tale continues, although the last new song   *Super Model* has been released a few years ago. While Olga has not sang the biggest hits herself, that hasn't stopped her for performing actively in 90's events and TV shows.

Corona live in 2018, published with permission of photographer Karine Sanche.

▶ *Double You*

London-born William Naraine (b.1965) was the face of the project Double You , which started already in 1985. Other members were musician Franco Amato and DJ Andrea De Antoni. This coalition faced a change when they met the producer guru Roberto Zanetti. First song made in Zanetti's hit factory, was *Please Don't Go* (1992), which stroke a chord with the general public and also managed to climb into charts. Gold record was given them from Germany, from Latin Americas every country and from many countries in Africa and Asia. William and company had struck gold, one of the key factors was Naraine's exotic outlook, which helped them to get success in many countries that eurodance artists usually didn't get much attention.

Published with the permission of DWA Records.

We All Need Love was similar to *Please Don't Go* and it gathered great positions all over the world. Album carrying the same name was brought to the public. But they still sealed their success with the more eurodancier LP, *The Blue Album* (1994). Singles like *Missing You* and *Part-Time Lover* enjoyed the embrace of the crowds. Especially the latter one was especially popular in Germany, where the group got to perform in the most important TV music shows. But only the single *Run To Me* opened up the doors to North America and enabled a tour there. However, they enjoyed biggest popularity in Brazil, because the second album sold 300 000 copies in a short time and earned them platinum records. During the Brazilian tour they performed in 64 different concerts in various venues.

A great deal faster single *Dancing With An Angel,* foreboded a new album. The song had recruited DWA regular, Sandy Chambers, to sing lead vocals. It was a big summer hit, especially in Italy.

DJ Andrea De Antoni left the band in 1996 to try out a solo career, while Double You's popularity remained strong in Brazil. Because of this, they embarked on a new tour there. To show their appreciation to Brazilian fans, Double You published their third album, *Forever* , only there. It sold 150 000 units and earned a golden status.

Somebody (1997) offered completely different Double You: it took its sound from dream house in the vain of Robert Miles, thus leaving eurodance to the background. This song wasn't featured in the fourth LP, *Heaven*. Its leading star was a disco/funk influenced song; *Do You Wanna Be* Funky. In addition to Brazil, this was released in Italy also.

After the millennium, Naraine has mainly released singles, like the absolutely perfect trance pop cover of Bryan Adams' classic, *Everything I Do (I Do It For You),*. He has also cooperated with the Italian DJ/producer DJ Rossi (Rossano Prini). There has been silence in the album front since 2011 (*Life).* He also released a couple of live albums in Brazil.

▶ *Alexia*

Published with permission of DWA Records.

Despite her small size (150 centimeters), Alessia Aquilani's (b.1967) voice is strong and multicolored. She started to show her singing skills already at the age of four and managed to achieve some rewards and glory. At seven, she joined a band, but soon left to sharpen her singing, dancing, and piano playing.

She got her first record deal from Zanetti's DWA Records. First song, *Boy*, came out in 1989. With this and a few other songs she got some chart success in Europe and Japan. In addition to this, she sang background vocals for two other Zanetti project, Ice MC and Double You. i

However, she wanted to continue her solo career, which turned out to be a good decision. In 1995 she recorded *Me And You*, in which Double You offered the guest vocals. The single bounced into number one in Italy.

But she reached real super stardom with songs *Summer Is Crazy* and *Number One*, which were done in the typical Robyx sound. But even their success was nothing compared to the absolute mania she caused with *Uh La La La* euro reggae. In some countries that single was released twice, that's how popular it was. For a fan of eurodance, it was quite depressing. The success of this song made Alexia to detach herself from eurodance gradually.

Having said that, the first album Fan Club was very tasty euro LP, although it was released in 1997, when euro was disappearing. It had many great dance songs like the opening song, *Virtual Reality.* It was released also in America with the name, *Fun Club.*

The unbelievable success caused by *Uh La La La* effected Alexia's second album: *The Party* (1998) was mainly euro reggae, like the single release *Gimme Love.* There still was a couple of fantastic dance songs like *The Music I Like* (which was confusing, that probably wasn't the music Alexia liked).

Both two albums sold well, over half a million copies each. Next, *Happy* (1999), was more of the same euro reggae. Especially the title song was self-plagiarism at its worst. *The Hits* (2000) collected Alexia's biggest hits and was a farewell to her first record company, DWA. A new deal was made with Sony Music and a new album *Mad For Music* saw daylight. It sold painfully little compared to previous chart

179

smashers. According to Danceartistinfo website, the reason for leaving Robyx, was that she said she had reached a point in her career, where she wanted to show her skills fully.

From that point on, a new era dawned for Alexia. She decided to concentrate on her home country and switched English to Italian. After her eurodance career, she had released several albums in Italy, the last one so far in 2017.

ALEXIA WITH OTHERS

Alexia's career in eurodance was much deeper than her solo career. Her liaison with ICE MC created euro hits like *Think About The Way* and she also sang all the female vocals in his *Ice'n'Green* album.

She didn't get to be the frontlady in any projects she had before her own solo. In Fourteen 14 project she sang, but in live dreadlock lady Sabrina Perugini lip-synched. Other singing credits for her are bands like Digilove, Cybernetica and Galactica.

It's a shame, that Alexia's biggest hits are euro reggaes. They are easy to chew for the masses, but their energy level doesn't even get near to her hectic and melodic dance songs.

▶ *Ice MC*

British Ian Campbell aka Ice MC earned his artist name in high school, where his initials IC were eventually transformed to ICE. After graduation he hang around on his home turf in Nottingham for a few years until he joined a breakdance group and embarked on a European tour with them. During these travels in 1989 he met the Robyx and in the same year they released a single *Easy*. It was made in the popular hip house style and it was giant success all over the Europe likewise the next efforts, the single *Cinema* and the album carrying the same name. It was hip house, but some house songs thrown in the mix. With the same style another LP was released, *My World* (1991), but it flopped because hip house wasn't that popular anymore.

Published with permission of DWA Records.

Ian decided it was time for a makeover, because eurodance had started to lift its head. First song done with euro sound was *Take Away The Colour* (1993) and it sure was a step in the right direction. A home run was achieved still with the song *Think About The Way,* which offered lyrics like *"bom digi digi bom digi bom"* . It enjoyed massive success in Europe. Refrain was sung by Alexia, while Ian offered the raggamuffin raps. Ian had also changed his appearance compared to his hip house era: previously he had shaved his head, but now he had handsome dreadlocks. Also, the raggamuffin rapping was something new. *Think About The Way* was especially popular in France, where it sold 125 000 copies.

Very similar single followed, *It's A Rainy Day*. This and *Think About The Way* got decent radio play even in America, latter one even got to be in *Trainspotting* movies soundtrack. Album *Ice'n'Green* was released also in US because of the radio play and club success there. It had several fantastic euro songs like the superhero-influenced *Dark Night Rider* and *Run Fa Cover*, while it had its share of more light and tiresome euro house like *Labba Ling*. It's the most sold album of Ice MC to date and also a remix edition of it was put out.

Everything wasn't still going according to plan: according to Eurokdj, in 1995 Ian sued his producer Robyx, because it wasn't mentioned in the credits that Ian had also wrote lyrics. For example, he didn't get any money from *Trainspotting* movie, because the songs had been credited to Robyx. Ian changed record company because of this.

After a small break, Ice Mc released a new song *Give Me The Light*, with Masterboy's guys in the production front. Despite the Robyx break-up, it become a hit in Europe, and soon a fourth album, *Dreadatour* (1996), followed which used also other producers like Nosie Katzmann in addition to Masterboy. The dispute with Robyx probably inspired the single, *Music For Money*. In this LP, Alexia had changed into another Italian female singer called Valentina Ducros.

According to Eurokdj, Ian regretted his leave from DWA Records. He said that he had wanted to change his style and that was one reason he left. New record company didn't want Ice MC to change his winning eurodance style, and that's why Ian felt that he was forced to work with Masterboy, which Ian thought copied Robyx's popular style.

Ian returned to England in 2001 and started to focus on his family and new projects, outside music world. The next year he and Robyx reconciled. As a token of this atonement, a new album, *Cold Skool* (2004),was released. It was probably the most natural album to him; it was mainly hip hop. Once again he changed his hairstyle.

Published with permission of Ice MC.

After *Cold Skool* he has released isolated songs for example with DJ Sanny J and also his biggest euro hit *Think About The Way* has been remixed and covered very diligently. He also does 90's gigs, although without dreadlocks.

▶ *Sandra Chambers* aka *Sandy*

Published with permission of Sandy and Off Limits Production

The most recognizable voice of 90's eurodance is without a doubt Chambers aka Sandy. Her voice has been heard in many classic euro songs, and she has also continued her career into a new millennium.

182

She first joined DWA Records as a backing vocalist. Her voice was so strong, that you couldn't hide behind other voices, so she was promoted to main vocalist in projects like Babyroots and Netzwerk. With her original name she did a euro single *Everybody's Dancing* (1994), but the next year she released a far superior and catchier *Bad Boy*. The latter one became a hit in Europe and Canada.

In 1995, two great things happened to her: she got to be lead singer in two major eurodance projects, Corona and J.K. Both acts superhits created more singing gigs and partners for her.

Sandy left Corona in 1998 because she had a baby thus minimizing her name in music business. But she was re-introduced to a new generation in the beginning of the 2000's by DJ Benny Benassi. Benassi fused together trance music and the then popular tek-house sound with his Benassi Bros project. Sandy sang some of the hits, like the absolutely mind-blowing *Illusion* (2003). It was number one in the French club chart. Because of this Benassi connection, she was able to continue her successful career and she has released a great number of singles during this new millennium. One of the most peculiar singing gigs has been with the legendary disco band Boney M: In *Boney M Remix 2005* album she sang the groups biggest hits.

Sandy was one of those unfortunate ladies, whose destiny was to stay only as a studio voice, while other people lip synched in live performances. Like Benassi, also the Swedish house project Sunblock wanted to bring recognition to this diva, by remaking Coronas mega hit *Baby, Baby* and hiring Sandy to sing again these vocals.

Sandys voice is so diverse, that it enables her to sing many kinds of dance songs. Also, her voice has depth and power, which is almost impossible to find in contemporary singers.

In The Spotlight

Sandy Chambers singer

You worked with many producers in the 90's. Who was your favorite and why?

I don't think I particularly had a favorite because I learnt a lot from all of the producers that I worked with . I think in the 90s I was so shocked by the fact that all these important producers believed in me and wanted to work with me....it was quite surreal!!!

From your own songs, which is your favorite from the eurodance era?

There are quite a few that I really love but the ones that spring to mind are *Baby Baby*, *Dancing with an Angel* and *Send me an Angel*

183

You sung many hits, but the frontmen used to be someone else. How did it feel to have someone else lip syncing to your songs?

Everything happened so quickly, and I was working so intensely that I didn't really have time to think how I felt about it! I can remember being at a big Italian music event and one of the featured artists was lip-syncing a song I had sung. It was a strange feeling!!!!!

How would you define eurodance?

Eurodance was a musical movement that was definitely unique and will never be repeated. In the eurodance era in the 90s, Italy was a hub of musical creativity and I had the fortune to be right in the middle of it.

You are one of the key singers of eurodance. Do you think that been good for your career or bad?

Eurodance was probably the best thing that ever happened to me!!!!! It launched me as a professional singer

Eurodance is a popular genre but is sometimes ridiculed. Have you experienced this?

I used to song jazz and blues and all of my musicians tended to look down on dance music in general. I believed then and I believe now that music is music!

Was it pressuring to make more hits in the 90's?

I made lots of hits in the 90s and loved every minute of it! I wouldn't change anything regarding my career then or today

Why do you think that eurodance was so popular and is so once again?

I think eurodance was so popular because it was really relatable. Everybody could try and do it.... everybody could sing to it and dance to it! It was good time music...summer music...happy and uplifting with strong beats and quick rhythms.

What led you to sing eurodance in the first place?

I started singing eurodance literally by pure luck. I was spotted in a bar and invited to do a studio session. And the rest is history...

▶ Co.Ro. / Taleesa

Emanuele Cozzi, Rolando Zaniolo and Maurizio Rossi put their musical talents together and founded a band called CO.RO. The name was created from Maurizio's and Emanuele's surnames. At first they were meant to record a cover version of Depeche Modes *Master & Servant*, but the female singer who was recruited to sing in it, didn't please them. Instead of her, Emanuelle Gubinelli (b.1971) aka Taleesa *Because The Night*. The men became infatuated to it so much, that they decided to smash-up: *Because The Night* but with *Master & Servant* melody.

Taleesa, who had a very masculine voice, was given more room: she also got to sing songs like *4 Your Love* and *There's Something Going On*, which were on the CO.RO debut album, *The Album* (1993). *4 Your Love* accomplished number one position in Israel. It's weird that Taleesa wasn't in the music video, the men are lip-syncing in it.

After the one and only album, they tried another female vocalist. With Lyen, they released quite adept and fast *Run Away* and a vinyl-only release of the David Bowie classic *Life On Mars*. In the end of the 90's they released more vinyl singles, both dry house songs.

In The Spotlight

▶II

Emanuele Cozzi producer

*Photographer: Gianfranco Brusegan, published
with permission of Emanuel Cozzi.*

Was there plans to make a second Album?

There was no plans to make an album because every one of us chose other thinks to do in life, after *Life On Mars* I left the group, the producer Stefano Secchi tried to produce other 2 or 3 songs under the name Co.Ro. but without success. Me personally, I went on singing and producing as you see as Paps'n'skar as lead singer, other productions as Sally Can Dance as lead singer, d.e.a.r., club (club deep inside) with the Italian DJ Giorgio Prezioso, in the last 6 years in collaboration with DJ matrix I had many Italian hits as *Voglio Tornare Negli Anni 90* (*I Really Wanna Go Back To The Nineties*) golden record in 2018, *Fanno Bam* with an awesome remix by Gabry Ponte as an example.

How did you meet Taleesa?

I met Taleesa in NTM studio, the first studio I went for my first production that was *Because The Night*. I already had a rough mix with the samples of *Master And Servant* by Depeche Mode. But something was missing so my sister Ramona suggested me to put the song *Because The Night* on the base I was producing, because the chords of the musical base reminded her of the song of Bruce

Springsteen and Patti Smith. So, we had to find a good singer and I met Taleesa for the first time

Why CO.RO eventually stopped?

The group broke up for various reasons, as often happens.

In 2019 i started my solo career as Paps with the brand new single in collaboration with Alien Cut and DJ Matrix - *Flex*

Taleesa live, published with permission
of photographer Karine Sanche.

Taleesa's career had started before CO.RO and she would also outlast them. In the beginning she wrote songs for Stefano Secchi and two of those become hits. This naturally helped her to start her own singing career. The biggest break was meeting CO.RO, which helped her make a name for self in dance music scene.

First solo effort (that was euro) was the great *I Found Luv* (1995). With a few eurodance singles she cooperated with different producers and also tried out some lighter euro house. As previously mentioned, her career lasted over the switch of the century and into the 2000's in the form of featuring for other artists and DJ's. According to Eurokdj, in 2011 she worked hard in her own media firm, Luv En Colors but music world draw her in once again, nowadays she is performing in 90's festivals.

▶ *Da Blitz*

Da Blitz is one of those Italian eurodance names, who should stand on the pedestal with the likes of Masterboy and Cappella. Despite their fantastic melodies and refrains, their Italian sound has little bit fell into oblivion...

In The Spotlight

▶II

Vivian Presutti *singer*

Published with the permission of Vivian Presutti

How Da Blitz was formed?

Da Blitz project was formed in November 1993. I was a professional singer working for Bliss Corporation and Simone Pastore was a musician and composer working for the label.

Simone chose a vocal sample from some of my previous registered vocals and with that sample he created the vocal of *Let Me Be*. It was the beginning of Da Blitz duo.

How would you define eurodance?

Eurodance is a genre that bases it success on easy vocals and lyrics and strong and powered sounds an arrangements. All that just to make people sing, dance and have fun on the floor. Italians are very good at making it! We ruled that genre for all the nineties. (1990/2000)

A kind of best of album was released in Japan called _Euromanic Trance_. Was there talk about a proper bigger album release?

No. We never made an album for other countries except Japan. That album was created only for Japan release, due to the fact that _Let Me Be_, _Take My Way_, _Stay With Me_ and _Movin'On_ were all smash hits in Japan. After many years, our previous Label (Bliss Co) decided to make a collection of hits from Da Blitz (called DA BEST OF DA BLITZ)

How would you describe Da Blitz sound?

Power Power Power : energetic synthesizers sounds and powered vocals.

Do you think that Italian eurodance has different characteristics than eurodance in other countries?

Yes of course. This is why all Italian eurodance licensed and sold all over the world. It is unique and completely different from other eurodance trends.

What made you come back with D.B.Reloaded?

I decided to open a publishing company and two labels. After many years involved in eurodance and dance productions I definitely had the abilities to become a talent scout. The first project I decided to give birth to it was our old project with a new name (we don't own the rights on our artist name and that's why we decided to choose a new one…).

How popular Da Blitz was in the 90's?

Very popular. We licensed all over Europe (except England where they preferred house genre) and east Europe, Japan, Latin America, and Canada.

What's the status of Da Blitz now, touring?

My ex colleague (Simon) left the label in 1998 and returned to the university where he graduated in pharmacy : today he's still working in that area. I left the label on 1997 and returned to live music with bands performing all round Italy and on 2002 I became a vocal coach, which is my main job now as now. Sometimes clubs and pr contact me to perform in Italy and abroad too with Da Blitz songs. I still make shows singing Da Blitz, but my main work today is to teach people how to sing : I also wrote a book about a singing method.

▶ Mo-Do

Fabio's portrait in the album's leaflet.

Mo-Do's frontman, Fabio Frittelli's, career started as a male model and a hard rock musician. But when he met Claudio Zennaro, dance project Mo-Do was born. Acts name was derived from combining Frittelli's hometown (*Monfalcone*) and his date of birth (*Domenica*, Sunday in Italian). Although the men were Italian, they decided that Fabio should sing in German, with authoritarian style. First single, *Eins, Zwei, Polizei,* copied the atmosphere from Falco's *Der Komissar*. Melodic and banging debut was a major hit and reached number one position for example in German and Italy.

Next and clearly more monotone release was *Super Gut*, but it didn't fare as good as the previous one, although it gained number one position in Finland. *Was Ist Das?* LP was released after these singles. In my opinion, it's one of the most overlooked eurodance albums: it has melodic ingenuity and it is so much more than the hit singles. Third single, *Gema Tanzen,* was remixed into a more fluid form comparing to the album version.

New material was released in 1996 with the utterly horrible *Sex Bump Twist,* but it was a flop. Closing the new millennium, Mo-Do released new versions from his biggest hit and in 2000 last new song, *Cyberdisco*, saw the light of day. It was of a different breed: it had modified vocals and the style was hard trance. According to Eurokdj, Mo-Do was dropped from the record company during this time.

Fabio's and Mo-Do's career ended in tragedy: Fabio was found in 2013 dead in his own apartment. He had committed suicide.

190

▶ Cabballero

Although Cabballero sounded like a German eurodance band, they were from Italy. Project was developed by musician Jama Johnson. Female vocals were provided by Sara Pola and Kristina Safrany of Future Beat fame. Stylistically they wore the same iconography as Pharao: Egyptian mysticism was used in music and record covers.

They stroked a hit with their second single, *Hymn*, which was a cover of synth-pop band Ultravox's classic. The song ended up number one in Germany and Italy. The producers thought that why change a winning formula, so they released another Ultravox cover, *Dancing With Tears In My Eyes*, which also turned out to be another great success. On the next one, they changed the band, this time they covered Camouflage, *Love Is A Shield*.

Naturally, an album was put out, called *Elements*. It's a wild mix of eurodance and happy hardcore. It also has an instrumental *Cabballero's Land*, which is the same song as Sonic Beat's *I Can Fly* without the vocals. The makers were the same in both. Last single from the LP covered Israel's national anthem, after which they went on a hiatus.

In 2004 the project woke from its slumber: house song laced with male vocals was released, *Sleepin' (Now That You're Gone)* (Rick Astley cover), which had nothing in common with the old energetic Cabballero. Their name was spoiled more in the 2010's with the perfectly boring cover, *Eye Of The Tiger*.

ITALO DISCO ARTISTS AT THE EURODANCE POOL

Italo disco artists turned their attention to eurodance, while their italo sound was left to the 80's. Eurodance was a chance to have more fans. Many italo artists released at least one eurodance single. The most famous of these was Radiorama, whose transformation into 90's euro act was perfect.

Den Harrow, who didn't really sing in his own songs during the 80's and 90's, grabbed the genre with songs like *Take Me* (1993) and *Universe Of Love* (1994). Den Harrow was more of a project than a solo singer. While the male model and dancer Stefano Zandri (b.1962) was the frontman (and the "pretty boy"), vocals were actually provided by several male singers like Tom Hooker and Silvio Pozzoli.

Not until 1998 he rose to the challenge and went to singing lessons and has since then sung himself (presumably) and re-sung the old hits. One of the voices behind Den, Tom Hooker sprinkled some eurodance magic on himself with his own solo act, *Runaway* (1994). There has been a grudge between Stefano and Tom about who is really singing the Den Harrow songs. There a documentary about this feud, called *Dons Of Disco* (2018)

Den Harrow and Spagna were easily changed to eurodance.

Fun Fun, Italian girl duo dipped their toes quickly into euro, with the fabulous *I'm Needin' You* (1994) and discovered that one song is enough. Fun Fun's leading figures were models and the real singers were something else, like Ivana Spagna. Ivana managed to make a successful solo career after being just a voice in the studio and released one of the biggest hits in the 80's, *Call Me* (1987). She dipped into euro with a couple of songs, of which *Lady Madonna* (1994) was the juiciest euro effort. Italian trance act Datura had the privilege to remix her song, *Why Me*, and succeeded on creating a most beautiful euro version of it. Spagna also wrote Corona's two hits.

They could have done a better job designing this cover...

Silver Pozzoli tested euro with the single *Don't Forget Me* (1994), which was quite average, because it didn't have typical wildness of Italian euro productions. Miko Mission aka Pier Michele Pozzetti on the other hand released a far better euro single *I Can Fly* (1993).

One of the most legendary italo disco legends is probably Ken Laszlo aka Gianni Laszlo Coraini. His euro career was much bigger than just a little splash. Their first eurodance from him was *Everytime* (1993) and after that he released a lot of euro music even in the end of the 90's, for example with Jenny Kee. These songs have been compiled into S.A.I.F.A.M–released album, *Dr Ken & Mr Laszlo* (1998).

▶ *Radiorama / S.A.I.F.A.M.*

Radiorama's 80's style.

Radiorama's trip from italo to euro is legendary. You can't tell their story without starting with the producers Mauro Farina and Giuliano Crivellente. Even at a young age, Farina showed great interest on music, especially playing the guitar. When he was six, he had all the Beatles songs memorized and started a band when he was 11. Also, Giuliano had a similar interest on music, but compared to Farina he was more introvert and interested more on playing the piano. When he was 16, Giuliano got to be in a well-known Verona band as a piano player. Three years later Italian producers asked him to accompany famous artists in the studio.

Giuliano was in a certain concert, where Mauro was performing. After the show he asked Mauro to accompany him in the studio in order to make a song together. Thus, began their musical friendship which would lead up to over 1000 songs. In 1979 they interested about two artists, who would be driving forces in pushing the electronic sound into the mainstream, Patrick Cowley, and Bobby Orlando. Both got excited about these two artists and decided to release their first dance single. Two years later they founded Factory Sound Studio and S.A.I.F.A.M. Both companies would be major players in eurodance.

These two friends started to achieve fame in the 80's with their italo disco productions. They got to produce songs for many dance artists like Miko Mission. But the biggest success was behind the corner. In 1985 they met two DJ/producers, Paolo Gemma, and Marco Brescia. These four men decided to set up one of the biggest italo disco groups, Radiorama.

First Radiorama single, *Chance To Desire* (1984) was an instant hit. Also, the next ones, *Desire, Aliens* and *Yeti* gathered fame all over Europe, Canada and Mexico.

Typically, also Radiorama used frontmen or ladies who didn't provide the real vocals. Actually, Farina sang most of the male vocals and Clara Moroni the female vocals (excluding the first single).

In the end of the 80's, italo disco had started to lose its power, so Mauro dropped out of the vocal duties and the band changed their style into fast eurobeat, which was a kind of combination hi-NRG and synth-pop. This style was especially popular in Japan.

Radiorama in the 90's, published with the permission of The S.A.I.F.A.M. Group.

Radiorama changed into eurodance act with *Your Love* (1994). After this they started to put out absolutely perfect euro songs like *Little Bird* and *Let Me Be* which shook off even the last traces of the 80's. Changing into a euro act was a good decision for the project. They released euro songs until the end of 90's, like *Beautiful Man,* although almost all the euro acts had given up the sound. 90's songs were compiled for the album *World Of Radiorama* (1999). I can't recommend enough this album, it's hard euro sound with lasting sounds from top to bottom, there's even a bonus mix of the old *Aliens* hit.

Project hanged on until the beginning of the 2000's. Last album *Yesterday Today Tomorrow* (2002) had a few new songs, remixed and warm-ups of their old hits.

Radiorama had many singers like another Italian project Cappella, it's not always sure who sings what. Although it's fairly certain to say, that Radiorama's 90's euros were sung by T.H. Express female singer, because that project is also Mauro's and Giuliano's.

▶ *T.H. Express*

Farina founded T.H. Express with the French record company, Ramdam Factory. The acts frontmen were Fauve and rapper Ramses, but it was very likely that they didn't really sing in their songs. First singles like *I'm On Your Side* and *Missing In The Rain* were club bangers for example in Spain, Japan, and South America.

Album soon followed, which is almost entirely eurodance. Farina has since released under the band's name some good songs over the years, but also really obsolete covers done in various styles ranging from dance to hip hop.

▶ *DJ Miko / Orlando*

4 Non Blondes rock classic, *What's Up,* ended up as a dance song in the hands of DJ Miko (aka Monier Quartararo Gagliardo b. 1973). The singer, British Louise Gard, sounded like the original singer Linda Perry. It managed to break into Billboard Hot 100 chart, but only to position 58. The song was still a hit in the UK, positioning at number five.

Miko continued with covers like *Hot Stuff* and *My Sharona* all through the 90's, but the album didn't come until 1999, *The Last Millennium*. It was basically a collection of singles released so far. He continued carefully and slowly creating new music until the 2000's.

According to Eurokdj, Orlando project was an answer to big 80's bands who had done a successful comeback in the end of the 90's: Modern Talking and Bad Boys Blue. There's still not much common ground between those acts and Orlando, only that they both had male vocals. It's a strange comparison, because Orlando began already in 1994, when euro was blooming, with *That's My Love*.

Farina's project continued with singles, like the quickly covered Haddaway hit, Rock *My Heart*. During BBB:s comeback, they covered one of their 80's hit, *A World Without You (Michelle)* in 1998.

Like it was common in many S.A.I.F.A.M. projects, there was actually two different voices behind the project, one of which had sung as Den Harrow. Orlando's singles were collected at *Number 1* album (2000).

In The Spotlight

▶II

Mauro Farina producer, singer

Published with the permission of The S.A.I.F.A.M. Groupin

SAIFAM has become a common name for italo disco and eurodance lovers. What made you to start this label?

Me and my partner Giuliano Crivellente founded the SAIFAM group in 1981 with the purpose to produce and manage our own productions.

Radiorama is one of your biggest successes. Can you tell me about why the project changed and started to do eurodance in the 90's?

I never wanted to fix my work only on a particular style, during my career I produced and wrote songs in several different moods: italodance, pop, house, techno, eurobeat.

T.H. Express has a same sound as Radiorama, did they share same singers too? What's the origin of T.H. Express?

Radiorama vocals were different from T.H. Express ones, T.H.Express project was born thanks to a cooperation with a French friend who wanted to make popular the italo eurodance in France as well.

197

Have you sung in your own projects?

Yes, all the songs under the artist name of Mark Farina were performed by me.

Tell me a little bit about projects Orlando and Wildside, how did they start?

Both of them are "studio projects ", they were born to meet the huge request of our productions especially for international markets (France, Spain, Far East, Australia and Japan).

Are there other eurodance projects you would like to mention (from your label) ?

We developed many artists and projects during the 80's and 90's, I like to name Bronski Beat, Delegation, Ken Laszlo, Den Harrow, Radiorama, DJ Miko.

What do you think is eurodance's legacy to today's dance music?

The current dance music has changed a lot comparing to eurodance, but a bit remains in creative part of melodies that keep the spirit of eurodance.

Music world has changed drastically since the 80's and the 90's, what do you think of the change?

I like all the changes and the evolution of the music as well. Music always accompanied the 60's, 70's, 80's, 90's generations and music will continue to do it. As fashion, cars, technologies changed also music had and will have to evolve and change!

HIGH ON A HAPPY VIBE - ENGLANTI

English brand of eurodance has certain levity. The beat is usually not so hard, and it doesn't necessarily have rap parts. It's also relatively happy and uplifting.

I feel that British euro is very hard to recognize because it has been blended so deep into other dance music genres like hi-NRG. For example, UK labels like Energise Records and Almighty Records release a unique blend of hi-NRG and eurodance.

That's why I have collected in this section the bands who had most euro in them, although many might think otherwise. I must also point out, that these bands or acts have other kind of songs too than euro.

▶ *Clock*

Clock's classy pose in Fly Away single cover.

One of the biggest names of British eurodance got its start from DJ and producer Stu Allan's idea. In the first single *Holding On* (1993) they sampled Bortolotti's house project 49ers song *Move Your Feet* (1991), in which Media Records Ann-Marie Smith gave her voice. The success turned out to be so huge that they started live performances. Because Ann-Marie was tied to other Media projects, Stu and another producer Peter Pritchard tried to find suitable live performers.

Finding the right leading figures wasn't easy. Stu and Peter tried different combinations, but they couldn't find the right one until they came upon ODC MC (Marcus Thomas) and Tinka (Lorna Saunders). ODC had his own dance group and Tinka happened to be on the same group. ODC had also practiced rapping, so the ingredients for good live performances were there.

Clock was especially successful in England, in 1995 they got three singles into Top 10 and album into Top 30. The biggest hits were from the first album, *It's Time...* (1995). In 1996 second Clock LP was released in Japan, called *Oh What A Night*. It got a more wider release next year with added songs, this time with the title *About Time 2*. It was an incredible mish mash of everything from funk and disco to happy hardcore and also featured some of the hits from the first one.

The project failed badly with their continued style of disco and funk. Last traces of eurodance were scraped out with the LP, *Boogie Sound*. Their last new song, *Sunshine Day (1999)*, was lighter than light house song. Their career was sealed with Japan-only collection, *Hits Around The Clock* (2000).

Clock has many similarities to Italian Gianfranco Bortolotti's project. Like with Bortolotti, Clock songs are performed by different artists and also samples were used. For example, *Everybody* borrows from disco classic, Hamilton Bohannon's *Let's Start The Dance* (1978).

I think that the Clock sound is best presented in the first album, because it was a great party feel and lots of energy. It also expresses eurodance's ideology better. I think that the Clock's latter songs could have been released with another project name.

▶ *Urban Cookie Collective*

Urban Cookie Collective was a positive band.

Rohan Heath (b.1964) is the main man behind British band Urban Cookie Collective. Before UCC he had experience in electronic music with the rave band Together. In UCC Rohan wrote the songs, played keyboards and produced.

He brought in the diva Diane Charlemagne (b.1964), who also had had a previous band, a jazz/funk/r'n'b ensemble called 52nd Street. She also got to write UCC songs. The two first singles from 1992 didn't bring any success, but the band struck gold with the third song, *The Key The Secret* (1993), which reached number two position in England and number five in Germany. The well didn't dry up after this because more fame was coming to them with the positive hits *Feels like Heaven* and *High On A Happy Vibe*. The debut LP was naturally also a success.

Like with many other euro acts, the fame didn't last long. Second album, *Tales from the Magic Fountain,* didn't offer any more super hits and so UCC eventually faded away...

The final single, *Mercedes Benz* (2000), was a bit dry attempt to imitate Vengaboys. Also, after the second LP, Diane wasn't the vocalist anymore.

Diane, who had sung also for Moby's and Goldie's dance hits, died of cancer in 2015, at the age of 51. For me, it was Charlemagne, who made UCC so great. Her magnificent vocals fitted perfectly to the bands uplifting sound. They were happy, without being too corny. Although the legendary lead singer has joined the heavenly dance choir, the band is still touring actively with a new singer, Danielle Barnett and with the blessing of the man himself, Rohan.

▶ *N-Trance*

N-Trance had really great eurodance gems, although their popularity was concentrated on the loose disco songs.

N-Trance began when friends Dale Longworth and Kevin O'Toole met and decided to set up a band in the beginning of the 90's. They had difficulty agreeing on a name, but eventually they ended up with the name N-Trance. Pete Waterman (Stock, Aitken & Waterman) took the band under his wing to his 380 Records record company. The soon-to-be mega hit was first developed in Waterman's stable, but it was soon realized that 380 Records wasn't the right way for success. They switched to AATW, where they are even in 2020.

Set You Free (vocalized by Kelly Llorenna) didn't become a hit easily. After a couple of re-releases, it didn't only end up tickling the Top 40 but got into top, number two. Eventually the single sold whopping 600 000 copies. In my opinion, it was harder to sell to general public because the song didn't have a straight beat and it had lots of techno/rave sounds, which were not familiar to most people.

Before the last and most successful *Set You Free* release, the band had put out a 100 percent eurodance song, *Turn Up The Power* (1994), which was sung by the fabulous Rachel McFarlane (of Loveland fame). A step to a completely another direction was a song sung by Ricardo Da Force, *Stayin'Alive*, which covered the well-known Bee Gees hit. It was a massive success and created a whole trend of remaking old disco hits into contemporary dance versions. For me this is one example how some of the biggest hits of eurodance bands are the most boring and phlegmatic ones.

The album *Electronic Pleasure* (1995) was released in the same year as their disco stomper. Luckily, it offered something for eurodance fans too like the euphoric club pleasers *(Just) Let It Go* and *Do You Wanna Rock?*, but it also threw in some completely unnecessary downtempo and hip hop. Also, the great *Turn Up The Power* wasn't in some versions of the album.

If you thought that the band had had enough of disco sound after this album, you were wrong. Next they covered Rod Stewart's old *Da Ya Think I'm Sexy? (1997)* and in the same year they revamped Ottawan's *D.I.S.C.O.* There seemed to be no end to these covers, because next a rock'n'roll classic by Guns'n'Roses was desecrated *(Paradise City)*. Although these previously mentioned songs are hard to listen to, their CD singles contain something noteworthy: they have bonus songs which aren't in the albums, like *Take Me Home*, which are from another planet compared to those derivative pop crowd pleasers.

While the public was showered with cover songs, N-Trance spilled out a second album, *Happy Hour*. Like the first one, also this was a mix of all kinds of genres. Luckily with this album also, there was a couple of melodic snacks like the club oriented trance song *Andare Con Me*. There was some weird shit too, like *Amadeus*, which combined rave with classical music.

Even in the turn of the millennium, they didn't want to throw out their disco shoes: five years after their first disco hit, they put out *Shake Ya Body*, which loaned from The Jacksons. After this they gave up the 70's and embarked on a whole new trip.

The next single release was a completely original song, *Forever,* which featured Kelly Llorenna. The song was in all its modesty euro trance done with the highest standards. They had probably got some influences from the new trance mixes of *Set You Free* (2001) and decided to do more trance: *Destiny*, *I'm In Heaven* and *Nothing Lasts Forever* (which sounded like their farewell song).

In 2009 they decided to release their third album in MP3 (it was an LP which never got an official release). It had some songs from the previous albums like *Mind Of The Machine*, but some new material too.

In the midst of house phenomena in 2005, O'Toole and Langworth had a project called Freeloaders, which gained a Top 10 single hit with a cover, *So Much Love To Give*. Also, Kelly Llorenna has had a successful solo career with hits like *Brighter Day, True Love Never Dies* and *Tell It To My Heart* , which are collected on *All Clubbed Up – The Best Of Kelly Llorenna*.

N-Trance as a band is a bit of everything, but their strength is without a doubt in their excellent eurodance/ trance songs. N-Trance had trouble balancing between pleasing the audience and creating what seems natural. That's why their albums and their whole line of songs are so mixed.

In The Spotlight

▶❚❚

Rachel McFarlane *singer*

How *Turn Up The Power* was born, how were you hired as a vocalist?

It was such a long time ago and I was new to the dance music scene. Everything was by word of mouth back then. N-Trance had heard me on a recording elsewhere and they asked me to record with them.

The video featured a totally different performer who lip-synced to your vocals, how did that feel?

Turn Up The Power was released many years later. It could be at least five years later? I was signed exclusively to record with Loveland at the time. Naturally, I don't like people miming over my vocals. I work hard and I am good at what I do and it's not right that someone else gets the credit for that. But this is the way of the music industry, even today! It's time we created a culture of honor and integrity in the music business and entertainment world, at large.

You also sang for Urban Cookie Collective. Were you supposed to be a more permanent member of UCC?

Yes, I recorded *Champagne Supernova*. As you know Diane Charlemagne had worked with UCC for years and she was coming to the end of her time with them. Rowan called me to vocal the track. I was lucky because Diane had already recorded it. I did enough to make it 'my version'. from what I understand it was never released due to unresolved conflict between label and Noel Gallagher. I've never wanted to be a permanent member of any band, to be honest. Which is why I've always gotten a 'featured' status on the track, where possible.

Tell me a little about your singing career and songs in the 2000's and forward to this day.

I developed Graves' Disease, an aggressive form of hyperthyroidism. I developed a goitre in my neck and was unable to sing for years. If I'm honest, I never thought I'd sing again. Naturally, it was a very depressing time for me. I had no plan B!! I turned to teaching vocals with local youth music projects. After some time, I would need to demonstrate to the young singers and had no idea that my voice would get stronger. Lee Monteverde from LMC contacted me in 2003 and asked to record, I obviously refused. But he asked me to come down. (Please check out my Behind The Music Vlogs on YouTube). I recorded *Take Me To The Clouds Above*- Number 1, BRIT nominated- absolutely mind-blowing experience!! I recorded their 2nd single *You Get What You Give* and then parted company with them.

I'm at a stage now where I want to do music on my own terms. I mentioned not wanting to be part of a band earlier. This is because I've always had a vision of being solo artist. I was promised my own deals if I recorded with this band or that and it never came to fruition. The music industry is a very different place today. You don't need to be signed at all (although it helps!!'). I've completed my debut album due to be released April 2020. I've gone back to my gospel roots and I'm remembering and celebrating all that has made me. I'll still record house music in the future but as an independent artist.

▶ Motiv 8

Motiv 8 is the golden name, which many people remember from its great remixes. There's actually one guy behind the project, Steve Rodway. His golden finger has changed many songs into energetic euro. Many hits from the 90's got a remix treatment, like Spice Girls' *Wannabe* but also many original euro songs like Dreamworld's *Movin'Up* and N-Trance's *Turn Up The Power*. Motiv 8 also produced many songs to Gina G's debut album.

Motiv 8 also had a few successful solo singles. There was never an album, but Almighty Records has released a collection of the remixes called *Almighty Presents: We Love Motiv 8*. Also, worth checking out is Australia-only collection *Motiv8tion (The Official Motiv 8 Remix Collection)* released in 1999, which has even more songs.

In The Spotlight

▶II

Steve Rodway producer

Published with the permission of Steve Rodway

How was Motiv 8 born?

I was releasing mostly underground tracks under different names in the early 90's. One of those tracks was an early version of *Rockin' For Myself* and it sounded much more commercial that the others. When the demand for underground techno began to fall off, I recorded a new version of *Rockin' For Myself* which became a massive hit in the clubs. Warner's then signed me. I remixed the track again and it became a top 20 hit on the UK charts – in the days when having a top 20 hit meant something. I therefore stuck with the name Motiv 8. Because of *Rockin'*'s success, Jarvis Cocker of Pulp approached me and asked me to remix *Common People*. That remix was huge and made the Radio 1 playlist. It played a big part in establishing Motiv 8 and led to many other high-profile artists requesting a Motiv 8 remix. The name Motiv 8 therefore just grew organically.

Do you see Motiv 8's sound as eurodance or something else? (I see it as British eurodance)

There are definitely other elements in the Motiv 8 sound that are outside eurodance. That's hardly surprising though, since I was just having fun making commercial dance music. I never analyzed other people's records, let alone eurodance ones. I just make the music and let others put tags on what style they want to call it.

Do you think that British eurodance has different characteristics than other countries' eurodance?

Yes. I think each country has its own brand of eurodance though sometimes the differences are subtle. The records coming out of Italy have their own sound as do ones from Germany, Belgium, Holland etc.

Why do you think that eurodance was so popular?

Because people will always want to dance – it's in our DNA. Add a great melody and you have a recipe for the dance floor.

The Motiv 8 sound is very upbeat and happy, is that something that comes naturally?

Yes, it's natural to me. I like emotional chord progressions. Take classical music for example - it's all made up of emotional chord progressions – whether somber or uplifting, it's emotional. I choose uplifting although I still use aggressive sounds within that - I'm not a fan of pure sugar. I'm also a drummer and a sucker for a great melody. So, putting melodies over beats comes naturally.

Motiv 8 is well known for its remixes. Could you describe the creative process in doing a remix?

I strip it back to just the vocals and discard everything else from the original version unless there's an essential element, (such as the guitars in the Doobie Brothers' *Listen To The Music*). Before I even begin a remix, I'll look at the song. I always start with the chorus. I'll loop the lead vocal and consider the chord progression on the chorus. I might make some minor changes or replace it completely. Once I've got that nailed, I've got the hook and know the direction I'm going in. I'll then start the remix. I begin with the kick drum because that's my anchor. It's a safe haven that will keep people on the dance floor. Next I'll build the mix up with the bass and the rest of the drums & percussion. The bass is a defining element so the sound and the bass line itself are crucial. I'll then work on the rhythmic keyboard parts. The idea is to create a counter rhythm that sits in the track and really adds flavor. As a kid growing up I was really into funk and disco, so probably a lot of my keyboard parts reflect this. It also makes drops and breakdowns much easier because you can expose these elements and feature them. I'm always mixing as I go as well – I see no point in trying to come back on another day to create a great "final" mix. Do it as you go and stay in the moment. Compress or eq that vocal or keyboard part there and then and get it sounding as you want – then move one. I work on each part of the remix separately i.e. chorus, verse, breakdown etc. Once I'm happy with each section, the remix is essentially done and can be run off.

Which remix is your best, in your opinion?

I honestly don't have a "best" remix, but the following have special memories either of where I first heard them, or the work involved on the mix itself:

Jellyhead – first heard it blasting out of the car next to me at traffic lights in Los Angeles.

Wannabe – working in the studio with the Spice Girls when they were still unknown was memorable.

She's On The Phone – I got invited to the Fridge nightclub in London specifically to see the place take off to this!

Listen To The Music - turning 70's American rock into dance was outrageous!

What do you think about dance music today?

To be honest, I am not impressed. Most of it is totally bland and devoid of melody. Any half decent dance tracks sound like they could have come from the 90's anyway. It's great that creatives can now release their own music, but the downside is that it has inevitably led to a reduction in quality. Today's music producer is also the A&R person and that's a significant challenge. Objectivity and creativity can be difficult to intertwine.

▶ Gina G

Australian Gina G aka Gina Mary Gardiner started as a DJ, until she decided to make her own music in the 90's. A song *Love The Life* (with Bass Culture) was a summer hit in Australia. In 1996 she decided to take her chances in the UK, where she found an old demo tape, which was going to the trash. This demo was *Ooh Aah...Just A Little Bit* (1996).

Gina G changed these remains into British single chart number one and also got to represent UK in Eurovision song contest with this song. She was number eight there. It was also a massive hit all over the world and a Grammy nominee. Motiv 8, known for its perky style, was behind the production. Further singles followed like *Ti Amo*, after which an album called *Fresh* was put out.

Gimme Some Love

After this great success she suddenly wanted to concentrate on her family and went on a break. A second long play wasn't released until 2005 (*Get Up & Dance*). Eurodance was long gone by them. She hasn't put out new material in the last few years, but she is performing e.g. in Pride events.

▶ Abigail

It's hard to believe that you could get a decent dance version of Nirvana's grunge classic *Smells Like Teen Spirit*, but Abigail Zsiga managed to do it. Abigail sang her first solo song in 1993: a cover of K.D. Lang's song *Constant Craving*. It was a hit in a few countries. The previously mentioned Nirvana cover was an even bigger strike to this young singer. Purest eurodance song from her is *Don't You Wanna Know* from her only album called *Feel Good*.

Like Gina G, having gained some fame and glory, Abigail also wanted to start a family. After the break she has released several singles over the decades, last she has featured on American tribal house DJ's songs.

▶ *Dymension*

Dymension, hosted by Dave Livingston, is one of the bands who has not received enough international attention despite their durable and high-class sound.

Dymension's original line-up.
Published with the permission of Dave Livingston.

In The Spotlight

▶❚❚

Dave Livingston producer

Published with the permission of Dave Livingston.

How Dymension was born and who are its members now and in the 90's?

Dymension had the foundations born in the late 1980's! I have always been writing music and songs from an early age so when I was at college and also for a time at the RSAMD in Glasgow I decided I needed a singer for my songs. Initially I was collaborating with friends at college, I joined a rock band playing keyboards but then I decided to move in a different musical direction.

So, I put an advert in a local newspaper and after a surprising amount of applications and auditions, the person who shone through for me was a singer called Hazell Taylor. She had the voice I had been wanting to sing on my songs. We got on very well and we worked on so many songs in a variety of different styles.

During the time we were working on songs, I saw a television program on a Scottish television channel, and it had an interview with a person I forgot I knew. The program was called NB and it featured an interview with a man called Bill Grainger who was talking about his new record label called Clubscene.

I first met Bill several years prior to this before I was at college probably around mid-1980's when he was a DJ at a Glasgow based radio station called Radio Clyde. He had a late night dance music show on late night every weekend and I was a fan. At that time I was writing a lot of tunes and music so one night after his show I telephoned the radio station and asked if I could write some incidental music that could be played in the background when for example music charts were being read out or other things talked about on air. He said yes and I composed a few tunes. When they were finished I called him again and we met at the radio station and I gave him copies of my tunes on cassette. He liked my music and he used them for the remainder of his time presenting his show at Radio Clyde.

So, when myself and Hazell had worked on some good quality demos and having seen him on television talking about Clubscene records, I knew he was the first person to get in touch with. I got in touch with him and he really liked our work and gave me guidance on the sort of style he would want to release on his record label. There wasn't even a band name at that point and after narrowing down a lot of options I thought of the name Dymension.

Not long after the initial meeting with Bill, I wrote the music and co-wrote the lyrics with Hazell for the first Dymension release on Clubscene, a track called *Don't Stop*.

Later that would be followed up with another five singles and an album released on Clubscene. After Hazell, the next person to join was my first MC, Neil Trotter aka MC Voyager.

Over the years the members of Dymension have changed a lot. After the release of *Don't Stop*, Hazell left to pursue other types of music as she never really was a fan of dance music. So that left me to find a new singer, which I did and thats more or less how it's been to this day. If someone decides to move on, I've been lucky to find great people to slot into the band.

Dymension have been playing live shows since our first single release and we still do with the fantastic current Dymension line up. When we play live shows on-stage alongside myself are my long time MC, Alan Laidlaw aka MC Madman, my outstanding singer Karina Smillie, my dancers Jade & Louise and my long time stage manager, Scott Morrison.

How did you get Hazell Dean to sing in one of your songs?

The collaboration with Hazell Dean happened after my ex-manager, firstly asked me about it then he got in touch with Hazell. Once the vocals were recorded, I decided to re-arrange the vocals and write fresh new music for the song. *Power And Passion* was released as the third Dymension single featuring Hazell Dean on Clubscene. It was well received with good reviews and got high up in the top ten of the Scottish dance chart.

How would you describe your music?

As an artist I write a lot of different popular styles. I write, produce, and compose eurodance, techno, electronic, synthwave and classical and I like to think that my music is well produced, well written, enjoyable and fun to listen to.

I'm very pleased how good the early songs still sound today. They have lasted very well and really do not sound dated or old. Even more so when the songs are remastered using todays techniques that I have learned as I do all my own production, writing and mastering in my own studio. I have also been able to remix a wide variety of artists in styles I enjoy working. My remix partner was an Edinburgh based DJ called Tom Wilson and together we created our remix partnership called The Dyme Brothers. The name came about because Tom was a huge fan of Dymension, he suggested to call ourselves that.

Sadly Tom passed away far too soon but together we worked on remixes for the majority of major recording labels in the UK and Europe and remixed many artists such as Scooter, Belinda Carlisle, Ice MC song *Think About The Way* from the film *Trainspotting*, Xpansions, Tom's own release Techno Cat, *The X-Files Theme* remix are a few out of many, many projects that we worked on together and always at my studio.

I've also written and co-written songs for other artists and created other remixes such as a One Direction song remix that I produced in a similar style I write Dymension songs today and the title track from Dracula Unborn feature film that was classical orchestral style. I've also co-wrote a number of songs in slightly different styles with my good friend Mike Wyzgowski, who was a writer on the well know song *Not Over Yet* by Grace. Most of these were along a more vocal / drum & bass styling but some pure pop. I met Mike through Tom as both of them went to school together.

I am really pleased to have released several albums, most recently an electronic album of instrumentals co-written with Steven Nelson under the name Transceive and a classical album I produced and co-wrote called *The Road To Trasanne* under the collective name of Fuasgail, which is the Scots Gaelic word for free. As well as being producer on other albums featuring guitar, electronics, and flute.

Of course, I am still busy writing Dymension songs and have many in the pipeline that I'm really excited about.

What kind of success did you have in the 90's? Sales, etc?

I was really pleased that we did well because I was signed to a small independent record label so there was always a limited amount of money available. My first single *Don't Stop* was released on 12 inch vinyl only and sold thousands of copies. Which was fantastic! This release also reached the number one position on the Scottish Dance Chart, which I was really proud of. I'll never forget hearing the chart position when I listened on the radio the first week of release to the chart countdown. *Don't Stop* was then licensed to a countless amount of compilation albums all over the UK and around the world for many years after the initial release.

The first single doing well allowed me to release a follow up single again on vinyl only called *Inside My Fantasy*; followed by *Give In To Me*; that also was released on compact disc. After that *Power and Passion*, *I'm The One You Need*; that was released on the three formats of the time, cd, cassette and vinyl and the last Dymension single release on Clubscene Records was *Move Into The Rhythm*; on cd and double 12 inch vinyl. And with more single releases the sales grew accordingly which I was delighted with.

Most Dymension singles have been licensed to compilation albums and some have been remixed and released and also covered by other artists. Another song unreleased as a single and after leaving Clubscene that I'm very proud of is called *Your Life* has had only one release on a compilation album to date.

It was due to my songs being licensed to compilation albums that led to us playing live at an amazing concert, one of the Mayday raves that was held in Budapest, Hungary. It was an absolutely massive event that was televised in Hungary. And again, due to compilation albums licensing of my songs, this let us play Heaven nightclub in London and also gain fans all over the world.

My remix career with Tom Wilson proved very successful. Our work was sometimes used as the main single and most of the releases got into the UK national top 40 and many were also licensed to lots of different compilation albums in the UK, Europe and other countries and territories.

British eurodance, do you think it has different characteristics than other countries eurodance?

I would say it has differences. Mainly in the bpm/tempo of the music here in the UK. In Scotland it would be slightly faster with an edgier slightly harder feel compared to England whereas Ireland is very similar to Scotland with regards to comparison. Again, England varies a lot with more northern areas having a similar taste to Scotland by differing slightly to areas further south.

I also think there are slight differences in instrumentation used and vocal styling depending on the region. Overall, I would say British eurodance is as tuneful, catchy and enjoyable as anywhere else when compared to other countries and the slight variations from the different countries can only be seen as a very positive thing.

Anything else you want to tell about Dymension?

I'm very proud to still be writing Dymension songs and we put on a great live stage show! When I was first signed playing live was never a thought I had. I always planned on being just a studio project, but my ex-manager explained how the dance scene was in Scotland and I jumped on the idea to play live and we've now been doing so for over 25 years. I'm really proud of the stage shows we perform. We don't perform as many shows as we once did and carefully select the shows that we're approached about. Over the past few years, we've played live at some excellent events and venues, such O2 and Barrowlands in Glasgow that we've played many times before, it's fantastic to still be playing those venues along with events in Newcastle and Preston in England. I try and make our live shows as exciting as possible by combining a unique video backing that I create to go along with the set of songs I've chosen for the show. A lot of artists now use video screens as backing for their live shows but as I produce it all myself I spend a huge amount of time and effort doing this and am very pleased when I look at video recordings, fan photos and video clips of our live shows.

▶ Q-Tex

Published with the permission of Scott Brown.

Scottish DJ and musician Scott Brown (b.1972), who has created a successful solo career for himself, was in the 90's a part of an assembly called Q-Tex. Scott recalls his time in the band:

"Q-Tex was born in 1991. I was at University and my friend / classmate / bandmate Gordon Anderson had been making music at home with some synths and keyboards we bought with pocket money. We managed to secure a booking at the University but didn't have a name. The venue we used to affectionally call the 'Tech', being in Glasgow we called it the G-Tech. We then changed this to G-Tex (a play of words on Manchester's G-Mex arena). We went through the alphabet ad stuck at Q! Simple as that :) "

Later the band was reinforced with Alan Todd and a singer Gillian Tennant, who would later be a part of N-Trance. Q-Tex released EP's and singles throughout the 90's like *Let The Love*, but their only album came out in 1997, *Into The Light*. It was an interesting combination of eurodance, happy hardcore and rave. Brown recounts: *"I actually liked writing both, and at the time in Scotland, it was a good representation of the music that was played in clubs and raves. Anything from commercial dance right up to hard gabber. "*

According to Brown, the band broke up in 1997 because of disagreements between band members, but Brown wasn't member any more at that time. There still has been some songs released under Q-Tex's name even in the 2000's. They also released a series of hardcore songs under the project name Equazion.

213

▶ *Johnna*

Published with permission of Johnna Lee Cummings.

Johnna Lee Cummings' career started as a member of a girl band produced by SAW in the beginning of the 90's.The band, Boy Krazy, lasted one album and a few singles, after which Johnna decided to go solo and wrote a record deal with PWL International Ltd. Her debut single, *Do What You Feel* (1996), raised some attention, even the big trance DJ Matt Darey ended up providing a remix for the single. Still the single didn't get any higher in the British Charts than 43.

The more emotional, *In My Dreams,* managed even worse, although the song is a really catchy dance stomper. Although the first songs didn't get good chart positions, Johnna still decided to release an album called *Pride*. The title song was released also as a single, and it was produced by Motiv 8 to increase the sales. The target group was without a doubt sexual minority. Even with Motiv 8's help, the single or the album didn't have chart success. Johnna coughed up the last single, *Let The Spirit Move You*, which instantly fell into oblivion.

It's a real pity that she didn't get bigger success, because the songs were absolutely remarkable eurodance. Also, the album is one of the best and most pure euro albums ever, because it doesn't contain any ballads, just dance music from top to bottom. Nowadays Johnna lives a normal life. Her current life after the fame can be viewed from a short documentary called Expect Less.

▶ *Deuce*

Deuce was a band of two women and two men. They were like pre-Steps, but Deuce's music is a step more euro. Tom Watkins, who also managed Bros and East 17, decided to set up a band after hearing his office worker Kelly O'Keefe's distinctive singing voice. Kelly hauled in her schoolmate Lisa Armstrong and Watkins recruited the boys, Craig Young and Paul Holmes.

Their first single effort, *Call It Love* (1994), is a perky dance song in the vain of Motiv 8, but with a more poppier outtake. Its biggest accomplishment was British single chart position 11. *I Need You* was up for representing UK in the Eurovision but had to settle on bronze although it had more success on the chart than the previous single. But still even the next one, *On The Bible*, didn't break into Top 10. The inevitable album, *On The Loose*, had to settle for position 18.

O' Keefe decided to leave the band after these moderate chart successes. Also, the record company was changed into label helmed by Mike Stock. O'Keefe was replaced with dancer Amanda Perkins. New single with new company was their biggest flop so far. Also, Craig Young left the sinking ship and he was replaced too in a little Australian tour.

Soon after these changes they broke up. Since then, Young has created a successful TV career as an actor, while Armstrong is nowadays a make-up artist (according to Wikipedia). Holmes has continued in the music business by writing songs for many pop stars.

▶ JX

JX's (aka Jake Williams) career was short but even more triumphant. He got his chance at the age of 16, when Red Jerry from record company Hooj Choons invited him in 1993 to his studio, because Jake had sent demos there. JX's first song, *Son Of A Gun*, was an absurd success and the second, *You Belong To Me,* continued with the same amount of fame. The 1995 re-release of *Son Of A Gun* got into British Top 10, but *Nothing I Won't Do* enjoyed the biggest praise by getting into number 4. 1997 release of *Close To Your Heart* was a step to a more trancier sound.

All in all, JX's singles have been sold over 500 000 copies, which is a huge accomplishment for a musician who is in the beginning of his career. In the dawn of trance pop, he was also a member of a project called Planet Perfecto, whose *Bullet In The Gun* sold over 200 000 units.

Jakes last JX release (so far) has been in 2003, when he made the rough trance pop song *Restless*. Nowadays he has musically gone into different direction with an alias Rex The Dog, through which he puts out electro/house songs and hardly even recalls his 90's sound, I think.

HEAVEN IS HERE - NETHERLANDS

▶ *2 Brothers On The 4th Floor*

Published with permission of Bobby Boer, picture: Ilona Hartensveld

Two brothers, Bobby and Martin Boer, had their first experiences in the world of dance music in their parent's residence, which located on the 4th floor of an apartment building. They hired a rapper Da Smooth Baron MC and singer Peggy to perform their songs as a live act. First, *Can't Help Myself,* was immediately an international hit with it's fashionable hip house sound. The next, *Turn Da Music Up* (sung by Gale Robinson), turned out to be another success and it would prepare the brothers for a bigger breakthrough in a couple of years.

After these two first songs, the project 2 Brothers On the 4th Floor (which was named after where the guys lived) was put on a break. Martin started remixing other artists under the alias Dancability, while Bobby concentrated on designing CD covers. In 1993 they started to work again together and out of these sessions, a single *Never Alone* was born. New leading figures were introduced: singer Desirée Manders (aka Des'Ray) and rapper René Philips (aka D-Rock). Revamping their old project was a good decision, because with *Never Alone* they earned many top positions in several countries like in Israel. The songs message resonates even today, urging people to dance as one, black or white. Encouraged by the song's success, they started to produce songs made in similar eurodance fashion, like *Dreams (Will Come Alive)* and *Let Me Be Free*. Single hits, including the first hip house ones, were packed into an album called *Dreams*. It also fared well and managed to get also positive reviews.

217

The band didn't want to get stuck in one style only, new singles like *Come Take My Hand* preceded happy hardcore craze, which many euro acts tried out. Bluntly named album *2* , contained only one classic slower euro song, *Fly (Through The Starry Night)*, which was released as a single. The act had graciously been reborn as a fierce and even more energetic band while still maintaining their natural characteristics. Their popularity continued steadily despite the style change; the singles grabbed many top positions in European countries.

The band continues to transform even after the second album. Sister Sledge cover *Thinkin' Of You* (1997) was a fairly light house, where their distinctive sound was still audible, the continuous snapping sound on the background. When the euro hip hop was getting more recognition (like Down Low and C-Block), 2 Brothers released the totally boring euro hop *Do You Know,* which used refrain from Diana Ross' *Theme From Mahogany.* Fortunately, they corrected this soon, by releasing *The Sun Will Be Shining,* which resembled their greatest hits. In 1999 they remade an old Stanley Foort eurodance hit, *Heaven Is Here*, which was a an even more joyous return to euro sound with a hint of trance. *Living In Cyperspace* gave us a great interpretation of Trans-X's italo disco song, *Living On Video*. Their last new song so far has been *Stand Up And Live*, which was influenced heavily by trance pop from the likes of Alice Deejay.

After this 2 Brothers vanished from the bigger audience, although they still toured in their homeland, Holland. In 2016 they made a big comeback with a collection *The Very Best Of (25th Anniversary edition)*, which collected their entire career and added an unreleased song, *Shine Like A Star*. There was also a totally unnecessary EDM remix of *Dreams.*

▶ Twenty 4 Seven

Stay-C and Li-Ann, published with permission of Stacey Seedorf.

Internationally famous dance band Twenty 4 Seven was put together by Ruud van Rijen (b.1964). He had awakened to a world of dance music after he heard famous DJ Ben Liebrand play his hour-long non-stop mix. Ruud got so excited, that on the next day he bought two turntables and started to mix songs together. He taped these mixes to a cassette and offered them to local clubs and they were liked a lot. Bit by bit he started buy more machinery to his home studio and finally even managed to win a mixing contest, after which he scored several wins in various DJ competitions. Events came full circle when after a certain competition Ruud's idol, Liebrand, came and complemented his skills.

Ruud also started to gig in different clubs and gathered some fame and money in order to find his own recording studio. First song from him was released through an alias, Drivin Force. The song was called *Rock This World* (1984) and although it was instrumental with some samples sprinkled on top, it did quite well. So, Ruud thought that a song with original vocals could have even more success and it would get into radio and charts. Twenty 4 Seven, was born.

Ruud van Rijen in the studio, published with the permission of Ruud van Rijen.

219

The first band member who Ruud brought in, was rapper MC Fixx IT, with whom he made a song, *I Can't Stand It*. Its original form was hip hop and Ruud sang the refrain through vocoder. It didn't gather much attention, so he modified it into hip house, which changed the song completely. For the new version he recruited singer Nance (aka Nancy Coolen, b. 1973). This remake sprang into Dutch Top 10. Also, a German record company expressed their interest towards the song, but they asked a different rapper. Ruud agreed.

Captain Hollywood came aboard to provide the raps (before his own breakthrough). It ended up being a number one hit in various countries. The next single, *Are You Dreaming?*, walked the same road to fame. They released an album called *Street Moves*, after which Captain left to concentrate on his own solo efforts (which turned out to be a great decision!). Stay-C (aka Stacey S. Seedorf) inherited Caps place.

First song with Stay-C and Nance was *It Could Have Been You*, but despite its great sound it was a flop. The band immersed themselves in the studio to make something better and so *Slave To The Music* (1993) was born. Embracing the new eurodance sound, this new song got incredible following all over the world, even in Australia and Asia. Follow-up singles like *Is It Love* and *Leave Them Alone* were also popular. They had found their distinctive sound, which was summery and joyful eurodance. The band exhaled positivity, which many of the contemporary artists lacked. The hits were collected on the *Slave To The Music* album.

Third LP, *I Wanna Show You*, was full of uplifting euro and single hits like *Keep On Tryin'*. Although they released a ballad called *Oh Baby* from it, even that was a success.

After the third long play they decided to have a bit of a break, during which both Stay-C and Nance released solo material. Nance wanted to stay as a solo act, so new female vocalist Stella (aka Stella Koedam) was hired. With the company of this new singer, their sound took some new undertones like the single *We Are The World*, which took its stride from happy hardcore and the new album, *Twenty 4 Hours A Day, Seven Days A Week* (1997) didn't even contain any typical euro songs. Also, it's weirdly stump, only seven new songs and a few remixes. Stella also left the act after her short stay, she wanted to concentrate on dancing and modeling, so there was no time for the band.

Before the new millennium, Nance came back for a one final single called *Né Né*, which relied heavily on the same sample as L.A. Style's *I'm Raving* hit. After this, the whole band went sleeping for a longer period...

...until Ruud started to gather up the band again. He had met Elle, who had an unbelievable voice, so Ruud wanted to hear Elle's voice in a new Twenty 4 Seven song. *Like Flames* (2007) was of a different breed, harder trance than eurodance, although it still managed to capture their distinctive style. Also, Elle didn't want to stay for long.

After Elle, Ruud met another great vocalist, Li-Ann (aka Lianne Lucia Van Groen), who was one of the winners of the popular Talent TV show in Holland. The winners of the competition formed a girl band, who broke up after a few hits. Li-Ann saw her chance and agreed to join this legendary euro band. Ruud also got Stay-C quite easily back to the band and so Twenty 4 Seven was alive again..

Stay-C and Li-Ann cooperated in *Slave To The Music 2010* and in a completely new song *The Reason*. Nowadays they are touring actively and introducing new generations to their happy eurodance.

In The Spotlight

▶II

Stacey Seedorf aka *Stay-C* singer

How did you end up in Twenty 4 Seven? Was it hard to fill Captain Hollywood's shoes?

During a European tour of Twenty 4 Seven ft Hollywood & Nance in 1990, their support act got sick and they needed another artist to support them. At that time Twenty 4 Seven was huge with their European hits *I Can't Stand It* and *Are You Dreaming*, so it was a dream to tour with them. That is how I met Hollywood and Nance and we had a great time. When Hollywood went for his solo career, they called me to take his place and I accepted right away of course! *Slave To The Music* was the first song I wrote for the group and it became a bigger hit than the once they already had. It went top 10 all over the world.

No, it was not hard to replace Hollywood, because I am my own artist with my own style. I never compare myself to other artists. But Hollywood and I are still good friends.

You have a great singing voice, but you rap too, which of these styles you love the most?

I love both, but originally I am a singer, not a rapper.

Twenty 4 Seven was one of the most popular eurodance acts in the 90's, what's the secret of your band compared to other euro acts?

Very hard to say, because many acts were very good and popular. But I think the combination of me, and Nance was unique. The people liked our energy, passion, and love for what we did.

Eurodance was starting to fade when you released your last album in 1997. Why do you think euro eventually almost died?

I think that eurodance was part of a very important period in time. Many things changed in the 90's. But also Internet bought a lot of different music to the world very fast and people had more to choose from. Also was it that the 90's acts worked and toured too much. The success was too huge to handle and many acts got personal problems because of that. Once the biggest groups stopped, the rest followed, and the fans switched to other genres. I am happy to see that fans never forgot eurodance and are still happy with the music we made in those years.

What's it like working with Ruud Van Rijen?

Ruud is a genius that knew how to inspire me to write good songs. He is the only one who got me to write at my best. I have worked with other producers, but never had the same creative click.

Do you miss Nance, would you like her to join the band again?

Nance and I had a great time and we worked hard for the big success. We were a great team. But since I work very successfully with my new colleague and partner Li-Ann I do not miss her. I worked with Nance three years, with Li-Ann now already 10 years.

You are touring the 90's festivals, what kind of audiences come to see you perform?

Basically, the same audience only everybody is a little bit older now. It is great to bring the fans back to a period that they love so much. This give me the thrills every time I perform and makes me love what I do.

In your opinion, what are the key songs or albums of eurodance?

Of course, our own album *Slave to the Music*! But also, albums of 2 Unlimited, Culture Beat, Haddaway, Alban and Cappella. But I loved them all!

▶ *T-Spoon*

T-Spoon was one of the biggest 90's euro bands, although their majestic sound didn't reach into every European country.

No Time 2 Waste (1993) kicked off their recording career by hiring Ingrid Simons (aka BB Queen), whose voice could be heard for example in Disney movies and her own successful solo career.

The debut LP *Joy, Life & Pain* was released after the brilliant *Where R U Now* single (ft. Jean Shy). Jean also participated on the Janis Joplin cover *Mercedes Benz*. In *See The Light* single they were joined by Johnny Kelvin, who had also his own solo career with eurodance song *Satisfaction Guaranteed*.

The band had a little transformation towards happy hardcore sound when Linda Estelle stepped in. Second album *Lexicon Of Melody* was put out in 1996.

In 1997-99 they had their biggest hit, when *Sex On The Beach* turned out to be an international phenomenon, for example in Japan number one position. In some countries they had to change the song into *Fun On The Beach*, because of censorship.

Before the dawn of the new millennium, third album *T-Spoon*, saw the light of day and even beyond 2000 they released a couple of songs like the reworked version of their debut song with Supreme Dream Team. In 2016 they put out a digital EP, *Back 2 The Wonderful 90's*, with new songs like *Big Booty Bitches*.

According to Eurokdj, in 2010 there was three different versions of the band touring the venues: one represented T-Spoon's past, one present era and one the future.

In The Spotlight

▶ǁ

Shalamon Baskin singer

Published with permission of Shalamon Baskin.

How T-Spoon was born, and what was the name based upon?

T-Spoon was started by myself (Shalamon Baskin) and Remy De Groot. I had written the first song *No Time 2 Waste* already but rewrote it for the first T-Spoon single. Officially T-Spoon was the two of us, but in reality, it was myself, Remy, Dominic Sas and Serge Ramaekers. The name came from one of the characters of a television show based on the Pony Express riders. His name was Teaspoon.

How long were you in T-spoon and why did you leave?

I am a founding member of T-Spoon. We started in 1993 and I stopped at the end of 1998, shortly after *Sex On The Beach* became a world hit. I left due to a culmination of internal group issues over the years. At a certain point I got sick of fighting every time a new single came out, a new tour was scheduled, or a new business opportunity came up for the group. It's difficult to steer a ship with three captains.

Do you like eurodance yourself and what is its legacy to today's dance music?

I've always liked some eurodance and I've even released several tracks in the past years as Lightwarrior. I've also written songs for other acts. My favorites from the

224

90's eurodance are the original Culture Beat, Snap and KLF. 4, As far as legacy, a lot of the sounds we used back then and even some of the songs are eurodance, just updated.

I am busy at the moment working on a new project with TOF and we will use some sounds from eurodance. I also have a project called Todaklop which is alternative hip hop - We use eurodance influences in that one as well. Both are unreleased as the moment but will be out soon.

Eurodance's big brother is techno music and it had a whole fashion style in clothes and in art. Do you think that eurodance has certain fashion style or art (for example in record covers)?

Hmmm techno. My first project HiTek3 was techno. I guess we were one of the first to use the girl singing/guy rapping combination in dance music. The first single from that project was with Ya Kid K (Technotronic) The second single and subsequent album the vocals were done by Perla Den Boer and myself. Perla was also a singer for T99. As far as a style of clothing - eurodance fans were divided. Happy hardcore or gabbers wore track suits and their hair a certain way. Other fans wore hip hop or new wave clothing. But there really was not a certain way of dressing for everyone. As for CD cover design, there was also no particular style. The first T-Spoon album cover and several of the singles were done by Peter Luts (Lasgo).

▶ *Good Shape*

If you had always wanted to know what a combination between a boyband and eurodance would look like, then Good Shape is just for you! It consisted of four handsome fellows (David Cantré, Geert De Meyer, Koen De Beir, Filip Vervaeke) , Good Shape caused a little commotion with their debut song, *Take My Love* (1993). In their homeland they reached number one position and in Spain and Israel number two.

The next single *Give Me Fire* was a bit easier to serve to the public with some success under the belt. It gained some fame, like the following songs. The album

Maniacs Of Love's cover gave a look that they were far away from the typical rebellious boybands by dressing conservatively.

While they were indeed in good shape during their first long play, the magic seemed to fade off in the next phase with the second album, *Closer To You*. All the singles released from this one flopped all over Europe and they vanished from the face of the Earth... ...

...until Regi Penxten of Milk Inc fame restored their glory by updating their biggest hit, *Take My Love,* in 2008. Good Shape even got to perform their updated version live and had a chance for a brief comeback.

Their sound was almost pure eurodance, but the bands appeal didn't last longer than the absolutely wonderful debut single and mediocre album. The competition was so hard that they were left in the shadows amidst all the vast eurodance content that came from Europe at that time.

In The Spotlight

►ll

Serge Ramaekers producer

Serge Ramaekers in his studio, published with permission of Serge Ramaekers.

In what eurodance projects you have been a part of? Name a few of the bigger ones and what was your role in those?

Confetti's : co-writer/producer/masterowner
T-Spoon : co-writer/producer/publisher/masterowner
Cartouche : writer/producer/publisher/masterowner
Orion Too : co-writer/producer/publisher/masterowner
Good Shape : co-writer/producer
Freddie Mercury : hit-remix of *Living On My Own*

What led you to produce eurodance? Was it a genre you like or was it a question of its popularity?

I started producing new beat and I just followed the 'flow'. And suddenly it was house that went into eurodance.

How would you define eurodance?

A lot of different influences brought together in a refreshing sound.

In your opinion what were the key songs or artists or producers in eurodance? And why?

Pump Up The Jam : it really brought Belgium in the picture. Other Belgian songs charted also internationally. 2 Unlimited with *Get Ready 4 This*, T-Spoon with *Sex On The Beach*, Cartouche with *Feel The Groove*.

Everybody felt for the "Belgian" sound.

Why do you think that eurodance was so popular in the 90's? And once again?

It was big fun ! All those big hits were happy songs with a powerful, catchy chorus. Easy to sing along with.

It was very common thing to use better looking people as a front of the band who didn't sing the songs in the studio. What's your opinion on that?

Those days, most of the performances were playback. So, it wasn't important who sing the song but who 'performed' the song. I'm happy that I can say that there were also a lot of exceptions like 2 Unlimited, Snap, T-Spoon,... They always did perform LIVE. And goes what,... they still do ! ;-)

Comparing 90's and today, which things in dance music industry have changed and what hasn't changed? Are the changes good or bad?

Music is always changing and evolving. But even in today's music, you still can hear some influences of the 90's.

The big difference between now and then is the format. The downloads and streaming ! It was bad in the beginning but it's going the good direction. Problems are getting solved and fixed.

Eurodance is a loved genre but also very hated. Have you seen that hate or loathing in your career? (from Finland's perspective)

No, I wasn't even aware of that.

Do you have a vision how kids today (millennials) see eurodance music?

Some records are timeless. I think that the new generation is open for older stuff as long it fits in their style of music experience. And the sound quality is very important for that. If the mix or production sounds outdated, it's going to be a hard one to sell.

What kind of music you are doing nowadays?

commercial/deephouse/R&B/hardstyle/techhouse/futurebass/trap.
I always worked in different styles.

▶ *L.A. Style*

Michiel Van Der Kuy (b.1962) of Laserdance, who had previously done space synth, was one of the founding members of techno/rave/eurodance duo called L.A. Style. Another member, Wessel Van Diepen, brought in more modern techno sound.

Wessel later produced songs for Vengaboys with an alias DJ Delmundo. Rapper Frans Mers aka FX was chosen as the frontman.

In the beginning of the 90's, techno and rave were the sound of now, so L.A.Style was founded to give audience just that. First song, *James Brown Is Dead*, was an instant mega hit all over Europe and reached Spain's single chart number one position. Big merit was also getting into US Billboard Hot 100. The song also inspired musicians to make their own counterpart to that song: for example, hardcore band Holy Noise released *James Brown Is Still Alive!!*

L.A.Style tried a more lighter euro sound with *I'm Raving/O Si Nene*, which had typical euro formula: female-sung refrain and man rapping. It was also an introduction of the vocalist Nicolette Suwoton. After the single try outs, they put out an LP, *The Album*. Like always, Japan got something extra: *James Brown Is Dead* EP was released there in the same year as the album and it had songs that weren't released in any other countries.

After techno/rave morphed into a more euro sound, also L.A.Style decided to try traditional euro music. Although *Got To Move* has a very generic refrain, it's one of the catchiest euros out there. In 1995 they released their last single, *Magic Trip*, with happy hardcore sound. It was produced by Sven Maes, who was going soon to be known from this trance project, Svenson.

After Frans Merx left the band, the whole project faded away. But you still can't underestimate the bands influence: in the beginning they sounded a lot like 2 Unlimited, which in 1991 was just starting up their career.2U managed to stay ahead of L.A.Style because of their radio friendly songs. While L.A. didn't manage to stay afloat, they were one of the introducers of combining techno sounds and rap, which had a huge meaning in creation of eurodance sound.

▶ *Sonic Surfers*

Sonic Surfers started out by trying out house and techno sound in the beginning of 90's. Even the legendary Jocelyn Brown joined them on the song *Take Me Up*. Although they are considered an eurodance band, they had lots of other genres in their production too.

In The Spotlight

▶️II

Vivian Black *singer*

Dorian Broekhuyse *producer*

Published with permission of Vivian Black and Dorian Broekhuyse.

How Sonic Surfers was born?

Dorian:

As a studio project with a live band and dancers. Quite elaborate I must say. With the first two tracks we were not involved. That was more a record company thing with a lot of input from the performing artists. We (Martin Trance and in a later stadium Enes Tvrtkovic) did the rest of the tracks on the album. So, with Jocelyn Brown etc. one thing special was the fact that there was a lot of variation in the background of the band members.

Vivian, how did you end up in Sonic Surfers?

Vivian:

A friend of mine, who at the time was the producer for Sonic Surfers, asked me to audition. I did and won. That's when we recorded *Having A Great Time*.

Your band had different kinds of songs including eurodance, was it a joint decision not to do just eurodance songs?

Vivian:

Yes, it was. We grew up with different styles of music and wanted to add a personal flavor to the album.

Dorian:

We all liked a variety of music.

Sonic Surfers released only one album, could you tell a little about the process of making that album?

Vivian:

We practically lived in the studio for two months. Prhyme was writing his lyrics at the spot. He worked fast and was so good at it. I didn't write any of the lyrics. At the time I wasn't experienced enough. We worked hard, laughed hard and worked some more. It was definitely the best time I've had in my career.

The album was released in 1994, how did it do in the charts?

Dorian:

I think it entered the top 40 but it didn't sell millions;-)

Are there other eurodance songs or acts you have been part of that you would like to mention?

Dorian:

We did a remix for 2 Brothers on the 4th Floor and some tracks with Ray Slijngaard (solo projects) from 2 Unlimited. A few releases with Victoria Wilson James (ex Soul To Soul) and participated on a multi-platinum album (in the Netherlands) of Total Touch.

What's your relationship to dance music, is it your favorite genre?

Vivian:

At the time I enjoyed making dance music, but it wasn't my favorite genre. Club music was and still is my favorite. But now I would love to go back to that era of eurodance and record a few more songs.

How do you think of your time in the band nowadays or the 90's music in general?

Vivian:

It was the best time in my music career. We had so much fun on and off stage.

Dorian:

Early 90's was cool. A lot of experimentation and a lot less rules to follow. Later on it was more and more streamlined and if you didn't use the 'right' kick or bleep suddenly the tracks were to experimental...

I really liked the 2step stuff at the end of the 90's. We had a track with Spark, *I Dream Of U Baby*. More of an underground hit, especially in the UK.

SS faded before reaching the end of the 90's, why is that?

Dorian:

The people involved wanted to do their solo thing. And that was it

Vivian, after SS, how did your career evolve from there?

Vivian:

After the Sonic Surfers I went solo and got signed at Arcade Belgium. We then recorded two songs. Shortly after I chose a different path and started to do musicals and theatre shows. Nowadays I help my children with their singing career by co-writing songs and coaching them. There are also plans to dive into the studio and record an EP.

෨

IT'S A LOVING THING - BELGIUM

▶ AB Logic

2 Unlimited, who gained worldwide fame and became one of the biggest euro acts out there, was surely a role model to Belgian AB Logic. Rapper K-Swing (Cedric Murril) and singer Marianne Festraerts though didn't face same kind of hysteria than 2 U did.

Marianne, who had a background in ballet, went to audition, where a singer was sought for a new dance project. She went to sing AB Logic's first song, *The Hitman*. K-Swing ended up in the band through same auditions and got to even write his own raps.

They managed to release only one album, which carried the band's name, and after that only two new songs, *Real World* and *Welcome To My Heart*. Their chart positions were not very good, even *The Hitman* only reached 60th place in Billboard Hot 100 chart. According to Marianne in an Eurokdj interview, the project ended because the producers didn't simply want to focus on it anymore. She feels that Ab Logic would have had so much more to give...

▶ CB Milton

Surinam-born Clarence Milton Bekker (b.1969) aka CB Milton moved to Netherlands at the age of six and began to show interest in the world of music at an early age. He participated in talent competitions and got some fame through those. In 1987 he joined Swinging Soul Machine band, who toured with the disco group The Trammps. This turned out to be a stroke of luck for CB, because the Trammps' bass player introduced him to Belgian producers Peter Bauwens and Phil Wilde. In 1990 CB left the band and began his solo efforts. 2 Unlimited's "father", Jean-Paul De Coster, saw Milton perform and joined forces with Bauwens and Wilde in order to produce songs for CB.

Send Me An Angel was released as the first single, and it gained international attention. He put out several singles, which succeeded at least in Benelux countries. *It's A Loving Thing* became the biggest hit, and it's no wonder: the catchy song really shows the best sides of his voice and it's a wonderful example of eurodance, where every little part supports the whole song. Its chart accomplishments include e.g. number three in Israel.

The two first albums, *It's My Loving Thing* and *The Way To Wonderland*, aren't just your basic eurodance, but there are lots of other shades too. CB's music is clearly more pop and lighter than 2 Unlimited. The third LP, *From Here To There* (1998), was a clear departure from euro, it was soul, r'n'b and a couple of house songs. The biggest commercial success was the first album, while the other two flopped.

At the turn of the millennium he decided to take a break from music business. Her mother's death and constant gigging had tired him. Because he was an adventurer at heart, he embarked on one year's adventure across the world. During this time, he faced some personal troubles, but found a savior from his old friend: music. He became a street artist in Barcelona. His voice got some attention in the right ears and he got to sing in a band called Playing For Change, through which he got his voice heard also in the US.

Nowadays he performs with his original name and sings mainly soul music. But DMN Records has brought him to him once again to the arena of dance music, and CB is once again ready to take us the dance floor.

In The Spotlight

▶❚❚

Clarence Bekker aka **CB Milton** *singer*

Published with permission of CB Milton.

Tell me a little about your career before you were CB Milton?

Before I was CB Milton I started doing talent contests on my 14th, from there I became at 18 year the lead singer of the Rotterdam based band Swinging Soul Machine and at 23 I signed a contract with Byte records and CB Milton was born.

How did you end up doing music with Peter Bauwens and Phil Wilde?

I was introduced to Peter and Phil by Stanley Wade bass/singer of The Trammps who used to play as a special guest member with the Swinging Soul Machine

Which songs were your biggest accomplishments, in your opinion?

Send Me An Angel, It's A Loving Thing

It's A Loving Thing was a huge hit; how did the song was created?

Peter and Phil had written it and was originally on our first demo.

Your first two albums were eurodance/euro house but the third one, *From Here To There*, was totally different. Why did the style change and did you have more influence in making that third album?

We started really writing together from the second album. The first album was written and produced by Peter and Phil except for *Send Me An Angel*. After the first album we wanted to create a more live and organic sound.

Eventually you disappeared from the music scene in the end of the 1990's, why is that?

I wanted to travel and took a year of. Then I wanted to play guitar and change my scene. I wanted to find a higher meaning of life went to Barcelona and became a street artist.

Do you have good and/or bad memories of the 90's music scene?

I had a ball during the 90's but I was yearning for a live band . I had my dancers around me, so I was never lonely, but I was craving to be around musicians and not tour around with a tape. It really became a bummer for me .

You have rebooted your singing career, what kind of music you make now?

I have never left the music scene after CB Milton. I toured with a band called 08001 (Barcelona world music) DJ Taito Tikaro and toured 10 years with the world famous band Playing for Change . You find me in a lot of their hit songs on Youtube where they have over more than 500.000.000 hits including the *Stand By Me* video which I starred as Clarence Bekker

Currently I just released an album with my own CLARENCE BEKKER BAND called *Changes*. A collection of all my musical experiences in my previous career

Have you ever considered making dance songs once again, has there been requests to feature on a dance song?

Now that I have settled and found where I belong I am open to all challenges.

Sure, I will be creating dance songs in the future and I am open to collaborations.

I am doing a collaboration with a band called Bleros from Belgium, *Sunshine Everyday*.

▶ Def Dames Dope

The sisters, Axana and Larissa Ceulemans, perform their old hits and 90's potpourris in gigs, on gigs, published with permission of Gilles Gobin and Star Entertainment BVBA.

Including 2 Unlimited and CB Milton, the Belgian producers Phil Wilde and Peter Bauwens, had other lucrative projects, like Def Dames Dope. The original DDD line-up consisted of Axana and Larissa Ceulemans and two dancers. The first song, *It's Ok, It's Allright* (1992), was an instant hit in Scandinavia and number one in Holland and Belgium, where they sold gold with their first LP.

After the album, Larissa got married and left the band and she was replaced with Yousra Lemaire, with whom DDD released new singles and a second album. After a few years Yousra got tired and left too. Barbara De Jonge (famous from her acting career) filled the slot for a one single, *Join The Party.* After this the band decided on a break...

...but came back soon in 2002 with a single *Beep Beep*, but it flopped. Today the band is touring with the force of the original sisters and nostalgia.

In The Spotlight

▶ ❚❚

Axana Ceulemans *singer*

Larissa Ceulemans *singer*

How Def Dames Dope was formed and what's the story behind the peculiar name?

Larissa:
Me and my sister Axana were influenced by Motown music, which was played a lot at home by our parents. When we started clubbing, the place to be was a well-known club in Antwerp called Funk You. We met a lot of dancers, singers and rappers who gathered there every weekend.

There were always dance and rap battles which fascinated us. So we started practicing and joined in. Most of our friends where colored, so at the beginning people thought we couldn't bring it, being white as milk. We learned from our friends, got better, got respected and started Def Dames Dope. We loved dancing, singing, rapping, we had nothing to lose so we just went for it. We were lucky to have found the right people to work with at the time. The name Def Dames Dope was a passage from a rap we once wrote, nothing more, nothing less...

You were produced by Wilde & Bauwens who also had huge success with 2 Unlimited. Did this create a kind of competition?

Larissa:

No, we were friends, sharing ideas, jammin' together, performing together, it was fun!!

How was it working with Wilde & Bauwens?

Axana:

At first we were a bit nervous, they had produced a lot of artists who made it big in the 90's and had a lot of number one hits. As we started working with them we felt a good connection, they knew how to push us to make the most out of every song. We worked hard and late hours, in the best atmosphere.

We loved what we were doing, we were thankful for the opportunity.

Are you touring again because of the huge 90's revival?

Both:

Hell yeah!!!! (laughing)

How would you define eurodance?

Larissa:

Eurodance will always be special!!

It's the era where music festivals were no longer for just rock bands. The technology was more advanced so that live performances became possible. It was a total experience, beats, singers, rappers, DJ's on stage, dancers, one big live dance video!!
Eurodance made dance music get out of the clubs to be shared with thousands of people, it was unique for that time!!!

What do you think about eurodance being so popular again?

Axana:

People are always searching for happiness, eurodance is happiness!! Recognizable melodies, easy to sing along with. Pumpin' beats, excitement, perfect party music!!

You were different than other eurodance acts because you were all-girl group. Was there a pressure to add a male rapper? Many eurodance acts had a rapper.

Larissa:

Euh... we never even thought about that...we had fun with the girls, did over 30 shows every month, no it never crossed our minds. Girl power!!!! (laughing)

Do you think that eurodance has influenced modern dance music aka EDM?

Axana:

I think that every music stream influenced another one, it had always been like that, guess it will always be...

Are you going to release new songs?

Axana:

No, we are not. The event organizations that book us do so because of the music we made back in the 90's. People want to go a little back in time, that's what we bring them!!! When we get on stage we bring our greatest hits combined with some fun 90's medleys!! Party hard on stage, get the crowed to throw their hands in the air, get them to sing a long, just have a great time!!!

ॐ

FORBIDDEN DREAMS - NORWAY

▶ *Stella Getz*

Norwegian had high hopes for Stella Getz (b.1976). They wanted her to be their international pop star. She performed first time publicly in a TV show called Casino, where she performed her first single, *Friends* (1993). Before this live performance, she had sent demos all over and soon Mega Records (famous for their dance music) took her under their wing. Producers Lars E. Ludvigsen and Mikkel S.Eriksen (later Eriksen would be half of the Stargate production team, e.g. Rihanna), went to studio with Stella and came up with *Friends*.

Stella got some wind under her sails from the television performance and the song soon became a hit gaining good positions in Norway, Denmark and Israel and got some moderate success also in Germany. There he joined on a tour with Dr. Alban and 2 Unlimited. The next song, *Dr. Love,* was also a minor success.

The album *Forbidden Dreams* was put out, but it also gave something else than the euro sound heard on the singles. Single releases *All In All* (downtempo) and summery reggae *Yeah Yeah* were truly of a different breed. Although she was titled as *"Norway's first lady of dance"*, her star faded away quite fast. Despite her title, she tried also a more rock approach with *Get A Grip*, but her career ended completely in Reel 2 Real copy, *Ta-Di-Di-Boom (1996).*

▶ Trancylvania

Although Trancylvania's name indicates something to do with horror, that is not the case. Actually, another euro project called Transylvania took its imagery from vampire mythology.

Trio composed of Svenna Mohaugen, Njaal Lie and Silvany Bricen, started out with *Tender Heart* (1994). To the next one, The *Colour Of Love*, they had managed to get the legendary Ricardo Da Force (of KLF and N-Trance fame) to perform raps.

They released only one album, *Compromise* (1995), which was only released in their home country, Norway. It's a pity because the album is one of forgotten eurodance gems. After this, they went off the grid.

▶ Hype

Sometimes you have to cut corners and rely on the power of sex. Norwegian Hype project had a leading lady Linda Johansen, who was a known nude model. She was exploited heavily in the record covers. There were also two male rappers in the background, but Linda probably took all the attention.

The other rapper, David J., had been a part of a Swedish dance project Black Label, whose Ottawan cover *Hands Up* (1995) ended up as one of the tracks from Hype. Surprisingly, the song grew out of its disco roots and was a quite good cover.

Apparently there were some efforts to launch Linda's solo career, because during Hype's short lifetime, also a single called Hype Presents Miss Linda: *Set U Free* was released, with the same producers. Hype's last single was, *All Of Your Dreams*, in 1997.

At the beginning of 2000's, Linda released a biography and took part in the local Dancing With The Stars contest but was the first one to go. Nowadays she has a job in cosmetics.

COME INTO MY LIFE – CANADA (CANDANCE)

In Canada, eurodance was such a big phenomenon, that there was a market for homemade variety of euro. They didn't want to acknowledge its existence, because it had no angst (like in rock), it wasn't cool and lyrical content wasn't so great. It's image in Canada was like rave cultures kookier, younger sister.

▶ JLM

In the countries relatively small eurodance scene, one of the biggest names was JLM, who got its name from the words *Just Love Music.* Belgian producer Peter Neefs took them under their wing and led them into fame.

Come Into My Life, their biggest hit, reached the Top 10 in many European countries and it was released in over 40 countries and 60 collections. Later an album with the same title was put out. Other merits are e.g. nominations in Juno Awards and Much Music Video Awards.

In The Spotlight

▶II

Jean Perruno producer

JLM is probably the most famous candance artist, published with permission of Jean Perruno.

How did JLM got started?

The band started in 1992 with me and my twin brother (Jean and Claude Perruno). We started writing all music, lyrics of the songs and finally found a female lead singer from Montreal (Shantal Maure) to complete our band.

Why did you choose eurodance as your genre?

To be honest, you did not choose a type of music in particular. Eurodance was the type of music which appealed to us during that period of time (90-97). Besides, as we were coming from Quebec City, the French speaking part of Canada, we were thoroughly influenced by European music culture. From what I remember, eurodance music was among only 7% of the music market in Canada at the time. This helped us to stand out of the crowd and consequently, we were first signed on Toco International and then, Epic. To our great surprise, we were signed and released in over 40 countries and appeared on over 60 CD compilations. In front of that success, we finally got signed with Sony Music Canada.

How would you define eurodance?

Eurodance music is a type of electronic music influenced by the use of warm melodic vocal lines combined with good melodic synth riffs, strong bass rhythm & melodic hooks. That is the core foundation of eurodance music for sure.

Are there euro artists who you look up to and who have influenced you?

I guess that eurodance bands were all influenced by each other at the time. In our case, we have been influenced a lot by Culture Beat, 2 Unlimited, Dr.Alban & the Shamen.

What makes eurodance so lasting genre that people still listen to it nowadays?

Because of the rhythm & melodic hooks which you do not found any more in dance music.

Why do you think that eurodance had so big effect in Canada?

Eurodance music was only 7% of the music market in Canada at the time. So, I don't think eurodance had a big effect on Canada at the time compared to the eurodance trend in Europe. Eurodance has always been marginal on the Canadian music scene.

Was Canadian eurodance different than it was in Europe?

Definitely. Although it was tremendously influenced by eurodance trend in Europe, we have always been obliged to adapt our product by launching different mixes specially done for the Canadian market.

You had a brief comeback in 2008 with one single, why did it stop there?

Yes, indeed but it did not stop there. We also released *Lift Me Up* in 2006 which did not work very well. Then we reached #4 in the top 20 in Canada with our single *Heaven Away*. We signed again with Toco International in 2006 but it was not lucrative anymore like it used to be in the 90's. On top of that, we had to produce ourselves the CD , videos & so on. One way or another, it has to be profitable somewhere. Otherwise, it gets really rough.

Have Canadian eurodance acts started to tour again because 90's is so big again? Or are you going to tour or make new music?

For JLM, eurodance is thing of the past and I don't believe we would tour again like in the 90's.

We are still active and writing music and songs for different artists. Our music style now is relating to different styles though. We are more influenced by pop music style of these days.

Have you gotten negative feedback because of your style of music?

Of course. Whatever style of music you do, you are always criticized. Especially in Canada, at the time, rock music was very popular and eurodance was not very well seen in Canada.

▶ *Capital Sound*

The girl duo Capital Sound got its name from the fact they were located in the capital city area. The leading ladies were Nathalie Page and Céline Guindon aka Katt, but in the background men were responsible for the music: Martin Brunet aka Bit Burn and Toasted Morgan, who was the main producer.

The first LP, *Sussex Drive* (1994), was a success in Canada and several hits were released from it like *In The Night* and *Desire*. Success brought them also several rewards: for example, they won Quebec Record Pool's Best New Dance Music Band category

Despite their success, Natalie wanted to embark on a solo career (which lasted for a couple, but pretty good euro singles). Donna Pearson was brought into Capital Sound. With this new singer they brought on the second long play *And The Party Goes On* (1996), which was surprisingly mixed together. From this, they put out their last single, *Your Love Is My Energy*. In the new millennium they sealed the project by releasing a 3CD collection of their hits and remixes. Also, Katt released a solo album called *Libre* that meant free.

▶ Emjay

Emjay started her musical career at a young age. At the age of 12, Ottawa-born Marie Josèe Riel (b.1974) became a backing vocalist for a local band. She learned a tough working morale, because she had to practice singing and different dance moves a lot. Her goal was to have her own solo career.

In 1994 her wish came true, when she recorded her first solo song, *Sound Of My Heartbeat*. That and the next singles like *Flying To The Moon* and *In My Arms* fared quite well, which led to the publication of her first album, *In Your Arms*. It's without a doubt one of the best produced eurodance albums out there flavored with some other sounds outside eurodance.

Marie became popular in her homeland. She got even an MuchMusic Video Award. In addition to that she performed in several high-profile TV shows and concerts.

We All Need Love (1998) was a new single from the upcoming second album, and it was supposed to begin a new chapter in Emjay's career. The song is a good updated eurodance song which took its influences from Sash!'s dream dance sound. Although she got to be a supporting artist for Backstreet Boys' Canadian tour, her recording career just fell into slumber...and second album never came. In 2020 she released a new song, a cover of The Supremes hit, *You Keep Me Hanging On*.

▶ *Nadia*

While Nadia wasn't as popular in Canada as Emjay, she put out the same kind of high-class material as her. Nadia's one and only album got released also in Japan.

In The Spotlight

▶❙❙

Nadia Robichaud *singer*

Published with permission of Nadia Robichaud.

How did you get involved with dance music ?

I don't really believe in chance; I believe more in the power of attraction and I think I threw it to me. At the time I was competing in competitive aerobics and in those days when you wanted to get music cut to create your own mix of music you had to go to a proper recording studio.

So, I started going to these different studios up paying engineers to cut music for my competitions. And being in that environment I guess it solicited like a desire in singing. I would see the whole set up and I just would get goosebumps. I really like the environment and I wanted to be a part of it not really knowing how.

And a little bit later on I was seeking someone to help me find music, someone who had a lot of music. I ended up through a referral at this ex DJ:s, Frank Terriers, house and he had wall to wall records. So, I went there for the afternoon and he played tons of music and so that I could choose some songs for my next competition. I started just being myself which is singing and dancing and not knowing that he was actually managing Emjay and Capital Sound. He then said I sing and dance well. He asked do I sing regularly. I said I have always sung, and my mom sung, and I've sung in choirs.

He was at the time developing a new project and he was looking for a singer so he offered an audition and he gave me his card and said he will call me, and I thought "yeah right". You know it's typical thing, you see it on TV. I really didn't think much of it, so I went home, and I thought whatever, he's never going to call me. A few days later he called me and asked to an audition at a studio. So, I went over, and I had the worst cold, I was really sick, but I really wanted to go so I took really good care of myself.

And it was on a Sunday and I thought, well will be what it will be, and I'll just do my best. It was *Live On Love* and it wasn't very complicated song. I sang the song in the recording booth and I couldn't believe it, it was a dream come true. Then I came out they and they really liked what they heard. The version which was released wasn't the same one I sang. Anyway, it was really cool. They took me on and then we got a record deal with company called Nu Music in Montreal.

Is dance music your favorite genre?

It is not my favorite genre. I remember a friend of mine (who teached aerobics with me) who went to Germany in the beginning of the 90's and came back with all this music I had never heard. It was dance music and it was really really good and I love that stuff. Then it became cheesy.

But when I was recording myself, I actually started going to raves and after hours and I really got into house music. I would have liked to sing house music myself but didn't get that far.

How was it like recording your album *Kiss Of Destiny?*

It was really fun. I love being in the studio I have to say. I prefer recording over performing. I mean I love performing but I prefer in when it comes to singing. I love the process of being in the in the studio, so I had fun, I liked it. But it was very busy time in my life: I was in university; it was almost my last year. I was teaching aerobics and full-time training, like 30 hours a week plus weight training and stretching. I met with the gymnastics coach, with whom I practiced my routines. I spent all my weekends in the recording studio and then the singles got released. I was on the road going to different cities to them to perform in bars or perform on TV and things like that.

I wasn't really able to super enjoy it, I kinda burned out. I got vocal nodules because I was straining my voice a lot especially in bars and things like that because that's usually where we would perform, or I would perform. I think I had enjoyed much more if my life wouldn't have been so full of everything. I just basically had no time for myself.

What happened after the album: basically, after making that album my contract finished it was like 1996? I tried to create other projects with other people but nothing really kind of took off. But I left the producers. I wanted to explore other things, I kind of made a decision. I had an opportunity to go to Los Angeles, I had a friend who moved there and I thought like if there's an opportunity to kind of see if I can really make a career out of this that it would be it. But then I realized what I was doing as a fitness instructor and with yoga was what I wanted to do.

Like I said earlier, I had a little burnout. That why I was drawn into yoga, I searched balance for my life. And I started taking yoga and then studying yoga and then teaching it and to me that resonated more I really wanted to change people's lives changed after doing all of these crazy things and that's why I came to yoga and I was looking for a balance in my life.

I would never complain that I got to do it that but it's not really a life either. I wanted a life. I wanted to be a better person. I wanted to have a full life. I wanted to get married etc. It was a great experience and I'm proud of the little success that I had, but I wanted more out of life than that, so I decided to not make a career out of it.

If you had the chance, what would you change?

I would be more careful with my voice and lighten my schedules for more downtime. I ended up with vocal nodules from singing in bars with bad sound systems that are not fit for singers. I was lucky that my singing teacher noticed so I got it checked out and had therapy, undetected it can become cancerous.

Are you still involved with music?

No. I run my own yoga studio where I teach. That's my career.

అ

U DRIVE ME CRAZY - FINLAND

As I am from Finland, I would like to tell you something about the eurodance scene here.

The Finnish attitude toward electronic music (and especially commercial dance) as a whole has been very problematic. Rock music has always been very dominant here and that is why anything done with computers has been frowned upon, even starting from the 1970's.The attitude seems to have loosen up a bit in the 2010's, when EDM started to conquer the whole world.

Eurodance was very popular here in the 1990's. Acts like E-Rotic, Basic Element, Pandora, Rednex, E-Type etc. dominated the album and single charts. Still the attitudes were there, in hiding or in plain sight. Even in school you didn't get much respect if you admitted to liking that kind of music.

Now the 90's euro has once again risen to the surface in the Finnish media, and the attitudes are still there. Even the people who in the media publicly identify themselves as eurodance fans, are making derogatory marks about the artists. Seems even they don't take the genre seriously. Their fandom is ironic, laughing to the whole phenomenon.

The whole attitude towards commercial dance music has mirrored what kind of acts has been born here. Many acts image is based on humor, like Hausmylly (but who eventually embarked on a more serious music journey) or Sikaduo (which mimicked Rednex, but with a heavier dose of adult humor). Even nowadays when a new Finnish song with eurodance title has been put out, it has mostly been in the style of hands up, which have got only the faintest traces of the 90's euro sound. Also, the singers have sometimes been old local schlager singers, to emphasize the humorous side.

Despite the awkward relationship towards dance music, there was still a couple of good projects or artists who wanted some international fame and tried to do things seriously. At this next part, these are best of the best, who got some success outside Finland.

▶ *Sound Of R.E.L.S.*

R.E.L.S.' first single covers had ravishing cover art.

Sound Of R.E.L.S. got the biggest fame with their euro reggae cover, *Raising My Family*. This is just one example of the convention of euro bands getting their biggest success with midtempo crowd-pleasers (like Alexia). Also the vastly superior euro songs were hits *Love Is The Powa!* and *Ee-Lie-Loe-Lie (If U Wanna Get)*. R.E.L.S. production team (the name composed of the guys surnames, Redford, Sam Eagle, Vinnie Lane and Guy Stoneman) also made material for other artists like Mira. Their main project Sound Of R.E.L.S was able to produce three albums and other minor hits like *All The Best Girls* and *Crazy Music*.

In The Spotlight

▶ꜚꜚ

Esa Mäkelä aka *Ressu Redford* singer

Published with permission of Ressu Redford.

251

How did Sound of R.E.L.S got started and who belonged in the band?

I wanted to do dance music again, although my own solo career was going so well (author's note: Ressu has had a very successful solo career in Finland, singing both Finnish and English). I have always wanted to change and try out new things. Rhythmic music and "eurodance" felt so fresh again. There was strong melodies and a strong beat. The record company executive said : "you are crazy because you are ending a very successful solo career ". Well, luckily the first Sound Of R. E. L. S record was a success in Finland and it fathered hits like *Raising My Family* and *Love Is The Powa* and gained also a gold record.

We had four ex-Bogart Co (author's note: Ressu's old 80's synth-pop band) musicians in various roles in addition to the first female singer, Alicia Johnston, later we had singers like Suzie Aldabbagh and Amina Hietikko.

Did you get success outside Finnish borders and with what songs ?

Love Is The Powa was a minor hit in Sweden in radio and in the dance chart. *Raising My Family* was in many dance music collections in foreign countries but there wasn't any international breakthrough for us. Although we did same successful gigs in our neighboring countries.

The second album, *Crazy Music*, was much lighter in sound than the first one, was this a conscious choice? And if so, did the contemporary trends affect that decision?

Yes, we tried to capture the sound of that moment, that was the whole point of the project. Club music and dance sounds have always been trendy, certain sounding at a certain era. You couldn't use any kickdrum, synth or bass sound.

Suzie was changed into Amina on the third album *Extra,* why is that?

Suzie met her current husband at a certain airport and fell in love. Then a new singer was needed, luckily, we found Amina.

A couple of your albums were surprisingly released in Japan, tell me a little about that?

I have no knowledge of any Asian releases.

Did you have idols when it comes to music?

I have always liked rhythmic music, so called "techno pop", pop, urban. I have had some influences from good artists and songs. Maybe not as role models but some influences, yeah.

Maybe some role models from dance music?

Not as performers or artists, but many successful dance act of that time influenced our sound and production. It's typical for the whole dance music genre. Big hits and different productions always work as influencers. You can take some influences, but it's no good to be a copycat.

Has there been any talk about comeback?

Yeah, there has been some talk about comeback once and a while and there has been some inquiries from different parties but so far my own solo career has been so busy, that we haven't reunited the team.

▶ Waldo / Waldo's People

Published with permission of Waldo's People.

Waldo aka Marko Reijonen (b.1967) started as a solo act in the middle of the 90's. With schlager star Merja Raski (the main vocals) and with his own Jamaican rap accent, he recorded *Feel So Good* (1995), which was a major hit and raised a little

253

international attention. Marko released two albums with the name Waldo, but the real breakthrough came when he brought more people into the band and changed the name into Waldo's People.

This new remade group had one foot in the old eurodance sound, and the other in the new progressive club sound á la La Cream. Also, lots of rock influences were added (because this was rock Finland, after all). The production got support from Sweden, from La Cream team. While Waldo's solo act was more camp, Waldo's People was a more serious effort. The music video made of their first song, *U Drive Me Crazy*, was the first video to be added in MTV Nordic's daily playlist.

Waldos People made three albums. Second one, *No Man's Land*, was even more giant leap away from euro, being done mostly with breakbeat sound. Waldo admits in an interview in 2019 that The Prodigy's sounds were the biggest influences on this LP.

The third album (and probably the last one). *Paranoid* (2009,) was once again step towards euro arena with emphasis on diva-like refrains in the style of E-Type. They even got to represent Finland in Eurovision with *Lose Control* in the same year.

Nowadays Waldo and his people are touring, but they don't want to make any new songs. They gig with the power of the 90's nostalgia.

▶ *Miisa*

Miisa, aka Miisa Päällysaho, was what Stella Getz was to Norwegian people: a hope for international breakthrough. She managed to get some recognition in USA, which is usually a tough place for dance musicians. *Set Me Free* rose to number nine in Billboards Hot Dance Music & Club Play chart. In Finland, her best position was with *All Or Nothing* single, fourth. The song was featured on a soundtrack of US comedy movie called *But I'm a Cheerleader* in 1999. The hype bubble burst when it was revealed that Miisa didn't sing in her own songs. Swedish singer Karin Strömfelt, was the real voice behind Miisa. Karin's voice was familiar from another eurodance group from Sweden, Dreamland.

Attitude is maybe the best Finnish dance album ever.

Case Miisa is just another example of the eurodance/dance music tradition, where the frontmen aren't the ones singing the songs. But in Finland this was unheard of, we are known for our integrity.

Having said that, I must conclude that her first album represents the best Finland had to offer in the euro scene. The producer Chris Owen has really embodied the essence of eurodance and created a timeless album. *Attitude* is full of hard dance beats and sheer joy of dance music. When the interest toward Miisa rose in the US, also her music changed into more house. Also, the songs from *Attitude* were remade into softer sound that they would suit US needs better. Those songs were recycled in two consecutive albums.

▶ *Ann Bell Fell*

Like Waldo, also Ann Bell Fell sought help from Sweden. Kati Lindtfelt (Ann) and Rauli Eskolin (Illusion Rake) were people behind the band and they got good productions from Pandora's team, *Around & Round,* and *I Feel It Coming* was done with Basic Element. The latter one seemed even to come straight out of BE's own catalogue, so similar it was (The single version had Petrus from BE rapping).

ABF released their first LP *We Come We Go* (1996) with a strong eurodance vibe, but the second (*Annbellievable*) released two years later was much lighter, housier and a little bit experimental. It's worth noticing that the latter one had a cover *Frost,*

255

which was the main theme of The Snowman, Christmas animation. They released this song about the same time when the Finnish metal band, Nightwish, did their version.

Nowadays the duo is on a break, probably indefinitely. They have been asked to perform on gigs, but they aren't really interested. Today Kati is a music teacher and Rake is a producer.

In The Spotlight

▶❚❚

Kati Mäkelä-Niemi *singer*

Rauli Eskolin *aka* Illusion Rake *producer*

The pics are released with permission of Kati Mäkelä-Niemi and Rauli Eskolin.

How did Ann Bell Fell got started and what does the name stand for?

Rauli:

Ann-Katrine Lindfelt was a find of songwriter Jukka Vuolle and they had been making demos together, one of which Jukka offered me to produce. The name was Jukka's suggestion and it became Kati's artist name. After the first record contract, we decided that ABF will become a duo and Ann Bell Fell will also be the band's name.

Ann Bell Fell was dance music, but what genre is/was close to your heart?

Kati:

This is hard one, because in my opinion all genres are really interesting. I have always liked good singers, simple folk style, jazz singers but also art pop. I loved Ann Bell Fell's studio work, harmony singing and seeking different ambiances and overtones.

Rauli, were you involved with other dance projects in the 90's?

Rauli:

I did several remixes and produced/co-wrote an album with Kristen Orre (Virgo) from Helsinki, Zen Garden released three singles but decided not to release an album. The material was ragged IDM with triphop / drum & bass influences. I also produced EMI's domestic 'spice girl' project, Sitruunapippuri's, album. In the 2000's I was in Campaus and Skydive.

How would you describe the dance scene in Finland in the 90's?

Kati:

The scene in the 90's was a little homemade, very enthusiastic and maybe childishly believing in the future. We were enthusiastically going abroad, that's why we wanted to sing in English. And the record company did have some contacts, we got to cooperate with Swedish producers and even got to be in a Japanese collection. Oh, and our first album was released in Japan.

How much success did you get abroad?

Rauli:

In Japan, the single *Around & 'Round* ended up on a collection called *Dance Now!* which sold well. That's why our first album was released in Japan and it sold about 20-30.000 copies – more than here in Finland.

Also, in Scandinavia they released some of our singles.

I Feel It Coming was done with Basic Element, how did this cooperation got started?

Rauli:

This happened mainly because of Finnish EMI's Wemppa Koivumäki (at that time he was marketing director); he had Nordic contacts. At first we made *Around & 'Round* single with Sir Martin Family (Pandora's production team) in Stocksund Studios/Productions. This was a world class big studio compared to the standards of the 90's at a society district in Stockholm.

During that same summer we managed to pull off a liaison with Basic Element and recorded the songs in Stefan Andersson's more down-to-earth cellar workshop. Although the mixing was done at EMI's own great studios.

How was it like to work with Peter Thelenius? (*I Feel It Coming*)

Kati:

I don't remember much about the recording of *I Feel It Coming*. I remember that we were thinking that the song must be surplus stuff from their own album. I was a bit amused by the songs ambiguous theme.

I also remember that he came to Finland and we did a joint gig in some TV show in fall 1996. The gig was set up to heat up the fading record and gig sales. Somehow I got excited in a live TV show to play a part of a dominatrix and pressed him onto his knees in front of me. Afterwards I thought that did I just do that. I asked him was it ok, but he wasn't bothered. After the show I went straight home and that was it.

The first album was mainly eurodance, but the second one lightened the sound, why is that?

Rauli:

Everything has to come to an end, sometime. Whilst making the second album, eurodance wasn't so current, I was more fascinated about house, big beat, trip hop and drum & bass, the more 'dirtier' lo-fi stuff. After that, I haven't been able to be so product or genre oriented, regarding my own projects!

Why ABF broke up or faded?

Rauli:

Partly the reasons I mentioned earlier, but also because we had children. Moving to Helsinki and founding and building Inkfish studios were the reasons behind my fading from the band. Also, the last phase had brought in real players in gigs (+hard drive) and this confused the musical focus of the project in my head. And also, I was interested in filter house and uplifting trance, which led me to Campaus and Skydive projects in the 2000's.

Have you thought about comeback?

Kati:

No. The life has led me to another direction. I have done lots of other things, music teacher, singing teacher, conductor, worked in musicals, but not in the public eye.

Rauli:

During the years I have recycled many of my songs and text, but when it comes to projects, my career has been linear for some reason.

After 20 years, how do you see the 90's music business and especially the dance music genre?

Rauli:

It was the time of internationalization, but we were so far behind, compared to e.g. Sweden. Our export efforts were groping, but we had strong will. At that time, the sales of dance collections were the motor, which helped single artists to break with a catchy hit single.

Video played an important role, but the productions which would fill the international standards were far beyond the reach of Finnish budgets. The media was surprisingly interested about Finnish dance artists, especially because of the success of Aikakone (author's note: one of the biggest dance acts in Finland in the 90's.). There were TV shows for 'live' performers like Jyrki. There was an also a lot of demand for gigs.

Is there something else you want to share about your band?

Kati:

The best thing in Ann Bell Fell was working in the studio with Rauli Eskolin, it was really inspiring. It was so cool when Rauli said that shall we do some parts and then we did overlap singing tracks, I loved it. Even today I'm proud of it. It has been great use for me later on, in studio I learned to sing in time, the computer just kept going on and wouldn't wait for me. Before I was a bit neglectful when it came to tempo of music.

The gigs were more painful, I would like to have performed with a band, not with a background tape in play or singback, first of all I felt that I was a singer, not a lip-syncer or a dancer. When we finally got a band together around the second album, none of the gigs were sold and so the booking agency forced us to go to tape. It was so wretched how the story ended.

Rauli:

Fun fact: our first single for EMI, *Around & 'Round*, was accused of plagiarism (Abba: *Summernight City*), and even Teosto's (author's note: Finnish non-profit organization, which administers and protects the rights of composers and music publishers) lawyer thought that it was a copy. The publisher of the song managed to get our song to Björn and Benny and we got a redemption from the highest place!

෭

SOMEBODY DANCE WITH ME – OTHER COUNTRIES

▶ **DJ Bobo** (Switzerland)

Published with permission of Marcel Obelholzer, Yes Music.

René Baumann (aka DJ Bobo) (b.1968) is the most productive and maybe the most sold eurodance artist ever, although his music hasn't been euro for a long, long time... With a distinct rapping and singing voice and the sturdy production of Axel Breitung, he has created his own empire.

When René graduated from college in 1984, he was interested in a career of a pastry chef but breakdancing and music called him even more. A bit by bit, he started to get some success and rewards with his dancing, one year he even won the Swiss show dance championship.

In addition to this he had started a career as a DJ, where he fared also amazingly climbing to the ranks of the best DJ's. In a club called Don Paco he got a lot of experience and self-confidence to finally start a music career. In the end of the 80's, Bobo released his first song, *I Love You*, after which he started a small tour in Swiss clubs. A couple of other songs followed, which caused a bit of commotion in his homeland. But international fame was just around the corner...

While his first songs were hip house, *Somebody Dance With Me* (1992) dipped into the rising waters of eurodance. The song was a partial cover of Rockwell's 80's hit, *Somebody's Watching Me*. The song threw the man to stardom all over the world, when it ranked in Top 100 while gathering gold records e.g. in Germany, Australia and Israel. The next single urged people to continue dancing (now that they had found a dance partner), in *Keep On Dancing*. Also, this was a same kind of mega hit.

Soon followed a debut album *Dance With Me*. Although the record was a huge success, it felt so quickly put together. There are some weird semi-instrumental songs, with Bobo's shouts in between, repetitions from the biggest hits and remixes, so that the album would feel longer. The poorness of this LP would be corrected on the next one. In this first LP, Bobo started a long lasting cooperation with a singer Christiane Eiben, who would sing the biggest hits of Bobo's career. In addition to this, Christiane's voice can be heard for instance in Urgent C (also a Breitung project) and in Centory.

Despite of its classic value, DJ Bobo's first
album is shoddily put together.

After the publication of the first album, they released more hits from it: *Take Control* and summery euro reggae *Everybody*, which success would influence Bobo's music even to this day. This reggae outing sold 500 000 units in Germany, platinum.

DJ Bobo's second phase started also with a success: *Let The Dream Come True* (1994) (with Lori Glori) was a very fast euro song. The second long play, *There Is A Party*, soon followed. It is probably one of the best eurodance albums of all time: it's loaded with perfectly catching euro euphoria, any which one worth a single release. The majority of it was straight forward dance songs, but the number of those would diminish in the several upcoming Bobo albums. With this album Bobo continued working with Breitung, who had done a successful career already in the 80's with his italo disco band Silent Circle (who also did eurodance in the 90's).

There Is A Party album gave birth to more hit singles like the album title song, which was once again euro reggae, in the vain of *Everybody*. The album has a much more superior reggae song, *Deep In The Jungle*, which should have been put out as a single. Also, *Love Is All Around* and *Freedom* kept the man in public consciousness by conquering the charts.

With this second album, Bobo started his massive tours, which have continued even to this day. *There Is A Party Tour'95* extended besides Europe, to Asia and South America. His background in dancing joined with dance music was a winning combination and that's why his concerts have gotten bigger and bigger over the time and grown into giant spectacles, comparable with Madonna's tours.

Before his third LP, Bobo offered a Christmassy treat in the form of *Just For You* CD. It wasn't a new album, but an EP, which contained a couple of new songs, like the ballad *Love Is The Price,* which gave us a glimpse of René's vulnerable side. There were also new remixes.

The new proper album, *World In Motion*, meant a big change in his music. He took a giant step towards pop stardom and started to separate from his contemporaries. There are only a few dance songs in *World In* Motion, like *Pray*. The main part is either slow songs or euro reggae and there's even a disco song, *Let Me Feel The Love*. At this stage, the childish positivity and world saving attitude of his music started to raise its head in Bobo's music. The fans didn't seem to mind, it broke sale records, for example platinum in Germany and in Switzerland double platinum. The more poppier approach appealed many. There is also a *Winter Edition* of this with a different track list, including *Radio Ga Gaga,* which was done for Queen Dance Traxx project. It was interesting to see *Shadows Of The Night* released as a single from it, because the single version was done with Wien Symphony Orchestra. This was a fine combination and showed once again that there is so much in common with classical and dance music.

Magic album (1998) continued along the same line as the previous one: lots of ballads and reggae but only a couple of dance songs. *Where Is Your Love* was closest to euro but even that had been done with a lighter touch. *Level 6* was put out in the eve of the new millennium and now a couple of songs had been produced by Jonas "Joker" Berggren from Ace Of Base. Although this too had a lot of downtempo, surprisingly much energy had been put to the single release *Together*, which had a big whiff of trance pop. At least Bobo showed that he still knew how to put out a good dance song. Energetic song was the first song on the album, and it raised expectations, but the disappointment was great, because there was nothing else on the LP that would live up to that. Although the two Berggren songs breathed new life into this dull publication.

The next, *Planet Colors,* was a concept album, in which every song represents a color and the spectrum of emotions. One of Bobo's favorite songs has always been Irene Cara's *What A Feeling*, and so he performed a new version of this in his new album with the original performer. Once again, besides a couple of dance songs, the LP was full of tear-jerkers and reggae.

Bobo is one of those few 90's dance acts, who have managed to put out an international hit in the new millennium, although *Chihuahua* (2003) should never have been released. It copied its style from Lou Bega's unbelievably bad *Mambo no 5* and offers only an unbearably foul earworm.

Another big moment for Bobo in the 2000's was when he was chosen to represent Switzerland in Eurovision with *Vampires Are Alive* in 2007. There was some controversy around the song when the Swiss Christian party collected 50 000 names to an appeal, where they demanded the song to be withdrawn from the competition because it promoted satanism and could agitate teenagers to commit suicides. Despite the hate towards the song, it was without the doubt one of the best efforts from Bobo and Breitung. Still it positioned only at number 20 in the song contest.

René has diligently reworked his old hits. In *Celebration* collection (2002) he dueted with other artists like Melanie Thornton and ATC with remakes of his old songs.

262

Another album done with the same concept, *Reloaded,* was irritatingly derivative because it used mainly electro house DJ's in the production side. Although his duet partners in this were big stars like Kim Wilde and Jessica Folcker.

Bobo is still a huge star, especially in his own country, but also in Europe. He continues making new music and albums, which are usually followed by a big tour. The latest album is *Kaleidoluna* (2018), which embraces once again faster dance music.

It's an undeniable fact that Bobo has outlasted many of these contemporaries from the 90's by changing his style into pop. It's reasonable but in the other hand you are irritated by the fact that the ballads and reggaes ate up much of the space in his records. In my own opinion, the best time for Bobo were the two first albums and a couple of singles released after these. Still he holds a special place in my heart because *Somebody Dance With Me* was one of the first eurodance songs I have heard.

▶ *Imperio* (Austria)

Adam and Eve of eurodance.

In the same way as Pharao took its style from ancient Egypt, Imperio got imagery from ancient Rome. The project producer Norbert Reichart had infatuated with old Hollywood spectacles, which described that era. Idea for the first song he got from a cigarette back, where the words read: *Veni Vidi Vici.* First he made it an instrumental, but vocals were needed. While clubbing, he met Manuela Ferisovic (aka Manuela Ray), who had tremendous amounts of energy and dancing skills. Norbert asked him to his studio where Manuela showed that she can sing too! It was a bit harder to find a rapper, but finally American Michael Harris joined them.

Rome theme appeared in record covers.

The first single, *Veni Vidi Vici* (1994), sold 250 000 copies. It contains the typical euro refrain, rap in between plus a low-voiced man who repeats the song name. After the second song, *Quo Vadis,* an album was put out, which carried the name as the debut song. Reichard was so strong in his belief to these two, that he set up another project for them, Decadance. The music was similar to Imperio's, the difference being the Mayan culture as a theme.

Michael had to leave after the album, and he was replaced with Lawrence Madia. Second album *Return To Paradise* (1996) was considerably different from the first one, because it had only one pure eurodance, *Never Go Away*. Other content was dream dance, which was popular at the time. Maybe because of that, the album didn't have much success and so the project faded.

According to Eurokdj, Imperio were to release a new single in 2001 called *Voices Of Eternity*, with album after. But there was just more silence from them, and they even haven't performed in 90's festivals in any formation.

▶ *Fish In Zone* (Israel)

One of the most unusual countries where eurodance was produced, is definitely Israel. There was at least two euro bands there at the time , one of them was called Insideout (who managed only to put out singles) and the more famous one, Fish In Zone, who released several singles and one album.

In The Spotlight

▶️‖

Eli Yona producer

Eli Yona second from right, published with permission of Eli Yona.

What was your role in the band and how did the band was born?

The band formed from studio productions. As a music producer I meet a lot of singers and musicians in various productions. This is how I got to know Gili Stein who was working on his rock production and told him about an idea I had in the dance style and he liked the idea and immediately offered to join in, and from various productions I worked with I took two wonderful singers Odelia and Orit and that is how the band formed.

Fish In Zone, could you tell me what does that name mean?

When we were looking for a band name, all the names sounded standard to us. One day I saw some movie and saw the phrase Fish in Zone. I said it sounded interesting and everyone agreed it was something more memorable and so it stayed.

Was there a demand for a domestic eurodance band in Israel in the 90's?

There was a demand for eurodance music. It was the most popular music in Israel. We are among the first to do it in Israel, was Dana International and us. We are the first eurodance band in Israel. Then there were some more dance artists.

When thinking about your sound, did you have other artists you mimicked or based your own music to?

We built our music and sound from our ideas and creativity. You can hear our sound. Of course, we are also exposed to what happened in the European arena and we loved a lot of artists .

Did you have success outside Israel?

Yes, we have had success in Italy, India, Japan and also in the dance parades in the UK.

You released your last singles in 2000, why did you stop?

Everybody turned to his business, so it somehow ended, and I did a many of other productions...

Your opinions on current eurodance scene, is there any?

I really like what's happening today in world pop and European pop. I do productions like this. A new international production will be released soon...

What is the status of the band now, are you doing 90's shows?

The band is currently inactive as I mentioned everyone is in his or her occupations but ... there is occasional talk about doing something.

▶ *Eurogroove* (Japan)

Eurogroove was not your usual euro project, because its producer, Tetsuya Komuro, was from Japan. To bring out more international vibe, there was also a production trio FKB (Bozidar Ristic, Tony King and Phil France). Their musical style had a definite Cappella vibe with luscious diva vocals and very melodic sounds.

The first singles were only released in Japan, like Dannii Minogue sung *Boogie Woogie*. Dannii wasn't shy to dance music, she has always been more into club music than her more famous sister Kylie (although her music has also elements from that genre).

But it was *Move Your Body* (1995) that opened up the road to Europe. The song obeyed all the conventions of eurodance to. It positioned in Israel at 21 and in UK at 24. Also, the most Cappella sound-a-like, *Dive To Paradise*, became a hit and got a wider release than any of the previous singles.

The world got to know better the project on an album *In The Groove*, which had different singers. There was the previously mentioned Dannii and a rapper Einstein (aka Colin Case), who was familiar from some of Technotronic's songs. There were different versions released of the album in different countries, for example Canada got a double album.

In Japan, they also released collections / mix albums under Eurogroove's name, where their songs and remixes were blended with songs by other artists. This was quite weird because they were easily mistaken as artist albums.

Eurogroove didn't outlast the euro era, with a whimper they vanished from the music world...

▶ *Rozlyne Clarke* (Australia)

Rozlyne couldn't hold it together.

Aussie Roslyn Howell aka Rozlyne Clarke (b.1966) started with musicals but soon ended on a solo career. She got her chance when her friend was supposed to perform to a French producer, Nikolas Skorsky. She couldn't make it, so she ended up introducing her musical friend Rozlyne to Nikolas.

Clarke's first, *Eddy Steady Go*, was a really big hit in France in 1991. Being the sound of that day, it was released also in Benelux countries and Japan. Strangely named debut hit were soon followed by *Gorgeous* and *Dancin' Is Like Makin Love*. Rozlyne's album, *Gorgeous,* soon followed.

So far Rozlyne had done house music, but in 1994 she faced a change: Belgian eurodance project Unity Power (Luc Rigaux and Patrick Samoy) remixed her old hit into new form. It was released with a name Unity Power feat. Rozlyne Clarke. New mixes gave new credibility for her.

She got excited and started to make new songs in the popular euro style. The new songs were for example *Take My Hand* and The Three Degrees cover *Givin'Up Givin'In*. However, the new album collected around the new style was only released in Belgium and it sold poorly. Nowadays the CD version of the album is really valuable.

Her last song so far has been *I'm On Fire* with Stevie H in 1997. Today she has given up music business entirely and works as a make-up artist under the alias Rozlyne Vidal.

ॐ

GO GO (LOVE OVERLOAD) – EURODANCE WANNABES AND CURIOSITIES

Many artists tried out eurodance in addition to those who were considered as euro bands. Especially 80's artists wanted be more credible by adopting a more modern sound.

Bad Boys Blue, which probably was one of the biggest synth-pop bands from Germany alongside Modern Talking, tried out thoroughbred euro on an albums *To Blue Horizons* (1994) and *Bang Bang Bang* (1996). The latter one had euro producers like Felix J. Gauder and Enrico Zabler, but in my opinion the previous one was far better effort with its trademark melancholic BBB sound incorporated perfectly into eurodance. The band continued working with Gauder into the 2000's. Nowadays John McInerney (b. 1957) is the only surviving member of the band.

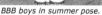
BBB boys in summer pose.

Another hard 80's project alongside BBB, was Silent Circle, who had accomplished only one album in the previous decade and a couple of hits. When the euro sound rose, they wanted to be more relevant. One of the band members was Axel Breitung, who is especially known for songs penned for DJ Bobo (plus many other

268

artists). While he had created Bobo a household name, he turned to his own old project and the result was absolutely wonderful dance music. Especially *Every Move Every Touch* (1994) was typical 90's Breitung with choir and all. The 90's sound carrier them a bit farther than the 80's, because they released a couple of albums with this updated sound. Although the latter one, *Stories 'bout Love* (1998), wasn't as good as the previous album (*Back!* , 1994) released in the best euro era.

London Boys falls into the same category than the previous two bands. They had some success in the 80's with their colorful outfits and dance moves and songs like *London Nights*. This male duo, Edem Ephraim and Dennis Fuller, stepped into euro arena on an albums *Love 4 Unity* and *Hallelujah Hits* (1995). The latter one is one of the most peculiar euro albums, because it's a cover album full of religious songs like *Kumbaya*, fitted into euro form. Their career faced an abrupt end: they both died in a same car accident in the Alps in 1996.

Babies, religion and eurodance were a strange combination.

After the Dieter Bohlen's and Thomas Anders' Modern Talking had quit in 1986 (they came back 10 years later with a bang), Dieter decided to set up a similar project called Blue System. With the same falsetto and queerly written lyrics, the legacy of Modern Talking continued even up to 13 albums. And of course, Dieter dabbled with euro. *X-Ten* (1994), *Forever Blue* (1995) and *Body To Body* (1996) had some great euro songs like the singles *Laila*, *Dr. Mabuse* and *Only With You*. He also produced projects like Major T, which had more clearer euro form with female lyrics and male rap. Their *Keep The Frequency Clear* channeled very clearly Intermission's *Piece Of My Heart* hits sound and ambiance.

Another falsetto singer, British Jimmy Somerville, had a very gay band called Bronski Beat. While Jimmy left the band, a new similarly sounding singer John Jon was brought into the band. The new sound had Italian Factory Team behind it and new album, *Rainbow Nation,* was perfect euro. Also new euro versions of the band's hits *Smalltown Boy* and *Hit That Perfect Beat* were released for the new generation of LGBT people.

Boytronic also dreamed of boy-on-boy love. While Bronski Beat relied more on hi-NRG and euro disco, German Boytronic took its stride from synth-pop. They tested out the euro sound with single *Send Me An Angel* (1994). The vocals are very reminiscent of U96 and that's no wonder: Ingo Hauss was in both projects, in Boytronic just for a while. The next year's *Blue Velvet* single was a much more harder euro with traces of trance music.

Paul Parker, who had collaborated in the previous decade with hi-NRG artist Patrick Cowley, was also fascinated in euro music and released a complete album of it called *Destiny* (1995). Gay community was also the target group for Paul and so the covers like *Riders On The Storm* done with a fabulous euro sound pleased the gays very much. Parker's 90's productions have been collected into CD Ian Anthony Stephens Presents Paul Parker – *The Definitive Collection* (Fantasia Records, 2013).

Cicero in studio 2018, published with permission of David Cicero.

Also, Cicero (aka David Cicero) had a one foot in the gay culture, he did synth-pop under Pet Shop Boys' wing in the beginning of the 90's. During the declining years of euro, he suddenly released two 100 percent eurodance songs, *Don't Worry* (1996) and *Summertime* (1997). It's a shame, that he released only those two.. Cicero comments those songs:
" *I was inspired by what was happening at the time with the club scene for Don't Worry, a lot of Italian disco was out at the time which got me wanting to do something like that. Summertime was again the same however it's all about when you go on holiday and fall in love, but it never feels the same when you come home.*"

Disco kitty's purring hit was transformed into euro.

Disco grandma Eartha Kitt started discoing at a late age in the 80's. Her purring hit *Where Is My Man* got some new power with a 1994 remix, which was very similar to Culture Beat's *Mr Vain* hit. Also, the French one-hit-wonder Rose Laurens updated her *Africa* in the same year in a similar euro style.

Canadian-Nigerian hi-NRG singer Carol Jiani (aka Uchenna Ikejiani) had created a semi-successful career in the 80's with hits like *Hit'N'Run Lover*. She wanted to try another genre in Canada, where eurodance was a relatively big thing. Album *Superstar* was released there, and it was eurodance mainly, with sprinkles of euro house.

271

While 80's artists were busy trying out eurodance, some 70's disco artists didn't want to be second best. They gave their hits to the hands of capable producers and wanted good euro versions of them. German disco collective   Dschingis Khan snatched   E-Rotic's producers for a couple remakes and the result sounded very similar to E-Rotic. Also, disco divas Thelma Houston and Amanda Lear turned to euro or in the case of Amanda, did completely new songs in that style.

American rapper Africa Bambaataa (aka. Lance Taylor, b.1957) is one of the 80's biggest hip hop names, so it's weird to think of him performing eurodance. But it's true: in the middle of the 90's he provided raps for songs like   *Feel The Vibe* and *Pupunanny*. These and other dance songs were collected for the   album called *Khayan & The New World Power feat. Africa Bambaataa: Jazzin.* He has done collaborations with electronic music artists also later on.

There was a fair share of arti(s)ts, whose physical appearance appealed the masses more than the music they made. The French Eve Vallois (aka model Lolo Ferrari) was especially known for having the biggest breasts in the world. She also had had a stunning amount of plastic surgery. These facts probably helped her in the music business, but only one single was released commercially: *Airbag Generation* (1996). Lolo (apparently) committed suicide in 2000.

These boobies just barely fitted into the cover.

Sabrina updated herself into the 90's, but where's the album?!

Also known for her rack was Sabrina Salerno (b. 1968) whose 80's banger Boys foreshadowed the rise of euro with brilliant rap part. So, it's no wonder that she released some euro music. *Angel Boy* (1994) represents the best of Italian production with absolutely stunning melody and beat and it is one of the best euro songs ever. *Rockawillie* from the same year only managed to annoy with its bad refrain.

Sabrina's contestant from the UK, Samantha Fox (b.1966), tried euroish production relatively late on an album *21st Century Fox* in 1997. Songs like *Let Me Be Free* and *Santa Maria* went further than your basic house. In the typical UK tradition, it was hard to say what was euro and what was not. There was also a new version of eurodance diva Nina's *The Reason Is You*.

Underwear model American Mark Wahlberg (aka Marky Mark, b.1971) gave us male cleavage and appealed more to females (and gays of course). He started his music career with hip hop and got a couple of hits with his Funky Bunch collective, like *Good Vibrations* (1991). With their two albums they flirted a bit with house sound, but it was still surprising that he turned to euro. With Alex Christensen (U96) and Frank Peterson in the production chair, project called Prince Ital Joe feat. Marky Mark was set up. A couple of fairly light but good euro singles were released: *Happy People* (1993) and *United* (1994), but they couldn't get the album more wrong: *Life In The Streets* is a mix of ballads, hip hop and there are only a few euro songs. This was soon corrected on a remix album where famous euro bands (or namely their producers) remixed the songs from the album. There were remixes for example by La Bouche and Fun Factory. Mark continued her own solo career for a couple songs, but eventually acting took him much, much further. Nowadays he is one of the biggest stars in Hollywood.

Prince Ital Joe and Marky Mark were buddies.
From the album leaflet.

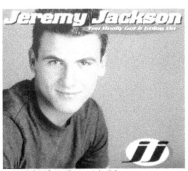
Hobie from Baywatch did some euro.

Jeremy Jackson (b.1980) is also an actor, whose most famous role was in Baywatch where he played David Hasselhoff's son, Hobie Buchannon. Inspired by the fame brought on by that popular show, he wanted to try out a singing career, although his singing skills were non-existent. The albums *Number One* and *Always* contain surprisingly European material, he probably targeted the same audience as Hasselhoff in his singing career in Germany. After the albums he released his best euro song, *You Really Got It Going On* (1997) with Twenty 4 Seven man Ruud Van Rijen. Nowadays he has exercised himself to a hard muscular form that it's hard to even recognize him anymore.

273

Pretty Wanda, published with permission of Fabio Spini.

Like Jeremy, also Wanda Fisher (aka Vanda Radicchi, b. 1947) couldn't hold a tune. Like Eartha, she jumped on the dance wagon quite late: *Meteor Man* (Dee D.Jackson cover) was released in 1993 while she was 46. After a couple euro songs, she performed *The Ride,* which Kim Sanders has also sung immensely better. Wanda pronounced herself as the queen of eurodance on the album released in Italy, *Euroqueen (Back To The 90's)* (2009), which had more new material alongside her 90's songs.

Scatman turned flaw into victory. (c) 1995 Michael von Gimbut,
Published with the permission of Iceberg Music Group and John Larkin heirs collectively.

Another fairly old guy to turn to dance music was Scatman John (aka John Larkin, b. 1942). He turned stuttering into a victory and released a worldwide hit in 1994 called *Scatman*. The song that combined scatting and eurodance blew up the charts all over the world and was one of those few songs that appealed to young and old. Producers were Italian Antonio Nunzio Catania and Ingo Kays, whose names can be found in many other euro productions. *Scatman* was such a big hit, that a

274

counterpart was released by a female singer called Scatgirl (not with the same producers).

John's first LP, *Scatman's World,* was a really unbalanced collection of dance songs, jazz and ballads, but he improved with the next one, *Everybody Jam*, which was a more in balance and a good quality combination of dance songs. There was even a Queen cover, *The Invisible Man*. But nothing could beat the fame of *Scatman* although he enjoyed big success especially in Asia after his biggest hit. The last dance album from his was *Take Your Time* (1999) and Catania and Kays had been replaced with Mr. President's producers. The times have changed by then, so it had no eurodance. In the same year, he died of lung cancer, diagnosed the previous year. A couple of years later the last recordings of John were released under his real name in the album *Listen To The Scatman*.

In The Spotlight

▶️❚❚

Tony Catania producer

Tony Catania and Ricardo Overman (MC Fixx IT, Cappella).
Published with permission of Tony Catania.

You have had hands on many dance and eurodance productions. Which are those you are most proud of and why? Are there stand-out tracks?

I have been producing records for over 35 Years now , every record I produce is a new experience, but I think one of my favorites is *Scat Music* from the album *Scatman's World*.

This record for me was the first experimental to combine free jazz and eurodance together.

We did a millions of sessions on this one , we had 500 piano improvisation, taken from John Larkin and finally we end up cutting piece by piece from each tracks to get one right. It was a never ending story :-)

Let's talk about Scatman John. How did you meet John and how the song *Scatman* was created?

By this time, I was a very successful producer before I produced Scatman John.

I have many club hits and I was working for Frank Farian also. BMG signed me and I became for many years a BMG inhouse producer. They offered me many different artists by the time, but one day they introduced me to Manfred Zähringer , he was John Larkin's manager at this time, and he came to my studios (Catania Music).

From VHS I observed John Larkin playing piano songs from example Ella FitzGerald, Louis Armstrong..

The sound was a little bit crazy but at the end of this tape, I remember it like yesterday, he starts his scat singing improvisation. I was thinking at the moment that this is a great idea. I say to his management, to bring John Larkin from L.A to my studio and in this moment, Scatman John was born!!!

In two days, we created the first single. Those days , the sounds were always the same, and I was coming up with an old jazz guy that had the talent to scat, something like that would shock the scene. I was right, Scatman John was a huge success worldwide.

I think the song *Scatman* appealed to both young and old, why you think is that?

In my opinion that song has a really strong message, I and John Larkin wrote the lyrics for old and young generation. Also, I think the track will go on to be an evergreen, because it's so catchy and original. On top of that, with old man singing dance music was not typical for the scene.

I think this is such a positive song, that encourages people to do something out of their life and the message is AGE DOESN'T MATTER:-)

Were you aware that there was a Scatgirl also?

I never have heart about a Scatgirl in my life, sorry.

I think that the second Scatman album was way more dance oriented than the first one and it appealed to me more as a dance music lover, why the second album was a bit more dance?

By the second album from Scatman John, we changed the whole equipment in the studio. I had bought a new synthesizer and I was working also with many DJ 's like Moguai, Da Hool, DJ Hooligan, Marusha and many more… so the second album I was more inspired by the DJ's, so it became more dance oriented.

You produced Casalla songs? How Casalla was born?

Casalla was born before Scatman John, I remember that a friend of mine Tim (Casalla, the rapper) came to my studios with a demo idea , and I told him that the song needs some better production work. He asked me if I would be interested to produce his group and I accepted the offer from him. And here we go, Casalla was born.

You made *Ta-di-di-boom* for Norwegian Stella Getz, how did that happen?

After my contract with BMG Records   RCA , I was signed by Motor Music. Tim Renner, the president, came to me with the idea to produce Stella Getz. I told that she is a good artist . This is how everything came together ....

You made some Haddaway songs too, but in the 2000's. What's it like working with Haddaway?

I met Haddaway over Coconut Records in Germany. The CEO invited me to his studio and introduced me to Haddaway. I was working during that time with Coconut Records on a different projects: London Beat, Weather Girls and many more…

How dance music has changed compared to 90's? Is something easier, something harder?

I think the dance music from the 90's was much more artist & producer oriented.

Now it's much more DJ's , we have no more bands or groups in these days.

The DJ's decide now which vocalist they want to use, and the focus is more on themselves.

K2, which was named after the Himalaya mountains, combined yodeling to their euro and used obscure samples from old German movies. The mix was without a doubt very weird and humoristic. They probably continued where the previous yodel/electronica band Edelweiss had left off. The man behind the project is Klaus Munzert, famous from his 80's italo disco project, Silicon Dream (which was also quite weird). *Der Berg Ruft* (1994) was K2's biggest hit. In addition to releasing an album with the same name they continued with various singles, each song being different than the other. Their better work is the previously named single hit and its tranceformation in 2000. Surprisingly, they came back with a new song, *I Wanna Yodel All* Night, in 2019.

Pompöös was a unique fusion was fashion and music.

Another curiosity was strangely named Pompöös. It was a brainchild of German fashion designer Harald Glööckler (b.1965) and Dieter Scroth (b.1948) and their one-of-a-kind attempt to marry together fashion and music. Baroque, contemporary outfits and dance rhythm were conjoined in a kind of baroque trance. Project was named after Harald's trademark crown pattern, where stood "Pompöös". The fashion guru got help from producers like Piero Brunetti. The result was an album, where current production techniques had been combined with various dance music styles (including eurodance) but also classical. Although the album was a whim of the designers, the music is something else. It starts with a fast eurodance and goes a bit by bit deeper into the world of trance and ambient. It's really one of the big surprises on dance or euro scene! In addition to the LP, they released a totally new single, *A Star Is Born*, after which they lost their crown and vanished completely from the music world..

Bonanza Techno Ska project released only one single, *I'm Waiting For You Honey* picture on the previous page), which combined Bonanza series' western theme to a hectic euro beat. In the middle parts female voice shouts out the name of the song. Production-wise it's really worth your while and done by Peter Ballweg (for example Future Beat and Riverside People).

Rednex in their original form, published with permission of Rednex Ltd.

Cowboys and cowgirls from Sweden aka Rednex, gave people a bigger slice of western atmosphere by connecting country music to a banging euro beat. The result was something between eurodance and bubblegum dance. Worldwide hits, *Cotton Eye Joe* and *Old Pop In An Oak,* broke the euro mold by letting a man sing the refrain while a woman sang the middle parts. Famous producer Patrick Edenberg (aka Pat Reiniz) first joined them on the stage, but soon discovered that he was better suited to produce and manage.

Rednex couldn't repeat the gigantic success of the first album, *Sex & Violins* (1995). Four years later ,when euro fever had been long gone, the single *The Way I Mate* tried to use the same formula as in the previous hits, but the results were bad. Second LP (*...Farm Out*), was put out in 2000, but was soon forgotten although they had recruited even Axel Breitung to produce. In the beginning of the noughties, they updated *Cotton Eye Joe* with trendy euro trance mixers. After this they have put out several singles in various formations, the most of them quite boring. The most recent one so far, *Manly Man*, has been a slight comeback to their earlier sound.

They also got some imitators. Stock and Aitken from SAW tried to copy them in their project 2 In A Tent *(When I'm Cleaning Windows)* and 2 Cowboys did their Italian version of country techno with *Everybody Gonfi Gon.* Also traces of Rednex's sound could be heard for example in Steps' first single, *5,6,7,8* (1997).

While Rednex was based on fictional characters like Mary Joe and Billy Ray, other characters wanted to break into the charts too. DJ Duckpower released only one single *Get The Duck Out Of Here (Move It!)* (1995) and in typical euro manner featured female vocals and male raps but also raps done with a kind of Donald Duck voice (!). Cuddly cartoon cat Garfield didn't want to be left out, so he also joined the party. Compared to Duckpower, there was more effort in this project. While the material was released under Garfield's name, he wasn't heard on the tracks, instead the British Rachel Wallace sang the songs. *Party Of Love* ja *Cool Cat* were the singles released from the LP called *Keep Cool, Cat!*

Garfield wanted to be cool eurodance cat.

Biggest hitmakers in doll world.

Zig & Zag were two alien-looking British dolls (from TV) who also dabbled with music career because they were popular amongst both adults and children. *Them Girls Them Girls* (1994) was a Reel 2 Real copy by DJ Erick Morillo, while *Hands Up! Hands Up!* took a page out of Rednex's book. In 2008 another doll Dustin The Turkey offered a euro throwback when it represented Ireland in the Eurovision song contest with a very stupid but catchy euro, *Irelande Douze Pointe*. Its flight didn't last even to the finals.

∼

ELECTRIC – 90'S ARTISTS' EURODANCE EXPERIMENTS / NOT EVERYTHING IS EURO

In the 90's euro was everywhere; many artists had an urge to do a couple of euro songs. Even some of the biggest names in dance music, like Pet Shop Boys (*Absolutely Fabulous*), did some experimenting. Many singers who did a couple of eurodance songs, were soon dubbed as eurodance artists, but that was not the case. For example, Whigfield is considered as euro, although she has technically only one pure eurodance, *I Want To Love*. Rest of it is euro house and/or bubblegum dance.

Two of the 90's big dance bands, Ace Of Base and Scooter are very often considered as eurodance. Although the Swedish foursome had very catchy songs like *The Sign* and a very definite euro flavor, most of their music was mainly euro reggae. They have only a handful of songs that could be considered euro in my opinion, like *Beautiful Life*. But the band still had a big influence for eurodance acts: many adopted their reggae style and planted some songs of that style between their eurodance efforts. Also, Scooter has probably been some inspiration for 90's dance musicians, but there's actually one eurodance song, where the leading man H.P. Baxter (aka Hans Peter Geerdes, s. 1966) has been, and that's in the Lovemessage collective's song *Lovemessage*. The band's regular style had encompassed almost every aspect of dance music, but not eurodance.

In the next part, I introduce some of the euro testers from the 90's.

▶ *Leila K / Rob'n'Raz* (Sweden)

Swedish Leila K (aka Leila El Khalifi, b.1971) started her musical ventures with a hip hop / hip house duo Rob'n'Raz by doing a joint album in 1990. Into proper superstardom she rose through her own solo career with album *Carousel,* from which hits like *Open Sesame* and *Ca Plane Pour Moi* were published.

Electric went well with Leila's image.

The biggest hit from the next album, *Manic Panic* (1996), was called *Electric* and it was pure euro energy. It also breaks the pattern of male raps: Leila raps and Jessica Folcker has the refrain. In its ferocity and aggressiveness, it encapsulates the best sides of eurodance. The album itself was a big disappointment: euro reggae, hip hop and rock. Since that she has come famous for her alcohol-fueled rock'n'roll life.

Rob'n'Raz featuring Lutricia and D-Flex.
Published with the permission of Rasmus Lindvall.

Leila's previous musical partners, Rob'n'Raz (aka Rasmus Lindvall and Robert Wåtz) wanted to get a piece of the euro action. They recruited the luscious USA-born Lutricia McNeal, with whom they released one of the best euro songs from Sweden, *In Command*. The band was evened with a handsome rapper, D-Flex (David Seisay). *In Command* had a very visual music video, where Lutricia's and D-Flex's best parts were exploited with humorous undertones. *Powerhouse* was another attempt at euro sound, it was a remix of a previous more housier song. It was clearly the weaker one of these two. Later Rob'n'Raz returned to hip hop.

Lindvall recalls: *"We always like to do different styles, and we were into hip hop and r'n'b a lot. But in the 90's eurodance was dominating the charts so it was almost impossible to do anything else at that time. So, we tried to put some soul into the euro, and did In Command and Powerhouse etc. "*. Lindvall states about the 90's eurodance era: *"It was a great time, and the 90's eurodance contains a lot of good melodies and is still very popular. Even among kids that weren't born after the 90's!"*

▶ *Tatjana* (Netherlands)

Tatjana Šimić (b.1963) was like a really cheap copy of the real bosom buddies, Samantha and Sabrina. She started as a model but soon moved on to become an actor, she has been in many comedies and TV shows. Like her idols, also Tatjana wasn't shy, so she posed in Playboy. Tatjana started to record music in the end of the 80's, but she got her biggest hit in the next decade with *Feel Good* (1993), who took its cue from Haddaway's popular *What Is Love* . In the cheaply made music video she cavorts on the beach with a male model.

Tatjana had the same provocative image as Samantha Fox and Sabrina.

Never Never was another eurodance from 1993, but it didn't even get to all the released versions of the *Feel Good* album. Surprisingly, the song got a cover version a few years later, when Bad Boys Blue did their own version of it, with better results. Tatjana's *Feel Good* album was a mix of several different styles, including songs from the 80's.

There were also some shades of eurodance visible in her next LP, *New Look*, from which *Santa Maria* single was released. Stock and Aitken-penned song became a dance hit. Around the same time, this song was remade by her biggest rival, Samantha Fox. The album also trifled with several styles giving air kisses to eurodance, being mostly house and hi-NRG.

Tatjana continued her recording career quite quietly by concentrating mainly on her home country.. *Blago Onom Ko Te Ima* song was a minor hit in Netherlands, and it was the first one from her that wasn't dance music.

▶ *Paradisio* (Belgium)

Summery Paradisio was born in 1994 when a man previously known from Unity Power duo (Patrick Samoy) fell in love with the Spanish Marisa Isabel Garcia Asensio's voice. The first effort with Marisa, *Un Clima Ideal,* didn't have much success, but the perky *Bailando* proved out to be one of the biggest summer hits ever. It sold millions of copies all over the world, and the project was personified to

Marisa and her pink wig in *Bailando* video. The debut album *Paradisio* had also a very similar song, *Vamos A La Discoteca*, which was a hit, but nothing compared to *Bailando*. Their music has traces of euro, but they are mixed up with a heavy latino vibe.

After the mega hit, Patrick started to change the leading lady very frequently. The original singer Marisa was replaced after two years and the current singer is Raquel Rodgers Rodriguez, and there were many other singers in between. In the 2010's they have been active again and released new songs and even new albums, although only in digital form. Paradisio is without a doubt a one-hit-wonder, which has stretched out its popularity and career further and further.

▶ **Mephisto** *(Italy)*

In The Spotlight

▶️⏸

Maurizio D'Ambrosio producer

Published with permission of Maurizio D'Ambrosio.

Your songs made in 1993-1995 could be considered as classical eurodance (like *You Got Me Burnin Up*). Where did you draw inspiration to these tracks?

I was inspired by the music that I was playing in that period in the clubs.

Were your first releases successful? Did they do well in the charts?

The first important release was *Euphemia*, this record sold 10.000 copies, but the radio didn't play it, and for this it was only in the club charts.

The first big success in Italy called was *State Of Mind*, it was number one in the spring of 1993 in the dance and sales charts and, of course, all the radio stations played a lot.

Eventually you ended up doing songs that were more house music like *Mystery Of Love*, why the change of genre?

I changed the style a lot of time in my life...because I don't like just one kind of music, I love every kind of music, and I produced what I feel in that moment....and not because I'm following one or another style just because is in the charts in that moment.

I produced, for example, Elgar *Sweetie Pie* in 2002 with Universal and it was completely another style....and very different with everything in that period, and it was a big hit in Italy.

2009 Mephisto *The Beat Of The Bee,* completely different.... with a very important music video. This is me; I produce just what I love to produce...when I love to do it.

NEW HIGH ENERGY – SMALL BUT IMPORTANT ONES

Besides all the acts and singers, I have introduced in the previous pages, there must be hundreds or thousands of projects who contributed one or two songs (or more) but failed to put out an album or create a longer career for themselves. Sometimes a well-known producer wanted to try out a different sound under an secret alias or some single experimenter was dreaming of his own eurodance hit, but got discouraged because he/she didn't get the same kind of success like Captain Hollywood or 2 Unlimited.

Although these following acts have released just a few songs, they all have a special place in my heart, so that is why this isn't a complete list of every performer out there.

GERMANY

One of the bands to come out of Germany's euro cornucopia, was 2 For Love with producers Johannes Lowien and Holger Grauel. The leading male and lady were Dwight Hayden (who rapped ragga style) and Jackie. The bands *Only For Love* (1994) is pure eurodance fantasy with its great melody and longing refrain. That's why it felt like a punch to the face, when they released their second effort, *Ding Ding (O Nana),* which couldn't be further away from the previous one with its happy and summery euro reggae sound.

One band that sang energy level to the maximum, was K.Da Cruz. There's no information about the female who sang the distinctive lead, but the rapper was Terry W.Cromwell. Their most aggressive and best song was without a doubt *New High Energy* (1993). This should have fared much better, but its best achievement was in Israel number six. The energy level tried to be stayed the same in the next ones like *Love Is Lifting Me Higher*, but they couldn't reach the same pure power. They also released a single with another project Push (NOT the one with Belgian trance DJ Mike Dierickx) called *Push*, which has a quite satisfying bassline. The video from that instead is really clumsy and cheaply done.

Slam, who quickly gave up eurodance, was consisted of singer Axinia Schönfeld and the two ragga style rappers, Sten Mehlhorn and Stefan Schleickmann. The men had known each other from childhood, and they had set up a raggamuffin band called Toasters. In Berlin they met Axina, who was studying there. Axina saw the boys perform on a club and decided to invite them to a studio session. She had soul music in mind but Sten and Stefan lured her into the world of dance music.

Slam's trademark was men with top hats.

Back To Music (1994), the first song, is very affective euro with gorgeous diva vocals. *We Get Around* continued with the same genre, but the singer in this one was Samira. In the third single, the style took a lighter turn and the result was *U Got 2 Know (Doodappenbadappen),* which cleverly (or accidentally) referenced Cappella's mega hit. Stylistically it was more euro house.

The positive vibe was continued with the rather abominable euro reggae *Big Fun*. *Crazy* instead copied   Reel 2 Real. In the *Crazy* CD single leaflet, they are mentioning an upcoming album, but nothing ever came out. Slam's career ended in a shockingly stupid Shaggy copy *If I Had A Hammer*. Axina's career continued in other music genres after Slam. She has performed for e.g. with symphony orchestras and even released a jazz album.

Berlin-born Samira Besic's career was rose to new heights, when she provided vocals for Maxx's mega hit *Get-a-way*. International success helped her in starting a solo career, and so she released singles like *I Look Into Your Eyes* and *Love Train*, which were really popular all over Europe. She also featured on a weirdly named G.E. Con-X-Ion's song *Gotta Have The Music*. Her career in dance music draw flatline after these songs, because the next one, *The Rain* (1996), was a soulful downtempo. She probably couldn't decide what her style was going to be, because the next one, *I Can't Get You,* was freestyle. The last Samira song, *It Was Him,* was once again downtempo, this time a vocal version of the Lenor fabric softener commercial song. In the 2010's she joined a rock group called Clic, where she still is today.

Technotronic's former member, MC Eric (aka Eric Martin), rapped under the alias Eric B in the one and only single of the project named Sirius *(This Is My Life)*. The refrain is sung by Michele, who is also known for her short solo efforts like *Love Is History*. The high-class production was by Christian Leibl, who also created another masterpiece with her other act, B-Cap. The act's main singer Aquila is unbelievably bad but if you forget that fact, their only single, *Send Me An Angel,* is one of the hidden jewels of eurodance. The song was a cover from Australian synth-pop band Real Life. The song had probably been loaned without permission, because the whole project collapsed after this one song due to legal issues with the original band.

A soulmate to the previously mentioned Leibl productions was Academia, which offered same kind of explosive energy with a song *Dance To The Music*. This was sadly the act's only single. Treasure 2 instead accomplished two singles: *Reality* and *Deeper And Deeper*. The former is the most appealing one and with a better availability (if you want to own the physical version). Songs are sung by a model Marilyn Mariani.

One could have wished that First Base had had a longer career. Their biggest song to date is *Love Is Paradise* (1995). Vocalist was Kristina Safrany (b.1972) and the producer is Michael Gleim aka DJ Wondermike. When the song was initially released, it really didn't get much attention, but when it was published a year later on a Canadian dance collection, it became a huge hit. Canadian markets had opened up, so they made more songs. Songs like *Heavenly* and *Can You Keep A Secret* ended up in a couple of collections there. Before 2000, the project released an EP there, which featured the previously released songs and a one new song.

The singer Kristina has also created a solo career for herself and she is still gigging because of her contributions to First Base and also to Future Beat. She also has a new eurodance project called Maxxima. She is joined by MC Fixx IT (of Cappella) and together with Andy Stead they are determined to bring the eurodance back.

Kristina Safrany, published with permission of Kristina Safrany.

Groovecult was a joint project of Markus and Michael Mohr, which mutated into a basic dance project after the first two euro singles. *Come To Me* and *Midnight Dream* were perfect euro, but the next offerings were something else: *Ultimate* was a boring euro house and *Bang To The Beat Of The Drum* (2000) was even more boring house. It's worth noticing that the Mohr's produced also B.G. The Prince Of Rap's last album.

Deviating from the typical eurodance formula, 3-O-Matic consisted of two women (Nancy Rentzsch and Tanja Geuder) and a rapper (George R.Walden III). The ladies had known each other since the 80's and had been Haddaway's background singers. They came up with a name 3-O-Matic when they united the number of band members to Tanja's car automatic transmission name, Variomatic. The band's first single, *Success* , foreshadowed their fame with its name, but they only succeeded in creating only two additional songs: *Hand In Hand* and *All I Want Is You*. According to Eurokdj, they recorded an album called *Senerata*, but it has never surfaced.

The party gets better, when there are fewer people, thought the members of 3-O-Matic, when they broke up and reformed into a girl duo 2 For Good in 1997. Nancy and Tanja's first single was *You And Me* and the producers were Nancy's husband Rene Baumann (DJ Bobo) and Axel Breitung. In the same year they also put out a euro reggae, *I'll Be Waiting For You*, and that was the end of that band too. But in 2014 Tanja joined forces with her former band mate George and they kicked up a project called 2-O-Matic and released only one song, *Harder Like Stone*, which is quite far from the lovely sounds of eurodance with its hands up trance sound.

Published with the permission of Tanja Geuder.

Strangely named Riverside People had a bit longer career, spanning five years but only four singles. Best of them is without a doubt the highly melodic *Fantasy Dancing*, where the singer's badness can be overlooked. Their last single *Come To The Riverside '99* was, despite its name, an update of *Fantasy Dancing* with trendy trance sounds.

Like in the case of Future Beat, Damage Control should have had a longer career. They did more remixes to other artists than released their own original songs. All their three songs are different from each other. The most serious and better one of them is *You've Got To Believe*.

Jesse Lee Davis drifted to Germany with the army in the 80's, like many other eurodance artist. The first one, *Get Up On This,* was a flop, but the next one, *Is This Love,* became a hit in Canada and Israel. He grabbed the essence of eurodance better with great songs like *Like A Flame* and *Round And Round*, which left people yearning for an album, which sadly never surfaced.

In The Spotlight

▶ll

Janina Mangold (Janal) laulaja

Published with permission of Janina Mangold.

How Janal was born?

Me and Al met in a little recording studio in Friedberg/Germany. This had been in 1992 when I was 12 years old and Al the age of 27. We released our first single *Don't Keep Me Waiting*, the project name had been DBX feat. Janina.

During that time, I got an offer for working with a professional and successful producer team in Cologne. Since working with Al was so much fun - and we had become good friends - I didn't want to continue making music without him. So, no discussion - he was as well on board and wrote the song *You Gotta Set Me Free* together with Buddy JD. Our manager presented our project Janal - a combination of our first names (JANina ALboom) - to some record companies and finally we got a record deal with Virgin Records in Munich. A dream came true for me by the age of 13.

Why did you release only one single?

The single release had not been that successful, to be honest. We did not reach a chart position. As well it had been very difficult for us to become known through live performances, because I was too young to perform in the evenings. The laws are very strict. Real promo work was almost impossible due to my age.

Are you still in music business?

I'm the singer of today's eurodance Project ,J.O.Y.C.E. Together with A.K.Swift from the massive successful project, Magic Affair, we already released two singles. *Let The Rhythm Take Control* and *Get 2Gether* at DMN Records.

In addition, I'm a singer in a rock cover band for almost 10 years, Agent Dee. Performing live on stage is fantastic!

How would u define eurodance?

For me eurodance is my youth. An incredible feeling of freedom and light-heartedness. The 90's were a great time, full of positive energy.

Why eurodance was the genre you chose to do?

It was THE music style that was hip - that so many people wanted to hear and celebrate. Together with my best buddy Al Boom it was a great chance to get part of that huge era.

Published with permission of Janina Mangold.

SWEDEN

Mach-7 wanted to reach the same demographic who liked fast eurodance á la Look Twice and Basic Element. They consisted of LA-Stevie (aka Stevie James) and women Ida-Jean and MaryLynn West. They kept up the heated pace all through their four singles and all songs were very enjoyable eurodance. Solid Base men Jonas Eriksson and Mattias Eliasson contributed to *Alacazam* while Pat Reiniz helped on *United States Of Japan*. If you want to get your hands on these singles, be prepared to pay a lot, the most expensive single is *Alacazam*. Anders Thorslund, who had penned the first Mach-7 songs, *Real Love* and *Dangerous*, had a one song project called H.R.Beat, whose *Hok Baba Jimmy* (1996) is one of the greatest euros to come from Sweden.

Basic Element was also the inspiration for E:Motion, whose *Get Up* (1994) is very reminiscent of BE's songs. It's no wonder that they both had the same producer, Stefan Andersson. The assembly also released some further singles like *Open Your Mind*, but the last one landed flat like a pancake: *Come Into My World* was a light house song.

Two significant dance artists, Nana Hedin and Jessica Folcker sang for Amadin. Collaboration between Kristian Lundin and John Amatiello used also a rapper called Swing in *Alrabaiye (Take Me Up)* (Swing also released his own euro single *Sweet Dreams* with Dr. Alban). Nana sang the refrain in *Alrabaiye* while Jessica was the main vocalist in *U Make Me Feel Alright*. Amadin released only one additional single, *Fonky*, which was house á la Nightcrawlers. Kristian and John have also produced music for instance for Dr. Alban and Herbie. According to Eurokdj, their liaison stopped because John didn't want to make music anymore.

ITALY

One name connects Italian projects Echo Bass and X-Ite: Brixt (Julio Ferrarin). X-ite released only one single, but what a song it is!! *Down Down Down* (1995) is energetic and fiercely melodic and one of my biggest euro favorites ever. It shares the same energy with Echo Bass' *Givin'it up*, which whisks you to heaven with the aid of a powerful vocalist. Echo Bass' three other songs don't even get near the same energy level as in *Givin'it up*. In these productions you can clearly see how good the Italians were in creating wonderful melodies. In that respect they are far above other euro countries.

Bass Expanders, which released songs quite slowly, consisted of rapper Christopher Sparacino and singer. Their three singles were released in three consecutive years, so you can observe the evolution of euro sound through these songs. The first one, *Beats Go,* is more raw techno, while *Party All Night* and *Bounce* are smoother.

House DJ Joe T.Vannelli (aka Giuseppe Troccoli) took a step into eurodance land with JT Company. She also founded a record company under the same name. Greg G was the rapper and singer in many of JT Company's songs, while the main female vocalist was constantly changing. They started with house and italo house like *Don't Deal With Us*, but eventually moved into greener pastures, into euro lawn.

Sometimes there was also male beauty in record covers.

Live My Life was their first pure eurodance. *Wet* continued with more of the same and sounded a little bit like Cappella. *Feel It (In The Air)* speeded up things and is their best one. *Baby Hold On* trampled the euro road, but *Miracle* (1996) returned the act once again to house music. In 2000, they surprisingly released a pure vocal trance song *Wake Me Tonight*, with a singer called Barby. While this was to be their last song, Vannelli has continued with his solo efforts to this day.

Beautifully illustrated Playahitty CD single cover.

If the voice on Playahitty's song *The Summer Is Magic* sounds familiar, the reason is that the voice belongs to Jenny B (aka Giovanna Bersola), who also delivered the vocals for the Corona mega hit *The Rhythm Of The Night*. Playahitty, which

294

composed of producers Emanuele Asti and Stefano Carrara, took their musical style from Corona but added a certain summery flavor to it. In the typical euro convention, they used lip-syncing models in live performances.

In consecutive years they released a few minor hits, but nothing could reach the same appeal as *The Summer Is Magic.* Their last songs in the end of the 90's were more house than eurodance. Playahitty has also a questionable honor to be in my trash list (one of the worst euro songs) with their absolutely childish and irritating *1-2-3! (Train With Me).*

The woman in the cover was just decoration,
the real singer was Sandy Chambers.

Jinny raised some attention in Italy, because it was the only Italian artist in addition to Black Box to get into US Billboard Top 100 chart. The song in question was a house song, *Keep Warm.* Eurodance was introduced with *Feel The Rhythm (U.S.U.R.A. Remixes)* (1993) where U.S.U.R.A cut off all the house stuff and left the hardcore euro/techno parts.

One More Time single was a commercial success in Italy. It had a very definitive British euro feel to it. Guys behind Jinny, Alessandro Gilardi, Claudio Varola and Walter Cremonini, decided to make more eurodance because of the success of that song. Eurodance regular, Sandy Chambers, was asked to sing *Wanna Be With You,* which is typical Italian quality. *Keep Warm* was rewarmed in 1995 with new Brit remixes e.g. from Alex Party and T-empo.

Eventually the project faded, maybe due to euro sound dying away, and their last commercially released song was *Memory* (2009). According to Eurokdj Jinny did comeback around that time: singer Lyv McQueen did some live gigs performing Jinny songs.

Producers Francesco Contadini and Fulvio Zafret set up an act called Night People. Fulvio's wife, Sylvia Zafret, was recruited as the singer and Tony Dyer as the rapper. With this line-up they released their first and best song, *In The Night (1994)*. You had to wait a whole year for the next song to surface and Renick was the new vocalist. Their last single, *We Want Good Sex Tonight*, once again featured Dyer. The title sounded very much something from E-Rotic album, but instead this was an awful US hip hop.

Also Mr. John was one of Zafret's projects. Its purpose was (according to Eurokdj) to be an act like Ice MC with ragga rap and Masterboy style. Nigerian frontman John Edokoplor had a very uncommon background: he could have been a prince in his homeland, but he abandoned the crown and became a businessman in New York. He moved into a more euro friendlier country, Switzerland, in 1992. His first single *U Gotta Move Me* (1995) was an instant hit, as was the next one, *Get It On*. The third one, *It's Not Too Late*, is the best one in my opinion. The original Mr. John's career ended after three singles, but Daniel Peyer (who had been involved in the project) owned rights to Mr. John's name and continued with the project. While eurodance was practically dead in 1998, another euro *Take Me Away* was put out to please euro music fans. Mr. John's works are collected in a digital album, *Dancemania My Party Album*.

HAD was a onesingle-wonder, but the song was great.

Also HAD (Human Athletic Dance) was a great example of Italians ability to make melody rich eurodance. Singer Nathalie Aarts and rapper Tony Dyer did awesome job with *Spirit Of The Night*. Both are well-known in dance music scene; Dyer was singing much for Zafret and he was in DJ Manian's electro house project R.I.O in the 2010's.

In The Spotlight

▶❚❚

Tony Dyer *singer*

Published with permission of Tony Dyer.

You've rapped/sung for many projects, do people recognize your voice from various hits?

People do recognize me as long as I use voices that they know like the *Shine On* - voice. But I have so many voices, sometimes you would not know it's me. I really have a lot of voices, so sometimes it's impossible to know that it's me. But if I use a voice that I'm very known of like I did when I sang *Shine On* or something from R.I.O. then people know it's me. But even then it's not easy for everybody because there are other people who also seem Jamaican. But for people to recognize me depends a lot on what voice I use.

Of your own songs, which one is your favorite and why?

My favorite song would have to be *Shine On* because that song helped me travel through over 60 countries and I'm still traveling because of it. It's my first evergreen song and it's still going to be there in 20 years. That's why every artist wishes to have an evergreen song. It's my favorite because it has so much power and has given me a lot and it has changed my life.

Would you like to have been part of a bigger stable eurodance group than jumping from project to project?

I don't think I would have changed anything in the past. I like how it was and everything was meant to be, so I don't think about ever wanting to be a part of something bigger or smaller because I take everything as it is. Everything happens for a reason, whether it's good or bad, in the end it doesn't matter. Important for me is, that I learned from everything, I learned from every choice and learned from everything that came out of that choice. That's more important than regretting or thinking it could have been better. I like everything how it is.

In the 90's I didn't jump from project to project. I am just a very fast songwriter and rapper. I could just rap, I don't need time. When I recorded songs, it was not for a project. It was just a song that some people bought and used them. I didn't know what for it was going to be for the moment I recorded it. I just rapped and rapped and rapped. In the 90's I wrote, I think, 60 songs in one day. I wrote them because somebody sent the beats and said they need it today and I sat down in the morning early like at 6:00 o'clock and I was finished in the evening and I wrote them. It wasn't for me it was for others.

Do you perform in the 90's festivals and/or still make dance music?

I do not perform at 90's festivals at the moment but it could happen in the future, I don't know. I have my own shows and I don't use songs from the 90's because it's too long ago. I have more successful songs today than in the 90's.

Anything else you want to share?

If there's one thing I don't like about my past it's that the most people I worked with were very good con artists. So, they were not truthful and that's why I'm a solo artist now with no contracts. I don't trust these people anymore because I worked with people who were going to take more money than they were supposed to take. That's why I quit all the projects that I've worked with because of them filling their pockets too deep. I'm not going to name any names, though.

OTHER COUNTRIES

French lady, Celia Gruss (aka Silja), spent just a little time in the euro arena. After telling her friend about her musical aspirations, the friend set up a meeting for Silja with a producer, who was responsible for example Enigma. After this meeting, Silja's debut single, *How Could I Find Love* (1994) was born. Further singles like *Time For Eternity* and *Flesh And Fire* continued with the same eurodance vibe, but after this a two-year long hiatus started, after which she changed her style completely. She moved on to sing pop music in French and even released an album with the same style. I have some doubt whether Silja is singing herself in the first two singles, because in *Flesh And Fire*, she sounds more different and worse...

Dutch Egma's name consisted of the first names of its producers, Ege Van Kruysdijk and Marcel Theunissen. Usually euro act started out as house or hip house act, but Egma started with techno. In the first single, *Let The Bass Kick* (1991), you could easily hear the soon-blooming euro sound. They were born anew in euro era, and a female vocalist Margo was recruited. Male singer and eye candy, model Henk Van De Weil was also brought to the band. First euro song, *Never Gonna Lose Your Love*, was a Europe-wide hit and spent 10 weeks at number one in French single chart. It's no wonder, the song has melodic beauty, the production has a kind of 80's nostalgia and longing but brought into the 90's. It's real weird that it wasn't a hit in their home country.

Never Gonna Loose Your Love.

Love Is took a happier tone and got to number one in Israel. After this the band changed their male to a new singer Michael Robby. With this new line-up, two additional singles were put out, after which the project vanished. These last songs brought some hardness to their previously light sound. The producers naturally moved on to other dance projects: Marcel did Central Seven and Ege created a girl band called Close II You. Egma faced a rather tragic end chapter in 2002: the original male singer Henk was murdered in Paris during a robbery.

In The Spotlight

▶II

Marcel Theunissen producer

Published with permission of Marcel Theunissen.

How Egma was born?

Egma was born by the cooperation of two producers, Ege and Marcel. Me and Ege were both DJ-ing at the same club in the south of Holland. We decided to meet and put all the equipment together to start producing. Egma – *Let The Bass Kick* was our first instrumental track. It became a club classic.

Why the band changed style (first you were making techno)? Why the change of male singer after a couple of singles?

After some productions (other projects, and remixes) we decided to produce more commercial dance music with vocals. Because of the experience we had with remixing other tracks, we tried to manage our own vocal recordings. That track became Egma – *Never Gonna Lose Your Love.* Egma was changed from a DJ act to

300

two singing artists, Hank and Ilse. *Never Gonna Lose Your Love* became an unexpected great hit. Because of the time between finishing a record and the release we experimented with several tracks and also with several artists. That was the reason that Margo was added to the second single *Love Is.* After touring Hank decided to stop singing and focus on his family and we started doing auditions for a new male singer.

Did other eurodance artists influence you?

I'm always a bit influenced, from that genre Snap! and Haddaway.

How do you see the 90's now, especially the music of that time?

Because of our job as DJ's we played a lot of eurodance music at that time. I can remember that *What Is Love* by Haddaway blew me out of my chair. It really felt as a huge track the first time I heard it. If I look at eurodance nowadays, you see that it became a part of history in dance music. At that time, a lot of people didn't like the sound of it and were against it. They said it was simply music from a computer. If you look at all the 90's parties which are still working well at the moment you can easily say those people were wrong.

ॐ

SAY GOODBYE – THE FADING AND LEGACY OF EURODANCE

The best years of euro were from 1992 to 1995. In 1996 you could see that it was trying to adapt to new musical surroundings and in 1998 new dance music styles had taken over although euro was in the heart in many of these genres. One of the executors of this eurodance metamorphosis was Ari Lehtonen. Artists that he produced (for example La Cream) had one foot in other genres than eurodance, but they had some common factors with euro.

The popularity of happy hardcore, which biggest performers were Scooter and Blümchen, also made euro projects to change their style. Artists and producers realized that the classical euro started to lose its popularity. For example, 2 Brothers On The 4th Floor's second album's dance songs are happy hardcore. Also, bands like Critical Mass balanced between eurodance and hardcore.

New projects born in the 90's (like Sash!) took the essence of euro but decorated it with a more club-oriented styles like trance and also got big hits with instrumental songs. Towards the end of the 90's, dance artists started to change into more anonymous acts without having a clear lead singer. Also, artists like Nomansland mixed euros fairly easy refrains into dream dance sound (*Fantasy*, 1997), which was a genre made famous by Robert Miles with his massive hit, *Children*. For example, Imperio's *Return To Paradise* (1996) album is a clear departure from euro. It has only one pure eurodance and all the other songs are done in the spirit of dream dance.

Around the turn of the millennium, trance music was very big. While at that time eurodance was basically dead, the producers united the melodies and refrains of euro to commercial trance sound and thus euro trance was born. One of the first representatives of this new genre was Alice Deejay with *Better Off Alone* (1998). Men behind this project were trance DJ's like Pronti & Kalmani. Alice Deejay was a massive success, so this brought on several other competitors like Ian Van Dahl, Lasgo, Kate Ryan and Sylver. Kate Ryan had classic eurodance producers behind her, like Phil Wilde (2 Unlimited). The musicians had adapted to the new trend. This new breed of euro trancers brought the euro sound into a new decade.

Other dance music genres started to take over the charts which had once been dominated by eurodance. That's why euro acts started to change and in the process started to lose part of their identity. For example, Culture Beat's fourth LP, *Metamorphosis* (1998), was a dried-up version of a hard dance band. It was mainly basic house. But there were also good transformations like Basic Element, which had a drastic change to a more poppy euro house sound but managed to get new hits and fans.

But there were a couple of artists who didn't want to give up the classic euro sound. E-Type continued recording new music even to the 2000's, in 2007 he declared himself as "Eurofighter". Also, E-Rotic continued to make euro sounds, although with a shade of euro trance and the Italian record company S.A.I.F.A.M released euro, most of them covers of popular songs.

The next two bands, La Cream and Reset, were signs of changing times:

▶ *La Cream* (Sweden)

With covers like these, of course you were only interested in music.

Short-lived La Cream was eurodance for a new era. The melodies, refrains and energy were from eurodance, but the music was produced with a more progressive club approach.

Singer Tess Mattisson (b.1978) and producer/DJ Andréz Abatte met at Dr. Alban's Dr. Records, where both of them were involved in different projects. They learned to know each other there and eventually started to make music together. They tried to bring sense of internationality to their music by using different languages like

Spanish and French alongside English. The first joint song was *Château d'Amour*. Ari Lehtonen and Freddie Hogblad were co-producing.

It wasn't until the second single, *You*, when people started to get excited about the band. One of the reasons was the music video, where Tess is shown in a very tight outfit. *Say Goodbye* was more of the same in music and in video. The cover of the old Dr. Alban hit, *This Time I'm Free* (now titles as *Free*) connected the band firmly to its euro roots.

As it was typical in that era, Therese probably didn't sing in the studio as much as was believed. The biggest proof for this is that you could clearly hear the original vocals from Martina Edoff in the Dr. Alban cover. In either case, the project's career ended after just one album. Tess went solo with similar trance pop sound. She released a few fairly successful songs under her own name.

In The Spotlight

▶❙❙

Ari Lehtonen producer

Published with permission of Ari Lehtonen.

How did you get involved with dance music and which songs were your first dance productions? What led you to produce Waldo ?

I began first of all as a hook writer, the production side of it all had to wait since when I signed with Dr. Alban back in 1994, he had producers like Kristian Lundin, John Amatiello (Amadin) and Peo Häggström. I had the privilege to learn from both

Kristian Lundin and Denniz Pop since I was allowed inside the studios while they were producing and mixing. After Kristian left Dr. Alban in 1995 and went over to Cheiron, I got my first chances to actually sit and try things out in the studio myself.

My first official dance production was Waldo from Finland whom we wrote the song *The Riddle*. I have no clue if that song was successful, but Waldo did return in 1997 to ask me for a full length album. That album became the first Waldo's People album which included the hit songs *U Drive Me Crazy* and *I Dream*, from there and on I did most of Waldos People's songs all the way up to 2009 ESC song *Lose Control*, which was Finland's official song.

My real producer career got started between 1995 autumn and spring 1996, that is when Dr. Alban was kind enough to get me a mentor who could show me how the samplers, synthesizers etc. worked, not to mention that back then everything was done on tape or a dat. We had to sample all vocals into the AKAI samplers and then play them from the keyboard in order for us to sync or pitch correct intonation notes. I still kind of smile when I think about those days, today I have both Protools and Logic X and everything is so fast and simple to do, almost too simple.

In 1997 I got into the dream house and trance scene, since euro style was almost out, so I decided that I wanted a project like that but then still add chorus melodies and vocals on top of more progressive productions, that is how La Cream came about. I teamed up with a fellow DJ friend Andrez Abatte and then a young dude who had been calling, bugging, mailing letters to Dr. Alban studios demanding a meeting, his name is Freddie Hogblad, who mostly was a trance guy with a huge appetite for dark sounds and he sure knew how to get a kick slamming. We had huge success with this project and meanwhile I did more commercial productions on my own such as Drömhus, Dr. Alban and various other projects.

La Cream and Waldo's people are half eurodance and half progressive house/trance, they have a very unique, hard but very similar sound, How did you come up with this, it's like the eurodance evolved into that?

Like I mentioned above, the La Cream sound was first of all an idea, since when I went clubbing in Stockholm, I noticed that only between 1994-1996 the DJ's started picking the darker remixes of all hit songs, no one played the radio or extended mix. I picked up on that, in 1996 Swedish Gilbey's Dance Music Awards was still going and much to my joy they had booked Alex Christensen aka U96 to perform. He played for like two hours and I was amazed over all the new songs he played and how he still got the dance floor cheering for every new song that kicked in.

That is where I understood that euro was dead and something new needed to happen, so I started to look for people to collaborate with. I met Freddie Hogblad who was a trance producer, even though he never released anything he had the sound and the knowledge of how harder club music should sound. He lacked experience in arrangement, melodies and adding vocals to his demos. So that is where we started from, I came with pop and commercial thinking, he came with club-oriented thinking and we just put our heads together.

I think it took about one month and we had done the whole La Cream album and began work on Waldo's People album which was done in three months after that.

You've also done remixes, how does it differ from making a whole new song ?

Remix is kind of a record labels idea to get fans and the sound from one producer to hopefully give them enough boost so that their record flies. These days you have to be a DJ, which is sad since I stopped DJ-ing in 2002, If I only had known what was around the corner.

I still do remixes for commercial projects since today's club music is so much more diverse so even a progressive record is commercial in its own unique way.

But the difference is, for me, to respect the original but still add some kind of a twist to it that caters to a new audience that the original mix does not attract. Also, mostly you get stemms, which is a perfect way to learn how other people think, I have learned more about picking sounds this way than ever before.

Are you involved with music nowadays? And if so, in what capacity?

Yes I am very much involved, I have revamped some of my old projects and remixed them into the 2010-2020 sound, mostly of my artists still tour both 90's nostalgia gigs and then normal club shows, I think it has to do with the fact that I am not afraid to try new things so I just jump in the studio with an old a cappella and then play around with it until it makes sense. We have managed to even stream gold status on some of these releases almost 20 years after they were hits in the 90's. For this I am proud.

What do you think of today's dance music (EDM)? Compare it to the sound from 20 years ago.

Today's dance music, especially with the EDM boom 2010-2015, I was amazed how much bigger everything became, I remember listening to the first releases of Steve Angello thinking, ok, this will probably get stuck in the late night slot in a club set. Much to my surprise I started hearing it earlier and earlier and suddenly people screamed when drops kicked in. By that time- I knew, ok here we go again soon they will add vocals to these drops and get huge streaming numbers, which happened. I absolutely adore what both Swedish House Mafia and Avicii did with dance music, but one must not forget, David Guetta's first releases had hooky vocals from Chris Willis which propelled David Guetta into stardom.

In addition to popular Aqua and Daze, there was an ever-growing army of other bubblegum bands who wanted success. Many had eurodance in their core, although it was laced with a more childish, soft sound. Bubblegum was an amalgamation between 60's gum pop and eurodance. Usually the main vocalist is woman and a male sings in between, rapping or normally. Naivety and happiness are the common themes in this subgenre and usually they sing about partying, candies, or fantasy characters. One of the first acts was Me & My, but it was Aqua who brought the genre into general knowledge with their international hit, *Barbie Girl*. Bands like the Norwegian Reset were part of that genre, but they were not so cheesy and had a more serious streak in them, closer to eurodance.

▶ **Reset** *(Norway)*

Photographer: Per Heimly, published with the permission of Camilla Alvestad.

Like La Cream, also Reset was like a missing link between eurodance and trance pop. Project was founded by Stig Antonsen. They released a pure euro, *U R My Dream,* in 1996, but the song went unnoticed. Two years later he was joined by Camilla Henningsen (now Alvestad) and Thomas Borgvang.

They updated their sound and released *Blue*, which sold 200 000 copies. They had added elements of eurodance, bubble gum and trance pop. The debut album *Play,* was sheer joy of dance music and is probably one of the best Nordic dance albums.

With their second album, *Calling You,* they stepped more heavily into trance pop form and at the same time started to forget their eurodance roots a bit. With this one, they didn't get as much success, so they decided on a break. Now, the band is active gain because of the huge demand for 90's bands.

In The Spotlight

▶ ||

Camilla Alvestad singer

photographer: Hanne Pernille Andersen, published with permission of Camilla Alvestad.

How did you get to be a part of Reset?

My Reset adventure started kind of by accident. I was hired in the studio to do a demo for a known dance act in Norway. The dance act decided to not to go for the song. So, producer, Stig Antonsen got inspired, finished the song, and got the idea to startup and old project called Reset. Thomas Borgvang was a radio host and Stig contacted him to complete the group. We teamed up in a week. Three first songs in a month. Six months later we released *Blue*. It went straight to number five on the Norwegian charts.

Reset's music incorporates sounds from eurodance and bubblegum dance. But how would you define your music?

dance, pop

Does Reset, as a band, have artists they look up to?

Well..we never had a band who we listened in the studio together. We are three different people with different preferences. We are inspired my music..all music!

There was a couple of years between the first and the second album, how would you describe the difference between these two albums?

I really can't tell you the difference other than new songs. The second album took longer cause of touring and success from previous album.

You were once a member of Solid Base? Could you tell more about it.

Yes, I was a member of Solid Base for some years (2014-2017). I also co-writed and recorded vocals on *Were Gonna Rock It* and *Coming Alive Tonigt*. The song *Wet* is also my vocal but no co-writing. These days I'm also doing shows with Turbo B from Snap! in Europe.

≈

EURODANCE NOW : FANS AND MAKERS

Now it's time to hear from the fans themselves and also the new artists of eurodance. In the next part, the fans tell about their relationship with eurodance, then we are introduced to a Canadian radio show Euro Nation, record company DMN Records and in the end of this part, we meet some contemporary artists who are making authentic eurodance music.

But next, four fans from all over the world speak out:

▶II *Henri Kumlander; Suomi*

Music enthusiast

How old are you and when did you begin listening to music and eurodance?

I was born in the middle of the disco era, 1977. In the 80's I was inspired by the pop and dance music of that time, and my biggest favorites were Samantha Fox, Madonna, Taylor Dayne, Whitney Houston and many Stock, Aitken & Waterman-productions, but it was until August 1993 when I started to study in a gardening school, I really got excited about eurodance when we listened to many dance compilations in the school dormitory. The first songs that really inspired me were. Snap!'s *Rhythm Is A Dancer*, M.C.Sar & The Real McCoy's *Another Night*, DJ Bobo's *Keep On Dancing*, Haddaway's *What Is Love* and Rob'n'Raz's *In Command*.

In school I was always shy and unsociable, and I was bullied throughout my school years, and I didn't really have any friends. So, I replaced the lack of social life with listening to music. I love energetic, electronic dance music and I don't like acoustic instruments except for piano and strings (excluding cello). I don't like basic rock or hip hop.

I am fascinated by the electronic, futuristic sounds of eurodance. Fast flow, hard beats and often anthemic melodies and catchy refrains. These are the reasons why

308

eurodance has stayed closest to my heart all these years. I constantly try to complete my 90's eurodance CD collection.

In what format do you listen to music, or do you stream?

In fall 1995 I bought my first CD album, Melodie MC's *The Return*, and March 1996 I got my first CD single, Leila K's *Electric*. I knew that I have found my format. CD is as its name implies, compact in size, and I like to flip through the inlay; read the lyrics, credits and thank you's.

I don't stream and vinyls will never be a part of my collection, despite their trendiness at the moment.

I am proudly "old fashioned" and will never part from my CD's.

Do you have any favorite artists or bands, and why do you like them?

I like the sound of many different projects by a few specific producers. Cappella and many other Bortolotti projects have a special place in my heart. The Italian eurodance sound is just so flamboyant and produced to perfection.

2 Brothers On The 4th Floor with their catchy, feel-good style. The Berman Brothers' soft and futuristic production for (M.C. Sar & The) Real McCoy.

Energetic hits of Axel Breitung and Robyx with powerful vocals. Loft's genuine Jamaican raps, Cyborg's production, and talented vocalists, Culture Beat starring Jay Supreme and Tania Evans and the strongly trance influenced sound of the project. E-Type and Martin Eriksson's amazing and catchy melodies with Nana Hedin's fabulous vocals are a killer combination.

Nosie Katzmann's beautiful melodies, that can be heard on many eurodance classics are always nice to listen to.

Finland's own artists or bands can't really be compared to all the great projects of other countries with our incredibly weak sound, and there are only a couple of artists worth mentioning; Sound Of R.E.L.S. and Aikakone.

Do you actively follow eurodance artists on the Internet?

Not very actively but I'm trying to stay aware of their doings.

How would you define eurodance? Is it just a 90's thing or do you hear it in dance music today?

The best days of eurodance were between 1992-1997. It is an energetic, synth-oriented genre with steady beat of 120 to 150 bpm. In today's music many songs are strongly influenced by eurodance, but otherwise dance music nowadays is an indistinct combination of many different genres.

Do you listen to other kinds of music as well?

I listen to many different genres of electronic music and danceable pop music from 1970's to this day. Most of my favorites are between 1975 and 2005. I don't really find today's dance music very inspiring.

My greatest favourites from disco era are Loleatta Holloway and many other Salsoul Records artists, Donna Summer, Gloria Gaynor, and Grace Jones.

Other electronic music favourites of mine are RMB, Dune, Blümchen, ATB, Talla 2XLC, Taucher, Mauro Picotto, Mario Piu, Gigi D'Agostino etc.

I also like many basic pop royalties like Madonna, Michael Jackson, Whitney Houston and Britney Spears, and sometimes I like to listen to country stars like Shania Twain and Dolly Parton.

Although I don't particularly love ballads, the downtempo sound and amazing voice of Josh Groban is a great soother.

Why do you think eurodance is so popular?

The music is easy to dance to, and the energy and catchy melodies impress people even today .

The best eurodance songs and/or albums in your opinion?

SINGLES Top 5

1. M.C.Sar & The Real McCoy : *Another Night*

2. 2 Brothers On The 4th Floor : *Fly (Through The Starry Night)*

3. Captain Hollywood Project : *More And More*

4. E-Type : *Here I Go Again*

5. Nina : *Until All Your Dreams Come True*

ALBUMS Top 5

1. 2 Brothers On The 4th Floor : *Dreams*

2. DJ Bobo : *There Is A Party*

3. Masterboy : *Different Dreams*

4. Culture Beat : *Inside Out*

5. Cappella : *War In Heaven*

ALBUM TRACKS Top 5

1. E-Type : *Will I See You Again*

2. Masterboy : *I Feel The Fire*

3. DJ Bobo : *Too Many Nights*

4. Solid Base : *Colours Of Your Dream*

5. Basic Element : *Somebody Watchin'*

REMIXES Top 5

1. Cappella : *I Need Your Love* (T.S.O.C. Mix)

2. Cappella : *U Tore My World Apart* (World Mix)

3. Eurogroove : *Rescue Me* (Clock Mix)

4. Victoria Wilson-James : *Reach 4 The Melody* (The Men Behind Mix)

5. 2 Brothers On The 4th Floor : *Dreams* (Twenty 4 Seven Trance Mix)

Eurodance holds this magic I can't explain. I will never get tired of listening to it.

▶❚❚ *Igor Dentov; Germany*

Fan/researcher/blogger (Eurodance magazine)

Published with permission of Igor Dentov.

How old are you and when did you start listening to music and eurodance?

I'm in my 40's now. When I was very young around 8-9 years old when I started to listen to music. One radio played some techno, I think that song was Inner City, later I found myself in eurodance, anyway in the 90's it wasn't called with this name they called it "euro", "euro-nrg", "dance floor" or "euro house"

Do you collect music in what form? Or listen stream?

I collect vinyls, CD's and listen streams.

Do you have favorite euro artists? Explain why you like them.

Well I have many favorites; I love Snap!, Ice MC, Dr Alban, DJ Bobo, La Bouche, Masterboy, ATC, Alexia, Loft

Snap! had such a unique style for that era.

Dr Alban also released some good catchy songs at the time, I like *It's My Life*, *Sing Hallelujah*, *Look Who's talking*, *Mr DJ*.

DJ Bobo, I love all his old songs.

Real McCoy with *Another Night* is good.

Ice MC, I think that this guy set some standard eurodance melodies later used by many others. And songs, *It's A Rainy Day* and *Think About The Way,* have always been my favorites.

Do you actively follow eurodance artists on the web?

Since old artists are not releasing new songs and albums I don't follow them too much. All these groups are reorganized with new members that perform old hits and only do concerts. So, I'm focused on new eurodance generation.

How do you define what is eurodance? Is it a thing of the 90's or do you see it in today's music?

That's a thing of the 90's, it can be returned only in original form with little bit modernized sound but not too much modern. The best eurodance is with female vocals and male raps. Eurodance as a whole is catchy music with nice lyrics that call you on dance floor.

Do you listen to other kinds of music ?

Yes, techno of the 80's to 90s, euro rap, ragga, italo disco.

Why do you think that eurodance is so popular?

It's popular thanks to unique sound and lyrics, that energy, vocals, raps and melodies not seen in any other genre.

Best songs and/or albums in the genre? And why?

Another Night album and song by Real McCoy

Sweet Dreams album by La Bouche

One Love Album by Dr Alban

Planet Pop album by ATC

Get Ready album by 2 Unlimited

Rhythm Is A Dancer song by Snap!

Think About The Way song by Ice Mc

It's My Life song by Dr Alban

Mr. Vain song by Culture Beat

More And More song by Captain Hollywood Project

Coco Jamboo song by Mr President

Captain Jack song by Captain Jack

Sweet Dreams song by La Bouche

Feel free to tell me something else about eurodance you want me to know...

Eurodance is not techno or house.

Eurodance is "catchy sound with nice lyrics that call you on the dance floor".

Eurodance started in the late 80's popularized by Ice MC,Masterboy,Snap!,Dr Alban.

Eurodance music is also created with Amiga computers and trackers

Eurodance was revitalized in 2000's by ATC.

▶II *Tanya Viitala-Crowder; USA*

Fan

Published with permission of Tanya Viitala-Crowder.

How old are you and when did you start listening to music and eurodance?

I am 43 years old. I've loved music all my life. I grew up listening to the melodic songs of Abba and an eclectic mixture of 80's music. In the 90's, a Finnish exchange student named Ville introduced me to the amazing world of Bad Boys Blue (to this day, one of my favorite bands) and Modern Talking. I actually remember the day I first heard a eurodance song. I was sitting in a restaurant with a friend in 1994 and *Mr. Vain* by Culture Beat came on. I said "Wow! What is this amazing song?" and found myself mesmerized by it. This started what was to become a lifelong love of 90's eurodance.

Do you collect music in what form? Or listen stream?

I do not collect music anymore per se, but I still listen to my 90's eurodance CD's or search YouTube for mega mixes or individual songs. I have also, at times, searched for eurodance streams on IHeartRadio or TuneInRadio.

Do you have favorite euro artists? Explain why you like them.

Some of my favorite eurodance artists include Culture Beat, 2 Brothers on the 4th Floor, La Bouche, Fun Factory, Amber and Captain Hollywood Project. I love how their songs combine a good dance beat with sensual lyrics.

Do you actively follow eurodance artists on the web?

I don't actively follow any eurodance artists on the web. I honestly don't know if today's eurodance would compare to that of the 90's and wasn't sure if any of the 90's eurodance artists still perform. If they do, I would definitely love to follow them and see their performances.

How do you define what is eurodance? Is it a thing of the 90's or do you see it in today's music?

Unfortunately, I do not see eurodance in today's music except for rare occasions. I don't think it will ever be as good as it was in the 90's. In fact, I started to see it changing as early as the late 90's (97/98) and it had already lost the power and feel that it had in 1995 and 1996 (which, in my opinion, were the height of eurodance). Two songs from this era that DO have a good eurodance vibe are *Titanium* by David Guetta and *Everytime We Touch* by Cascada. Those two songs pop into my mind as capturing the essence of 90's eurodance. I would define eurodance as a melodic journey about love and sexuality combined with powerful beats and a touch of reggae and rap.

Do you listen to other kinds of music ?

Nowadays I mainly listen to hip hop, Lady Gaga, and some Top 40 music but in honesty, I am usually always listening to music of the past - 80's music such as Samantha Fox and Duran Duran, 90's music like Pet Shop Boys, Erasure or Enigma (and of course eurodance), and hip hop from the early 2000's. The music of today doesn't capture my interest as much.

Why do you think that eurodance is so popular?

I think eurodance is popular because we can relate to its emotions - lost love, sexual desire, heartache, lust and even seeking meaning in the world. I find it also has a bit of a metaphysical or supernatural feel to some of it. It's our innermost thoughts and emotions put into music, and our subconscious mind translated into beats and lyrics.

Best songs and/or albums in the genre? And why?

Songs: *Rhythm of Love* (DJ Company), *Close To You* (Fun Factory) - both of these songs capture the longing of love. They are my two favorite eurodance songs. I also love *Omen III* by Magic Affair and *Dreams* by 2 Brothers on the 4th Floor due to their supernatural feel. I think the album *Sweet Dreams* by La Bouche is one of the best because EVERY song is excellent and beautifully done. The 20 Fingers *Compilation* album is also an excellent variety of sensual eurodance music.

Feel free to tell me something else about eurodance you want me to know...

Eurodance music of the 90's helped me through some difficult times in my life when I was really trying to find myself and required courage. It fills my heart with joy and always uplifts my spirit. I think it is an overlooked genre of music and is so much more than "*What is Love? Baby don't hurt me...*" It is the music of our lives and a celebration of life and love. It takes us back to the days of the dance clubs, the discovery of love and who we really are and want to become. It seduces our souls.

▶II *Geoffrey Cavin; France*

Fan/entrepreneur (Eurodance 90's CD Shop)

Published with permission of Geoffrey Cavin.

How old are you and when did you start listening to music and eurodance?

I am 38 years old. Throughout my childhood, my mother listened to a lot of music and often bought vinyls. This is where my passion for music began. I watched the music shows on television, with a special interest for Rozlyne Clarke, Snap!, Black Box, U96... It was during a school trip to Germany at the age of 11 that eurodance became a real passion. *No Limit* from 2 Unlimited and *Rhythm Is A Dancer* from Snap! looped on radios at that time. My parents bought a CD player, and I started buying CDs with my pocket money. When my parents went shopping, I went into the disc department and watched the new CD releases, noted the prices on a notebook to buy them later at the best price. It was the beginning of a collection that is still relevant today.

Do you collect music in what form? Or listen stream?

I only collect music on CD's because I have always been fascinated by the object. When I was a child, as soon as I had a new CD, I inspected it to the smallest detail, the booklet, the pictures, the lyrics. And I feel the same excitement today when I find a CD that I have for the first time in the hands. I do not particularly like the digital format, but I save all my CDs in mp3, to be able to listen to my music everywhere. And I never really liked the vinyls, the sound that cracks a bit, the irregular speed according to the turntables. The object is pretty, but I prefer the clean and flawless sound of the CD. I also have some audio cassettes in my collection, but it's only because the object reminds me of memories when I had a Walkman.

Do you have favorite euro artists? Explain why you like them.

There is a lot, it would be difficult to list. I give a lot of importance to the voice. One of my favorite voices is Sandra "Sandy" Chambers and all the eurodance projects she has sung. There are also Lyane Leigh of E-Rotic, Beatrix Delgado and Linda Rocco of Masterboy, Tania Evans of Culture Beat, Anita and Ray of 2 Unlimited, Franca Morgano of Magic Affair, Kyra of Pharao, Alexia, Taleesa, William Naraine of Double You, Ice MC, E-Type, Haddaway, Lori Glori, Vivian B of Da Blitz, Jenny B, Plavka, Nina, Kim Sanders, Melanie Thornton of La Bouche, Linda Meek of Maxx, Michelle Weeks, Annerley Gordon, Clara Moroni... In fact, there were so many eurodance projects with playback, or the person on the cover was not the person who sang, that I have a big preference for recognizable "real voices", and therefore the associated artists.

Do you actively follow eurodance artists on the web?

Yes, a little on Facebook, but much more on Instagram. I really like the humble and sincere way in which they communicate. They had a huge success in the 90's, which was probably chained with a little empty period for some. And to see their joy to return on stage, to please their fans, to be grateful to them, I find it very beautiful and touching.

How do you define what is eurodance? Is it a thing of the 90's or do you see it in today's music?

For me eurodance is above all an extremely positive energy. A music with sometimes not very deep words and a repetitive melody, it is for these reasons that this music was a little criticized in France in particular and qualified as commercial. But we cannot deny the effectiveness of this music intended above all to dance. Although I listen to a lot of other more current music, I often listen to eurodance, because this music cheers me up, motivates me.

It is a typical style of the 90s, even if more and more artists are inspired by it and even start sampling famous titles of the 90s, but in a much more current style. And rare are the old or new artists who dare to make music as at the time, and it's a shame. Masterboy has released a great new single *Are U Ready* that sounds like in the 90's and it was a fantastic gift for their fans.

Do you listen to other kinds of music ?

Yes of course. I listen to a lot of electronic music and indie rock. I like the fact that music is harder to categorize today. The genres mix, and in the same title we can find rock, electro, and hip hop. I like to be surprised by the music, and I appreciate the risk taking of the artists who make the music exactly the way they want, regardless of the categories.

At the moment I'm listening to artists like The Blaze, Flavien Berger, Robyn, Polo & Pan, Tame Impala, Kompromat, Superpoze, Apparat, Son Lux ... That would be too long to list.

Why do you think that eurodance is so popular?

Because it's a joyful music full of energy. The lyrics are easy to remember. Even today in the evening with friends, just put Corona, Gala, La Bouche, Reel 2 Real or Technotronic and everyone wants to dance. Some songs are really part of the history of music, and everyone remembers it and associates it with a part of their past, often a happy part.

Best songs and/or albums in the genre? And why?

Too much for all to mention but I will focus on the albums I've listened to hundreds of times and that I like to listen to from beginning to end.

- E-Rotic *Sex Affairs* : I'm a huge fan of Lyane's voice, whom I had the chance to meet a few years ago, after a S.E.X. Appeal concert. E-Rotic has always fascinated me with their music, their lyrics, their album covers and their video clips in animation, created by Zoran Bihac.

- Masterboy *Different Dreams* : Whenever I hear the intro of the album version of the track *Different Dreams*, it projects me to a happy memory. I was admiring Beatrix and happy to see her in the Dance Machine concerts that were broadcasted on TV in France.

- Cappella *War In Heaven* : Gianfranco Bortolotti produced a big part of the italo dance music, but Cappella was really a project of great quality, an efficiency in music, with intense climbs and crazy energy.

- Magic Affair *Omen, The Story Continues* : for the melodies, the voices of Franca Morgano and the excellent rapper A.K.-S.W.I.F.T.

- T.H. Express *Love 4 Liberty* : I am a huge fan of italo dance produced by Mauro Farina and the Factory Team in general. The sound is very recognizable, and the album of T.H. Express is the perfect demonstration.

- God's Groove *Elements Of Nature* : Rather in a trance style, but I love the consistency of this album and the way it is built. *Back To Nature* remains one of my favorite tracks of all time, I love it's power and it is an album that I still listen regularly.

318

- RMB *This World Is Yours*: This album is completely crazy. Rolf Maier Bode was pleased in the choice of sounds, melodies without concession. This album, that I sometimes listen to while playing sports, is extremely motivating and pushes me in my efforts.

There's also *Ice N Green* from Ice MC, *Inside Out* from Culture Beat, *Pharao* from Pharao, *Alpha Centory* from Centory, *Visions* from Activate, *The Rhythm Of The Night* from Corona, *Made In Sweden* from E-Type, *To The Maxximum* from Maxx, *Welcome To Tomorrow* from Snap!, *Club Bizarre* from U96, *Herzfrequenz* from Blümchen...

There are also many artists I would have liked to have released an album, like Egma, Antares, Space Master, J.K., Le Park, Netzwerk, Wienna, Zhi-Vago, Anticappella...

෨

In The Spotlight

▶II

Mauricio Castano host (Euro Nation)

Published with permission of Mauricio Castano.

How long Euro Nation has been on air? Why the show started, was there a demand for it? Current and past hosts?

Euro Nation has been on the air since 2013. Before that we were called Euro Status which started in 2009. We had large local listener numbers then and even did our own all ages event. Eventually we got serious and started focusing on just music and playing the music to a worldwide audience. I don't think there was a demand per say but there is always a niche audience for all types of music. We do it because we are fans of the music and we want to play our favorite music and share interests with people all over the world. As for hosts, it's just me Mauricio Castano. I am from Toronto, Canada and have enjoyed this music since I can remember, there is truly no other music like eurodance. We have had special guest DJ's occasionally like Quickmixin' Nick from Chicago, Johnny Mastermix from Florida, & a few others.

Your definition of eurodance?

Eurodance is indescribable, its uplifting and it's timeless because there is very little music out there that is just as happy and promotes a loving message.

What kind of feedback you get?

The feedback we get is all positive, it's pretty awesome because we have listeners in literally every continent.

It's pretty insane because what started off as a hobby has gathered attention from people all over the world much including yourself. I think the main driver is YouTube which everybody is on, so they find out about our show.

Most requested songs or artists?

The thing about our radio show is we not only play eurodance, but we play what evolved from eurodance which is euro trance, vocal trance, some house and all that and hands up. We like to switch things up that's why on our show you can hear that we play a lot of old stuff which gets requested a lot like 2 Brothers on the 4th Floor, or Real McCoy but we also play harder stuff like Scooter and Milk Inc.

Something else you want to share?

It's great to see the show growing and our podcast being on every platform, but I'd like to see it grow even more. I would like Euro Nation to organize and lead eurodance and dance music concerts one day and host it in a different place each year, kind of like Tomorrowland. We know the support is huge in Europe still for this music and would love to get on that level of events. At the same time, we do air live on the Internet, but it would be nice for radio stations around the world to syndicate our show and pick it up for airplay which would get more exposure.

In The Spotlight

▶❚❚

DMN Records

Published with permission of DMN Records.

(*DMN Records' representative wishes to stay anonymous in this interview*)

How DMN Records was born ?

DMN Records was born in the summer of 2012. the first released artist was Shilton. All early singles were only eurodance and later we started with house music too. The idea about the label was born after having many contacts with artists mostly from the 90's scene who needed a label and management, and I decided to start working for them.

How have you managed to get so many eurodance stars on your label?

The list of eurodance artists has grown up in different ways. At first I had music promotion service and used to promote many of them. As a result, we built some good connections and later they started working with the label. A huge number of artists I contacted personally later.

I don't know if I can collect all names I worked with but can list some of them :

Regina, Lane McCray of La Bouche, Stay C and Nance of Twenty 4 Seven, Shamrock and Linda Estelle from T Spoon, James and Debora from 2 Unlimited the 3rd Generation, Ice MC, AK Swift, BG The Prince Of Rap, Will G, The Outhere Brothers, Pamela Knight of Spike, Tanja Geuder and George Walden of 3-O-Matic, Linda Rocco of Masterboy, Janina of Janal and many more

We also release many newborn eurodance groups from our times not from the 90's as Free 2 Night, Soundstream, Joyce, Unlimited Friends, Flash Point, J&V, Experience of Music, Real 2 Day, X Tension, Pulse of the Beat, E Bomber, BPM, Acting Lovers.

Also, to add Lori Glori, Fun Factory, Rozalla, Kyra from Pharao, General Base and U96.

How would you define eurodance?

Eurodance music is evergreen, one of the best and successful styles of dance music ever. It's still very beloved in many countries outside Europe as Chile Peru or Russia.

What makes eurodance so appealing even nowadays?

Eurodance is very energetic and happy music, with lovely lyrics in the songs, with messages to the people and with amazing live artists presenting the bands.

In The Spotlight

▶❚❚

Digital Base Project

Published with permission of Digital Base Project.

Why did you choose eurodance as your genre?

D-BASE:

We wanted to do something that no one at that time did. At the time when our project was formed (2011), there were only few real classic eurodance projects left in the world that would make new songs.

FREEZE:

Well, I've chosen eurodance, because it's very melodic and eclectic, combining rapid raps with soothing vocals, bright and optimistic melodies with a thumping techno beat. That's why we've thought it had to be revived

How would you define eurodance?

DAGOTH:

Eurodance was popular European electronic dance music since the end of the 1980's. The music was created using synthesizers, drum-machine, sequencers with bpm from 90 to 155. Eurodance song usually includes melodic female vocals in chorus and male rap parts in verses.

FREEZE:

Eurodance is energy, pure and simple.

Were you eurodance fans in the 90's? If so who were your favorites?

D-BASE:

Yes, I have been and remain a eurodance fan.

DAGOTH:

I have many favorite eurodance artists. Each of them was unique and interesting. I can name DJ Bobo, Cappella, Masterboy, 2 Unlimited, Basic Element, La Bouche, Captain Jack, Captain Hollywood Project, Fun Factory, Centory, Culture Beat, E-Rotic, E-Type, ICE MC, Magic Affair, Maxx, Twenty 4 Seven, U96 and many, many others. I had more than a hundred audio cassettes with eurodance music and listened to them every day.

FREEZE:

I was born in '93 and didn't catch the euro vibe at its heyday. I've discovered eurodance much later, around 2006-07 and was thrilled! However, I've never considered myself a fan, my passion lies a decade ago, in the 80's. But no one can argue that eurodance music brought us a lot of memorable bangers! My fav artists are Ice MC and E-Type, aside from them I love A LOT of tracks from various one-hit wonders.

Have you gotten negative feedback?

D-BASE:

Of course, we had negative reviews. But all the same, we hear more words of support, and this gives us the strength to continue our creativity.

FREEZE:

Of course, there is some negative feedback, but it isn't that significant, because the positives surely prevail. We know that you cannot be loved by everyone.

Why eurodance was and is so popular?

DAGOTH:

Eurodance was so popular because it combines beautiful, romantic, tender female voice and hard, fast male rap. It's like Ying Yang – male and female energies. It was very hard time for the world in the 90's. So eurodance was the one hope for people to live in love, peace and harmony.

FREEZE:
I believe that eurodance is the music of love and peace and there are times when the world REALLY needs love and peace. It was much needed in the 90's, and it's needed more than ever now. That's why we can see the vibes of the past coming alive again!

In The Spotlight

▶II

Free 2 Night

Published with the permission of Victor Plotnikov.

How Free 2 Night was formed and who are the current members?

Free 2 Night was formed by three members: Oleksandr Hrytsiv (aka Real Thing), Victor Plotnikov (aka Viper, Freeze) and Irina Bogryanova (aka Ira Vain) and was founded on 25th April 2012. Also, we are working with the stars of the 90's (Lori Glori) and new talented singers such as amazing Timi Kullai.

How did you end up on DMN Records?

Founder of DMN Records wrote to me and offered to release our tracks on his label.

Do you have favorite eurodance acts you draw inspiration from?

Of course! 2 Unlimited - first of all. La Bouche, Loft, BG The Prince of rap, Ice MC, Pharao and many more.

I've listened your *Best of Collection* and it's hard to imagine that your music is new, it sounds so authentic 90's eurodance! How you managed to accomplish that sound?

Thank you! It is the main goal for us - to sound as our music was released in the 90's. So that people might think that they missed something in their eurodance collection. It is a long and hard work to listen, to search, to synthesize and to select right sounds and instruments on hundreds VSTi plugins.

What are your future plans?

We are planning a new pure eurodance tracks and to make a video clip on some of our last songs with Timi Kullai if all will be well for us, I hope.

In The Spotlight

▶II

Acting Lovers (answerer Patrick Thomson)

Acting Lovers aka Kathryn McCunningham and Patrick Thomson, published with permission of Patrick Thomson.

Who are the members of Acting Lovers?

At the moment: Kathryn McCunningham and myself.

Acting Lovers takes its tone and imagery from E-Rotic. Why is that? How did your band got started?

It all started back in 1999 when I thought that it would be nice to do a eurodance project myself. So, I started composing songs and stuff but had the problem: Who's going to sing it? It took some years to find someone who dared to sing this stuff. But in the end it wasn't what we had in mind. So, we kept on searching and found first singer Madeleine. It worked well so we did a solo album with her as well.

She would've continued to work with us but put her family first and became a mother.

So, we changed to Kathryn in early 2009. Since then she's been our singer. And a great one.

The inspiration for our project was two meetings with David Brandes, in 2002 and 2006. We made some fun about songs and titles with rhymes (e.g. *Rock my cock*). And yeah, that's how it all started. We did the comic stuff because none of us was brave enough to put his/her face on the cover.

How would you define your style, eurodance, euro trance or something else?

I'd say it is pure eurodance with a little bit of modern touch.

How would you define what is eurodance?

I'd say eurodance is the musical way of love.

Who draws all the graphic covers?

The covers were drawn by Jack Summers.

Besides E-Rotic, is there some other projects you look up to?

Phew, there are some, so I just tell you those who influenced me the most (as a producer):

Scatman John, Rednex, Whigfield, Das Modul, Blümchen, Masterboy, Mr. President, Culture Beat, Twenty 4 Seven, Bad Boys Blue.

And of course, some great musicians: Meat Loaf, Chris Norman, Kenny Rogers...

Why do you think that eurodance was so popular and is so once again?

I think eurodance has all aspects and can give you just every feeling that all other music genres can. It is highly danceable; you can weep during a nice eurodance ballad. You can also use this kind of music to make statements (e.g. *Love Message*).

Have you performed live?

Once in 2012. But it is hard to fit live gigs with our daily business.

In The Spotlight

▶ ||

Newborn 90s

Published with permission of Newborn 90s.

Who are the members of the band and how the band was born?

Jack:

Newborn 90s is a new 90's eurodance project from the UK. Our mission is to revive the 90's eurodance scene and reach out to the huge audience who still love this style today.

The group consists of Freya (vocalist), Mambo (rapper) and myself (producer). It all started in 2019 when I had a vision to make new music in 90's eurodance style. I'd reached out to Freya and Mambo and the group was born. I have known my friend Mambo since 2009 because we used to work together at the same company back then. I knew about Mambo's passion for music, especially hip hop and he's been writing lyrics for a long time. Freya and I have known each other for a while through music. I already knew that she had a great voice, so I approached her and presented the project idea which she really liked and wanted to jump on board. I'm lucky to have found and be working together with these talents.

I'm from Hungary originally, moved to Scotland 16 years ago. I have been DJ-ing since I was 15 years old, organizing and playing on regular parties in the local area I grew up in (local pubs/youth club and house parties). I completed a DJ course and acquired an official Club DJ certificate in Hungary. After moving to Scotland, I was running a club night for over a year with three other DJ's and also had a few other club gigs afterwards. I have been solely focusing on music production for 10 years.

Freya:

I'm from Newcastle, started out as a backing vocalist for a band and outgrew my position after a few months to lead vocalist. I performed at Clubs and festivals for 7 years whilst doing my BA Hons degree in music and that's how I got into recording and writing. I can sing all styles, but dance music is my roots.

Mambo:

I'm half Scottish half Cameroonian, was born in Africa and moved to Scotland when I was 15, studied music and audio tech, and music and writing is life and breath to me. Working on a project with a friend on something not quite in the hip hop comfort zone is very intriguing, and exciting.

Your relationship with eurodance? Did you listen to it in the 90's?

Freya:

I was inspired by 90's through and through. That era was mind-blowing, and every track was fresh. Jam & Spoon, Culture Beat, Cappella, QFX, so many influences.

Mambo:

I have not listened to eurodance much in the 90's but I remember the craze. I'd heard of a few artists such as QFX and their songs though. I was more into hip hop and gangsta rap back then. I started listening to more eurodance since Jack approached me with the project. The hip hop/rap element is really cool in these songs and I'm glad that I was able to rise to the challenge.

Jack:

I grew up partying in the 90's. Those were my teenage years, so I was listening and partying to eurodance an awful lot. I feel very lucky to have listened to all those hit songs back in the day when they were released. I have never stopped listening to eurodance. As Freya said, it was a great era for dance music and those artists created something new, they had their own unique sound. Our biggest inspirations are eurodance heroes such as 2 Unlimited, 2 Brothers On The 4th Floor, Masterboy, Cappella and many others.

You are Scottish? There seems to be a very vibrant dance music scene in Scotland, with many bands like QFX, The Time Frequency and you, why is that?

Jack and Mambo:

We're based in Scotland, Freya is from Newcastle, England which is just across the border. Scotland has a very vibrant dance music scene in different genres nowadays, it's because there are quite a few venues which cater for different type of club nights and dance music genres so there are good opportunities for both DJ's and promoters. This also applies to the UK. Also, dance music is very popular everywhere in the world today. Of course, back in the 90's the club scene was also very busy, possibly even more vibrant, especially the rave scene with the famous

Ultra-Sonic and the emerge of bands like QFX and The Time Frequency. Dance music just caught on and has gained a lot of followers since and it was destined to stay.

Freya:

We had a massive scene in the UK and lots of underground gigs wearing fluorescents, rubber jackets and gloves. I think it did so well over here because it was so different to the usual stuff.

What is the current state of eurodance music, in your opinion?

Freya:

I feel it's been left behind but we want to change that.

Mambo:

Music has evolved a lot since the 90's and eurodance became the thing of the past with that progress, unfortunately.

Jack:

I think eurodance music is nostalgia today. There are still quite a few 90's eurodance parties/concerts around the world where big names from the era perform live for the audience which is quite nice. I have heard new songs in the past decade which were made by some of these artists. I think a couple of songs were good and they were made in the original eurodance style however they did not have a proper follow up. Other artists updated their sound to follow trends therefore they did not make new eurodance music. Our plan is to keep producing new tracks in eurodance style and not to stop. We do a lot promotion and marketing in order to reach out to a wide audience because there's still a huge eurodance audience today. Also, there are many people who try to keep the eurodance spirit alive by sharing the old eurodance songs in social media sites and we're really glad that they do. These people also help us spreading the word about Newborn 90s and posting our songs to their audiences.

Anything else you want to say for your fans?

All:

Thank you very much to each and every one of you who are supporting us in our journey. We are very happy that we were welcomed by the fans from the beginning and have received positive feedbacks and kind words from many of them already. We can promise that we will keep the eurodance spirit alive and release a lot of new songs in the future for you to enjoy.

(Author's note: check out Newborn 90s' absolutely fantastic songs: *I Feel Alive* and *No Time Lost*)

In The Spotlight

▶II

Experience Of Music (answerer Frank Winkelmann)

photographer: Helge Vokening, published with permission of
Frank Winkelmann (on the left).

How would you compare 90's dance music to today's dance music? What has changed, for better or for worse?

In many cases the dance music of today is a music without soul and passion, in my modest opinion. I really miss the good old catchy synth hook lines and a clear song structure, so I am not a friend of those EDM tracks full of crazy sounds but no real melodies.

But a good progression of the music nowadays is the brilliance of the sounds and the good productions. There are easy and never ending possibilities to express a project's sound & style.

Lyane Leigh has sung in couple of your songs, is she one of your favorite eurodance singers? How did you get her involved?

Yes, I know Lyane personally for about 19 years now. She sang on our classic tune *Hardhouse* in 2001/2002 and later on the follow-up *(Do you think it's) Magic?*. I made an instrumental track with a really catch synth hook, like I most did in the mid 90's. It was 1999, but around 2000 I thought that it would be better with some vocals on the track. I was looking for help. So, my companion Gregor G. Schydlo and I got to know Marco Quirini who signed some hits for EMI Electrola also in the 90's (Magic Affair etc.). After his EMI time he built up his own record company Quincy Records in Cologne, the city where I still live. He also preferred a female singer on that high potential track. I liked the tracks and the voice of the E-Rotic band. So, I got in touch with Lyane who was also open to sing my vocal writings on *Hardhouse*. The rest is history, haha ☺ .

Eurodance's big brother is techno music and it had a whole fashion style in clothes and in art. Do you think that eurodance has specific fashion style or art (for example in record covers)?

Ha-ha, I never thought about an eurodance fashion style. Was there a style for this? Techno was a special niche at the early 90's, so techno also had a specific fashion style. Eurodance was a mass phenomenon for normal people. I really liked the CD artworks, which were fantastic (most of them...)

Favorite producers and artists in dance music and why?

I was totally impressed by the old German Cyborg/DMP production team around Tom Keil, Michael Eisele, Giora Schein (and others) that produced hit acts like the Captain Hollywood Project, Intermission and Loft. They had lots of their unique synthesizer sounds and melodies.

My dreams to establish also an eurodance project with CD releases and well known artist featurings luckily became true through all the years later. Till now, we celebrate more than 200 appearances (on CD or digital) on companies like ZYX or Warner etc. We featured 90's stars like Lyane Leigh, Franca Morgano, The Outhere Brothers, Michael " MIC" K., Richard Williams, Elyse Rogers a.k.a. Linda Meek, Shalamon Baskin and worked with producers like my friend Frank " Quickmix" Hassas, P. Rossini, TN'T Party Zone and many others.

Your thoughts on eurodance's impact on today's music?

Like it is a law of nature, everything will come back any time. Many hook lines, samples or choruses appear in today's tracks. And don't forget, almost all acts of then are still active or active again because eurodance is a feeling. I never cared about what others said about eurodance (many negative thoughts), and we do our own thing – till today. That's the secret of success, to do your own thing constantly.

In The Spotlight

▶️❚❚

Maxxima (answerer Andy Stead)

Published with the permission of Andy Stead.

Tell me a little about your musical background and how did you become an artist in DMN Records?

I began producing music back in the 90's when I was a teenager! I used to rent my brothers friends' studio and just go and make dance tracks and remixes. I never made anything for release it was purely for my own benefit. After I completed college I decided that i wanted to be a performer and started working as a vocalist onboard cruise ships and when I returned to the UK I toured a lot in shows and bands. I then got the producing bug back and wanted to start making music but eurodance and euro house music had disappeared and that was what U wanted to make. I started messing around with remixes and that's when the track with Linda Rocco happened. DMN was the label that had been chosen to release the track as they had great connections with Linda and a passion for eurodance and 90's nostalgia.

I think DMN didn't want me at first as I was not a regular name on the remix circuit, but a chance remix happened for BG The Prince Of Rap on his *So Special* track. I made a euro mix and it went crazy! From there DMN regularly asked for mixes and so since then I have remixed for La Bouche, Corona, BG The Prince Of Rap, AK Swift, Linda Rocco, Soundstream and many others. I would have to say my favorite euro mix has been for *Once You Have Me* – BG The Prince Of Rap, Timi Kullai is so powerful on vocals and BG is still sounding awesome.

Maxxima and the song *No More Chances* is a great nod to 90's eurodance and especially to Cappella, how did you come up with this song? And how did you get Kristina Safrany and MC FIXX It to the project?

So, to the Maxxima project! Maxxima was going to be a one single 90's rave project but then I started making a track which is now known as *No More Chances*. Tina agreed to do some vocals for the track, and I started searching for a rapper as I wanted the authentic euro/italo dance sound. We tried a couple of the recordings with a rapper from Australia, but it was missing something and that something was

333

MC FIXX IT! I contacted him and from the first demo of the track he was on board and joined the team. Now that we had the original Cappella/AntiCappella/Twenty 4 Seven rapper, and the powerhouse vocals of Kristina Safrany, all of the tracks now sound like we have pulled them direct from the 90's.

Is there going to be a Maxxima album? If so, do you already have ideas for it? Are Kristina and MC FIXX IT stable members or are they going to chance from song to song?

Maxxima is no longer a one track project. Kristina and Ricardo have worked hard with me to finish a full album. As far as I am concerned, Kristina Safrany and Ricardo Overman are Maxxima! This was always going to be a solid project once they joined and I couldn't see anybody else replacing them.

Your euro favorites?

Okay so this is the hard bit, my favorite eurodance songs! From my younger days I listened to a lot of Technotronic and fell in love with the basslines and kick drums so my first would have to be *Get Up (Before The Night Is Over)*. 2 Unlimited then became my obsession and I have a very large collection of rare and signed releases from them. But the song that changed everything for me was *Move On Baby* by Cappella. The synth, arpeggios, kick and then the vocals and rap parts just create such a perfection! Gianfranco Bortolotti and his team for me, got everything right! The sound, the promotion and the faces of Kelly and Rodney. From there on I became obsessed, not with the group but with learning the tricks of Media Records and how they produced records. Maxxima is the produce of many years of research of producers Rossini, Picotto, Bortolotti ect. Finally, I can't wait for everyone to hear the forthcoming singles and album from Maxxima, it's been a pleasure to work with everyone involved.

At the music video shoot of No More Chances. Published with permission of Andy Stead.

༄

OUTRO

Nowadays eurodance lives in the web, like anything else. New projects are making authentic 90's eurodance, but they only release it as download or stream. Although from a collector's viewpoint this is pretty frustrating, but this has enabled artists to have a bigger fanbase than in the 90's. It's very positive but at the same time it's a shame that only a handful of these end up in some physical format. I still believe that eurodance's popularity in the 2010's has been increased because of downloading services and social media, where new and old projects are strongly present.

As for eurodance's visibility in media, in my homeland Finland it's still considered as humor music. They acknowledge its nostalgia value, but people react to it with a demeaning overtones. Even some public figures in Finland, who name themselves as euro fans, make fun of it.

But when thinking globally, there are a lot of real fans, who listen to this genre without prejudice and collect it in some format. They are really interested about the artists and music and the classic euro artists are revered. Also, these fans are interested about the rarest euro songs and albums, although the mainstream media tells only about the most famous acts.

When it comes to eurodance's influence in modern dance music, it's largely nonexistent, in my opinion. Sometimes there are bits and pieces visible in some songs, but in the dance music's most popular subgenre, EDM, there seems to be no respect for the old classics. While EDM relies only on technical gimmickry and joining together different parts with stupid " melodies", eurodance flows naturally with a clear melody and devoid of overly technical tricks. Euro was organic and easy-going while modern music is made to serve web age people, the songs are all over the place, they are created to please everybody. They are completely without personality.

The worship of modern DJ's today has gone off the rails. In the end the 90's singers and artists started to fade into the background while the DJ was promoted to the limelight. In the 2010's the worship is almost manic in the EDM culture. The wonderful dance music singers who raised dance music to its fame in the 80's and 90's have been put aside, and they been replaced with ever-changing squad of pop stars, who want to cash in with the popular EDM sound. Also, the young generation of EDM DJ's seem to have no respect or sense of history towards old dance music. They might loan pieces of old dance hits into their own songs but do it without one sense of dignity towards the classic, they just want to make a hit as fast as possible.

The old 90's stars are still respected outside the mainstream in social media forums. While their new songs won't become chart hits, they tour with a fervor in many 90's festivals and club tours. Also, many old star has found a new home in the gay circuit, and they are common mainstays in many Pride festivals and gay clubs.

All in all, eurodance was revolutionary music in its hedonistic boldness. It crossed all borders and joined people in a universal dance movement. It didn't matter who performed the song, who produced it or in what country: the most important thing was the music and the aggressive pulse in the heart of it, which took people to the dance floor.

Although it was clinically electronic, it had a lot of emotion. The songs expressed feelings and they flowed naturally. The artists really poured their heart and soul into the song, you could see right away that it was so natural, they really must have put a lot of work in it. Euro was sometime criticized as being cold, but in my opinion that was not the case. Compared to contemporary music, a really big part of today's music has been produced to cash in as fast as possible. Of course, the 90's had its fair share of that kind of projects, but the songs were mostly born out of sheer joy of creating.

For me, eurodance means youth and freedom to be myself. It has been a great comforter at hard times and an escape from the cruelty (and stupidity) of the modern world. The biggest liberator in euro is its ease and straightforwardness, it doesn't mask itself to be something it's not, its dance music, pure and simple. It's strongly melodic, infectious and uses repetition only when it sounds good. For many people songs are connected to certain times in your life, so it is for me too. For example, E-type's *This Is The Way* creates a sense of independence in me.

Although I had a phase when I couldn't even think to listen to eurodance anymore, now I feel that the circle has closed, and I have come back home from my musical ventures. These last years I have listened euro intensely, it has some indescribable magic, something you can't find in modern music.

I hope that you have found the same magic of eurodance between these pages.

...Let the beat go on!

THANKS:

Biggest thanks to my darling, who helped in many ways, especially in technical details. Thanks to our lovely cat Selina, who always brightens up our day! I love you both so much!

Thanks to my family for understanding my book project.

Thanks to Antti Mäkijärvi, Karine Sanche, Luke Skys and Alexander Avram that I got to use your pictures.

And biggest thanks to all the artists, who had some part in making this book! I have such gratitude toward you, it's wonderful that you took part and finally helped to put the history eurodance between the covers. And most of all: THANK YOU FOR THE MUSIC!!!

And no thanks to Kevin O'Toole from N-Trance and Sin With Sebastian, shame on you and grow up!

CHECK OUT THESE SONGS

THE ROAD TO EURODANCE

Songs that have influenced the creation of eurodance sound, but are not euro themselves:

Donna Summer: I Feel Love (1977)
Cerrone: Supernature (1977)
Michael Zager Band: Let´s All Chant (1977)
Giorgio Moroder: The Chase (1978)
Sabrina: Boys (1987)
Inner City: Big Fun (1988), Good Life (1988)
Black Box: Ride On Time (1989)
Technotronic: Pump Up The Jam (1989)
Mysterious Art: everything they have made
Modern Talking
Bad Boys Blue
Snap!: The Power (1990)
C + C Music Factory: Gonna Make You Sweat (Everybody Dance Now) 1990
Opus III: It's A Fine Day (1991)
Cappella ft. Loleatta Holloway: Take Me Away (1991)
L.A. Style: James Brown Is Dead (1991)
The KLF: Last Train To Trancentral (1991)
Gat Décor: Passion (1992)
Dance 2 Trance feat. Linda Rocco: Power Of American Natives (1992)

FAMILIAR STUFF

2 Brothers On The 4th Floor: Never Alone, Dreams, Fly (Through The Starry Night), The Sun Will Be Shining
2 Unlimited: Let The Beat Control Your body, No Limit,The Real Thing, Jump For Joy
Ace Of Base: Beautiful Life
Alexia: The Summer Is Crazy, Number One, The Music I Like
Amber: This Is Your Night
Basic Element: The Promise Man,The Ride, This Must Be A Dream
B.G. The Prince Of Rap: The Colour Of My Dreams, Can't Love You, Rock A Bit
Cappella: Move On Baby, U Got 2 Let The Music, U & Me, Turn It Up & Down
Captain Hollywood (Project): More & More, Only With You, Flying High, Impossible
Captain Jack: Captain Jack, Little Boy, Another One Bites The Dust
CB Milton: It's A Loving Thing, A Real Love
Centory: Point Of No Return
Clock: Everybody, Holding On 4 U
CO.RO: 4 Your Love
Cool James & Black Teacher: Dr. Feelgood, Godfather, Rhythm Of The Tribe
Corona: The Rhythm Of The Night, Baby Baby, Don't Go Breaking My Heart, When I Give My Love
Culture Beat: Mr. Vain, Anything, Crying In The Rain, Under My Skin
Cut'n'Move: I'm Alive

DJ Bobo: Let The Dream Come True, Somebody Dance With Me, Take Control, Let The Dream Come True, Freedom
DJ Company: The Rhythm Of Love
Double You ft. Sandy Chambers: Dancing With An Angel, Run To Me, Feel The Rhythm, Long Time Ago
Dr. Alban: It's My Life, Let The Beat Go On, Look Who's Talking
E-Rotic: Fred, Come To Bed, etc. almost everything made by them
E-Type: Life, Angels Crying, This Is The Way, Set The World On Fire, Life
Fun Factory: Take Your Chance, Prove Your Love
Gina G: Just A Little Bit
General Base: Base Of Love, Poison
Haddaway: Rock My Heart, Life, Waiting For A Better World, What Is Love
Ice Mc: Thing About The Way, It's A Rainy Day, Take Away The Colour'95 reconstruction
Imperio: Amor Infinitus, Nostra Culpa, Veni Vidi Vici
Intermission ft. Nina: Honesty
Intermission: Piece Of My Heart, Six Days
JX: You Belong To Me
Jam & Spoon ft. Plavka: Right In The Night
La Bouche: Be My Lover, Sweet Dreams, You Won't Forget Me
La Cream: You, Say Goodbye, Free
Le Click: Call Me
Leila K.: Electric
Loft: Hold on, It's Raining Again, Mallorca
Look Twice: Go Away, Feel The Night, Move That Body
Lovemessage: Lovemessage
Magic Affair: Energy Of Light, Omen III
Masterboy: Feel The Heat Of The Night, Generation Of Love, Feel The Fire, Is This The Love, Show Me Colours
Maxx: Get-A-Way, No More (I Can't Stand It)
Melodie Mc: Climb Any Mountain, Anyone Outthere, Dum Da Dum
Mo-Do: Eins, Zwei, Polizei, Gema Tanzen
Motiv 8: Rockin For Myself
Mr. President: Up'n'Away, 4 On The Floor
Nina: Until All Your Dreams Come True
N-Trance: Electronic Pleasure, Turn Up The Power
Pandora: Don't You Know, Shout It Out, Trust Me
Paradisio: Bailando
Patric: Love Me
Pharao: I Show You Secrets, There Is A Star
Playahitty: The Summer Is Magic
Prince Ital Joe feat. Marky Mark: United
Real McCoy: Another Night, Runaway, Automatic Lover
Rednex: Cotton Eye Joe, Old Pop In An Oak
Rob'n'Raz: In Command
Scatman John: Scatman
Sin With Sebastian: Golden Boy
Snap!: Rhythm Is A Dancer, Do You See The Light (Looking For)
Solid Base: You Never Know, Together, Let It All Be Sunshine, Katie'
Sqeezer: Scandy Randy
Stella Getz: Friends, Dr. Love
Tatjana: Feel Good
Technotronic: Move It To The Rhythm, Recall, Hey Yoh, Here We Go
The Free: Dance The Night Away, Lover On The Line, Born Crazy

Twenty 4 Seven: Slave To The Music, We Are The World
Urban Cookie Collective: Sail Away, Feels Like Heaven
U.S.U.R.A.: Drive Me Crazy
U96: Love Religion, Inside Your Dreams
Whigfield: I Want To Love

RARE TREAT

2 For Good: You And Me
2 For Love: Only For Love
2 Raff: Don't Stop The Music
3 II One: Make Love
3-O-Matic: Hand In Hand
49ers: Keep Your Love
100%: Power Of The Light
A.B.Free feat. Linda Rocco: Go Deeper
AB Logic: AB Logic,Real World
Absolutely Fabulous (Pet Shop Boys): Absolute ly Fabulous
A.D.A.M. feat. Amy: Memories And Dreams
Abigail: Don't You Wanna Know
Africa Bambaataa Presents Khayan & The New World Power: Feel The Vibe
Alana Dante: Take Me For A Ride
Alpha Base: Heaven Help My Heart
Amadin: Alrabaiye (Take Me Up), U Make Me Feel Alright
Antares: Ride On A Meteorite
Anticappella: Express Your Freedom, Move Your Body, I Wanna Love You
Academia: Dance To The Music
Alter Ego feat. Daisy Dee: Dance! (If You Cannot)
B-Cap: Send Me An Angel
Bad Boys Blue: Go Go (Love Overload)
Bang Gang feat. Conchita: Bang Gang Night
Bass Expanders: Beats Go
Beat System: Dance Romance (Chapter 2), The Lights Of America
Berri: The Sunshine After The Rain
B.L. Lover: Time 4 Love
Black Baron: Girl, I Love You So
Black 4 White: Cannibal
Black Rose: Melody
Blue System: Dr. Mabuse, Laila
Bonanza Techno Ska: I'm Waiting For You, Honey!
Cabballero: Dancing With Tears In My Eyes, Gimme Gimme More And More
Capital Sound: In The Night
Chase: Love For The Future
Cicero: Summertime
Club Factory: I Think I Wanna Rock
Clubmen: All We Need Is Love
Clubzone: Hands Up
Crosstalk: Love Is The Reason
D4S: Wild Wild West
Da Blitz: Stay With Me, Take My Way
Damage Control: Don't You Feel My Pain, You've Got To Believe
Daddy K: Voulez-Vous Coucher Avec Moi?

Darkness: In My Dreams
Datura: Eternity, Passion
Daydream: Thinkin' About You
Decadance: Save My Soul
Den Harrow: Take me, Universe of love
D.I.P.: Give Me Your Lovin
Diva: Everybody
DJ Duckpower: Get The Duck Out Of Here (Move It!)
DJ Miko: Rhythm
Dreamworld: Movin'Up
E:Motion: Get Up
Echo Bass: Givin'It Up
Eclipse: (You Just Got) Let The Rhythm Move You
Egma: Never Gonna Lose Your Love
Energy Go!: There's A Music (Reaching Out)
Eurogroove: Dive Into Paradise
Fanny Cadeo: I Want Your Love
First Base: Love Is Paradise
Flexx: Flexxible, The Good The Bad And The Ugly
Free 2 Dance: Piece Of Heaven
Future Beat: It's My Party
Future City: Only Love, Let Your Body Free, Infactuation
Garfield: Party Of Love
Goddess: Spirit In The Night
Good Shape: Take My Love
Groovecult: Midnight Dream
H.A.D: Spirit Of The Night
H.R.Beat: Hok Baba Jimmy
Herbie: I Believe
Hype: Find Another Way
Hysterie: Call Me, Midnight Hour
Indra: We Belong Together, Anywhere
It's 5 To 12: Survival Game
Janal: You Gotta Set Me Free
Jeremy Jackson: You Really Got It Going On
Jesse Lee Davis: Like A Flame
Jinny: Wanna Be With U
J.K.: My Radio, You & I
JLM: Come Into My Life
Johnna: In My Dreams, Do What You Feel
Joée: Angel
JT Company: Feel it in the air
K2: Der Berg Ruft
Katarina: Calling All Cars
K.C. Linn: Got To Get It On
K.da Cruz: New High Energy, Push
Ken Laszlo: Everytime
Ketty DB: Spacer
Kim Sanders: Ride
K.L.J: Fly Away
Kora: Night Is Alive
Kuttin' Edge: I Believe In You
L.A. Style: Got To Move
La Verdi: Vinger

Lena: Something In My Heart
Lian Ross: Keep This Feeling
Linda Carriere: Is This Life
Lip Service: It's A Miracle
Loft: Live It Up
Logic Dream: Get To You
Lolo Ferrari: Airbag Generation
Love 4 Sale: Do You Feel So Right
Mach 7: Alacazam, Real Love
Mad feat. Jennifer Romero: Think Of You
Maduar: Mystic Party
Magic Motion: Don't Fly Away
Ma-radscha & The Sham: Right Now
Mars Plastic: Find The Way
Major T. : Keep The Frequency Clear
Matrix: Can You Feel It
Metrix: Slow Down
Michéle: Love Is History
MC Erik & Barbara: It's Your Day, U Can't Stop
Mimmo Mix feat. Nicole: Love Me Baby
Ministry Of Sound: Let's All Chant
Mister Soul: Sex Machine
Mix Factory feat. Gill Jackson: Miracles
Motiv 8: Searching For The Golden Eye
Mr. John: It's Not Too Late
MTS: All I Wanna Do
Nadia: Beatman
Natascha Wright: Lovely Lie
Newton: Sky High
Night People: In The Night
Noizefactory feat. Tanya: Reach Out
N-Trance: Electronic Pleasure, Turn Up The Power
TNT Partyzone: Das Omen Teil 1
Miko Mission: I Can Fly
Molella: Confusion, Change
Navayah: What About My Love Boy
Nymfo: Move Your Lips
Ondina: Into The Night
Ova Steel: In Love With You (Baby, Baby)
Paco: Lollipop...Is Cool Man
Paul Parker: Can You Feel The Love Coming
People Of The World: In Heaven No Limit
Pompöös: Pompöös Part 1
Radiorama: Cause The Night, Little bird
Rage: My Cryings Done
Reggy O.: Move My Body
Reset: Get Me, Blue
Riverside People: Fantasy Dancing
Safe: Love Is All We Need
Samira: When I Look Into Your Eyes, Lovetrain
Scatgirl: I'm A Scatgirl
Secret Dream: Call Of The Wild
S.E.X. Appeal: Sex Is A Thrill With A Pill, Voulez Vouz Coucher Avec Moi
Sharif: Pearls Of Peace

Shift: Remember The Time
Silja: How Could I Find Love
Simone Angel: Let This Feeling, Walk On Water
Silverscreen: Honolulu Baby
Sabrina: Angel Boy
Sirius: This Is My Life
Slam: Back To Music
Sonic Beat: I Can Fly
Sound Of Seduction: A Love Like 7
Space Master: World Of Confusion, Jumping To The Party, Step On, In The Name
Of Love, Everybody Sing, Hold Me Baby
Space Tribe: Better Be Alright
Spagna: Lady Madonna
Superfly: Is It Love?
Swayy: On And On
Swing feat. Dr Alban: Sweet Dreams
Systematic: Love Is The Answer
T Zone: Movin'Up & Down
Technocop: The Miracle Of Life
Ten Minutes: Your Toy
Texture: Power Of Love
T.H. Express: Missing In The Rain
The Immortals: Mortal Kombat
The Lovers: Go Just Get It
The Lovers: Love Me To The Limit
Time Cut: El Verano
Timeshift: Don't You Feel The Beat
Tokyo Ghetto Pussy: Everybody (On The Floor)
Total Control: Be What You Wanna Be
Trancylvania: Tender Heart, Colour Of Love
Trey-D: Higher & Higher
T-Spoon: Where R U Now, Take It 2 The Limit
Treasure 2 : Reality
Tuff E Nuff: Yo Yo
Unit: Live It Up, Move Your Body
Unity Power feat. Rozlyne Clarke: Eddy Steady Go, Dancin' Is Like Makin' Love
Unlimited Nation: Move Your Body
U.S.U.R.A.: Drive Me Crazy
Wanda Fisher: Meteor Man, The Ride
West Inc: I'm Gonna Get You (Anyway), Rhythm Takes You Higher
X-Fade: Dance
X-Ite: Down Down Down
X-Pression: This Is Our Night
X Stress: I've Got The Feeling
Zoo Inc: Lay Down
Zulu: Pain In My Heart

BIGGEST FROM FINLAND

101: Haluan extaasiin
Aikakone: Aarresaari, Odota
Allekirjoittanut: Ei pysty joraan

343

Ann Bell Fell: Around & Around, I Feel It Coming
CatCat: Piirtelet mun sydämeen, Yksin sateeseen
Dance Nation: Freed, True Conviction
Hausmylly: Ikävä lokakuu, Kaiken saat, Putoan pilviin
Ho-Dads: Show Me (Secret dreams)- The Way To The Exstazy
Minna Björn: 1 sekunnin vain
Mira: Paha
Movetron: Romeo ja Julia
Optical 2: Move On Up, Let The Rhythm Move You
Quicksilver: See The Light
Rama: Light My Fire, Cryin Out
Soittorasia: Tanssin (olen tulessa)
Sound Of R.E.L.S.: Love Is The Powa!, Eee-lie-loe-lie (If U Wanna Get)
Tino: Dance In The Rain, Maxximum Energy
Waldo: Feel So Good, Move Your Body, The Riddle
Waldo's People: U Drive Me Crazy, I Dream, Lose Control

THE ALBUMS

2 Unlimited: No Limits!, Real Things
Alexia: Fan Club
Bad Boys Blue: To Blue Horizons
Basic Element: Basic Injection, The Ultimate Ride
Cappella: U Got 2 Know, War In Heaven
Captain Hollywood Project: Animals Or Human
Captain Jack: The Mission
Corona: The Rhythm Of The Night
Culture Beat: Serenity, Inside Out
Dance Nation: Dawn
DJ Bobo: There Is A Party
Dr. Alban: Look Whos Talking
Dymension: Fantasy
E-Rotic: Sex Affairs, The Power Of Sex
E-Type: Made In Sweden, Euro IV Ever
Factual Beat: Groove Your Soul
Flexx: Flexxibility
Fun Factory: Nonstop! – The Album
Future Beat: Destiny
Hype: Provocative
Johnna: Pride
Kikka: Remix
Loft: Wake The World, Future World
Masterboy: Different Dreams, Generation Of Love
Maxx: To The Maxximum
Miisa: Attitude
Mo-Do: Was Ist Das?
Molella: Originale+Radicale+Musicale
Mr. President: Up'n'Away -The Album
MTS: Let It Go
Pandora: One Of A Kind, Tell The World
Paul Parker: Destiny
Pharao: Pharao

Radiorama: The World Of Radiorama
Real McCoy: Space Invaders
Silent Circle: Back!
Taikapeili: Suuri salaisuus
Tears'N'Joy: Enjoy
T.H.Express: Love 4 Liberty
The Free: Crazy Worlds
Weather Girls: Thing Big!

REMIXES

2 Unlimited: Here I Go (X-Out In Club)
Bingoboys: Sugardaddy (Nocturnal Club Remix)
Culture Beat: World In Your Hands (MKM's Danish Flex Mix)
Eartha Kitt: Where Is My Man (Remix 1994)
E-Rotic: Help Me Dr. Dick (The First Aid Remix)
Fargetta: Your Love (Remix)
Haddaway: Life (Mission Control Remix)
Hithouse: Jack To The Sound Of The Underground (94 Remix)
Jinny: Feel The Rhythm (U.S.U.R.A remix)
M-People: Sight For Sore Eyes (Lee Marrow Remix)
Saint Etienne: She's On The Phone (Motiv 8 Remix)
Technotronic: Recall (On Stage Mix)
Victoria Wilson-James: Reach For The Melody (Men Behind Remix)

BEST EURO REGGAES

Ace Of Base: All That She Wants, Happy Nation, The Sign
E-Rotic: Help Me Dr. Dick
Heath Hunter: Revolution In Paradise
Mr. President: Coco Jamboo
Loft: Summer Summer
Pandora: Tell The World

THE LEGACY OF EURODANCE

Activate: Spotlight
Alice Deejay: Who Needs Guitars Anyway? album
Basic Element: Touch You Right Now
Benassi Bros ft. Sandy: Illusion
Cascada everything
Corona: Queen Of Town
Culture Beat: Can't Go On Like This (No, No) , Mr. Vain Recall
DMN Records productions as a whole
Dustin The Turkey: Irelande Douze Pointe
JLM: Heaven Away
J.O.Y.C.E ft. A.K. Swift: Let The Rhythm Take Control
JX: Restless
Lady Gaga

Newborn 90's: I Feel Alive, No Time Lost
Nomansland: 7 Seconds
Magic Motion: Show Me Heaven
Reset: Calling You
Sunblock ft. Sandy: Baby, Baby
Tony Moran ft. Ultra Naté: Destination
Van: Classica

AVOID THESE (If you like real euro sound)

Alexia: Uh-la-la-la, Gimme Love
Bushman: No One Else
Culture Beat: Metamorphosis album
Dr. Alban: Prescription album
Look Twice: Celebrate album
Pandora. Changes album, I Won't Look Back album
Playahitty: 1-2-3 (Train with me)
Sabrina: Rockawillie

SOURCES

Digital:

2 Brother On The 4th Floor official homepage
https://2brothersonthe4thfloor.nl/wordpress/bio/ _(Retrieved 14.7.2019)_

BBC.com 29.10.2016 Urban Cookie Collective singer Diane Charlemagne dies at
51, https://www.bbc.com/news/entertainment-arts-34666593 _(Retrieved 6.10.2019)_

Bubblegumdancer https://www.bubblegumdancer.com/info/ _(Retrieved 24.4.2019)_

Complex : A Brief History of House Music https://www.complex.com/music/house-
music-history _(Retrieved 9.8.2020)_

Danceartistinfo http://www.danceartistinfo.com/ Niklas Adolfsson

Dart, Chris, CBCMusic, 24.2.2015: Emjay, Love Inc and beyond: remembering
Canadian eurodance, https://www.cbcmusic.ca/posts/11874/emjay-love-inc-and-
beyond-remembering-canadian-eur _(Retrieved 13.8.2019)_

Dennizpopawards.com : The legacy continues
https://www.dennizpopawards.com/the-legacy-continues/ _(Retrieved 27.6.2019)_

Discogs: https://www.discogs.com/

Diskoteka Festival homepage Diskoteka.ro: Mr President
https://diskoteka.ro/en/artisti/mr-president/ _(Retrieved 19.6.2019)_

DJ Bobo official homepage: Biography https://www.djbobo.ch/en/biography/dj-
bobo/ _(Retrieved 24.7.2019)_

DWA Records homepage 2007
http://web.archive.org/web/20070317192056/http://www.dwarecords.it/dwa-
artist-doubleyou-bio.asp _(Retrieved 2.7.2019)_

Dyer, Chris, Dailymail.co.uk, 7.11.2018,
https://www.dailymail.co.uk/news/article-6363695/Two-construction-workers-
tortured-death-singer-Happy-Lucky-hostel-Berlin-jailed.html _(Retrieved 6.10.2019)_

Ettelson, Robbie 28.4.2015 Cuepoint: Gettin' kinda hectic: Snap! and Chill Rob G's
epic "Power" Struggle, https://medium.com/cuepoint/gettin-kinda-hectic-snap-
and-chill-rob-g-s-epic-power-struggle-cc545a1b2fce _(Retrieved 29.6.2019)_

Eurodance Encyclopedia https://www.eurokdj.com

Eurodance Encyclopedia : Marianne Festraets (AB Logic) The Interview 1/2009
https://www.eurokdj.com/interviews/marianna_interview.php _(Retrieved 25.3.2019)_

Facebook Activate official page,
https://www.facebook.com/pg/ACTIVATEofficial/about/?ref=page_internal
(Retrieved 15.6.2019)

Facebook B.G. The Prince Of Rap official page
https://www.facebook.com/pg/bgprinceofrap/about/?ref=page_internal *(Retrieved 29.4.2019)*

Facebook Captain Hollywood Project official page
https://www.facebook.com/pg/CaptainHollywoodProject/about/?ref=page_internal *(Retrieved 17.7.2019)*

Facebook Dr. Alban official page
https://www.facebook.com/pg/dralbanofficial/about/?ref=page_internal *(Retrieved 3.8.2019)*

Facebook E-Type official page 18.6.2018
https://www.facebook.com/pg/etypeofficial/about/?ref=page_internal *(Retrieved 20.6.2019)*

Facebook Haddaway official page
https://www.facebook.com/pg/haddaway.eu/about/?ref=page_internal *(Retrieved 9.4.2019)*

Facebook Ice MC official page
https://www.facebook.com/pg/IceMC.co.uk/about/?ref=page_internal *(Retrieved 6.7.2019)*

Facebook Melodie MC official page
https://www.facebook.com/pg/realmelodiemc/about/?ref=page_internal *(Retrieved 15.7.2019)*

Facebook Real McCoy official page 29.5.2019
https://www.facebook.com/pg/realmccoyofficial/about/?ref=page_internal *(Retrieved 9.8.2019)*

Facebook Sandy Chambers official page
https://www.facebook.com/pg/sandychambersofficial/about/?ref=page_internal *(Retrieved 7.7.2019)*

Facebook Snap! official page https://www.facebook.com/snapofficial/ *(Retrieved 29.6.2019)*

Facebook Solid Base official page
https://www.facebook.com/pg/solidbaseofficial/about/?ref=page_internal *(Retrieved 29.6.2019)*

Facebook Technotronic official page
https://www.facebook.com/pg/technotronicofficial/about/?ref=page_internal *(Retrieved 17.7.2019)*

Facebook Twenty 4 Seven official page
https://www.facebook.com/pg/Twenty4SevenNL/about/?ref=page_internal *(Retrieved 17.7.2019)*

Gina G: Official Page
https://www.facebook.com/pg/gina.g.music/about/?ref=page_internal *(Retrieved 18.2.2019)*

Hirn, Jouni V2.fi 23.11.2007 "Pandora käärmeissään Kylie Minoguelle"
https://www.v2.fi/uutiset/viihde/1528/Pandora-kaarmeissaan-Kylie-Minoguelle/?quotecomment=1661 *(Retrieved 6.6.2019)*

IMDB: Lolo Ferrari biography https://www.imdb.com/name/nm0274097/
(Retrieved 31.1.2019)

International Music Summit : Gianfranco Bortolotti 6.3.2017
https://www.internationalmusicsummit.com/ims_speakers/gianfranco-bortolotti/
(Retrieved 5.2.2019)

JLMMusic: Artists http://www.jlmmusic.com/ *(Retrieved 20.6.2019)*

Kauppinen, Ina, Iltasanomat Is.fi 8.7.2018, Ysäritähti Pandoran uran mahalasku
paljastui keikalla suomalaisessa pikkukylässä – "Tunsin itseni liian hienoksi siihen
paikkaan" https://www.is.fi/viihde/art-2000005746373.html *(Retrieved 6.6.2018)*

Kauppinen, Ina Iltasanomat 30.12.2018 Tiedätkö, kuka oikeasti lauloi E-Typen
hiteissä? Lahjakas laulaja jäi täysin pimentoon ja ajautui alamäkeen – "Vaikeaa
olla ylipainoinen tällä alalla" https://www.is.fi/viihde/art-2000005736907.html
(Retrieved 23.6.2019)

Kilpoinen ,Anna: Rap-musiikki on vaikuttamisen väline 17.12.2006 Kaleva
https://www.kaleva.fi/uutiset/kulttuuri/rap-musiikki-on-vaikuttamisen-
valine/120926/ *(Retrieved 21.1.2019)*

La Bouche Official website, Bio 2018 http://www.officiallabouche.com/bio.html
(Retrieved 14.6.2019)

Neverending Dream movies' homepage, http://neverendingdreammovie.com/
(Retrieved 17.1.2019)

Marotta, Tony, La Gazzetta Italiana : Alexia (The powerful voice of a petite
singer), February 2011, https://www.lagazzettaitaliana.com/entertainment/7639-
alexia-the-powerful-voice-of-a-petite-singer *(Retrieved 15.6.2019)*

Martela, Olli (2016) : 90-luvun suosikkilaulaja Miisa menehtyi 46-vuotiaana.
Iltalehti 16.7.2016. https://www.iltalehti.fi/viihde/a/2016071621918182
(Retrieved 6.10.2019)

Mason, Andrew: Tom Moulton and his extended disco remix forever changed
recorded music 28.6.2013, Wax Poetics
https://www.waxpoetics.com/blog/features/articles/tom-moulton-disco-remix/
(Retrieved 6.10.2019)

Milestone artist homepage, 26.3.2019 https://milestoneartist.com/u96/ *(Retrieved
19.6.2019)*

Murphy, Ben (2016) : 10 classic Hip-House tracks you need to hear.
https://www.redbull.com/gb-en/hip-house-best-tracks-10-breaking-classics
(Retrieved 18.1.2019)

Nanahedin.com official home page: Denniz Pop Award
http://www.nanahedin.com/ *(Retrieved 27.6.2019)*

Neate, Rupert Telegraph 9.7.2008
https://www.telegraph.co.uk/news/2274009/Worst-lyric-of-all-time-Im-serious-
as-cancer-when-I-say-rhythm-is-a-dancer.html *(Retrieved 29-6-2019)*

Pandora.se official homepage: Pandora: Biography
http://www.pandora.se/biography/?lang=en *(Retrieved 4.6.2019)*

Pandora.se official homepage: Pandora: The History
http://www.pandora.se/press/the-history/?lang=en *(Retrieved 4.6.2019)*

Pulkkinen, Henri: Eurodancen paluu 3.12.2013 Yle.fi
http://vintti.yle.fi/yle.fi/musiikki/c-puoli/henri-pulkkinen-eurodancen-paluu.html
(Retrieved 6.10.2019)

Rapila, Senja: Waldo's people, miksi ette ole levyttäneet 7 vuoteen? 26.8.2016
Voice.fi https://www.voice.fi/musiikki/a-124117 (Retrieved 2.11.2019)

https://rateyourmusic.com/genre/Eurodance/ *(Retrieved 17.1.2019)*

Rawo.info, Clarence Milton Bekker, http://rawo.info/clarence-milton-bekker/
(Retrieved 26.4.2019)

Rozlyne Clarke unofficial homepage rozlyne.clarke.free.fr *(Retrieved 12.3.2019)*

Ruud Van Rijen official homepage : About Me
https://ruudvanrijen.com/aboutme.html *(Retrieved 17.7.2019)*

Räsänen, Mikko : Muistatko ysäritähti Ann Bell Fellin ? Missä hän on nyt?
26.9.2014 Voice.fi https://www.voice.fi/musiikki/a-71226 *(Retrieved 28.1.2019)*

Räsänen, Mikko Retroperjantain biisitilastot julki – tässä ovat ysäribiisien top50
9.1.2018, Voice.fi https://www.radionova.fi/uutiset/musiikki/a-157017 *(Retrieved
6.10.2019)*

Sanche, Karine: What is eurodance, https://www.eurokdj.com/faqs.php *(Retrieved
17.1.2019)*

Sommar, Heidi Sound of R.E.L.S ,Yle.fi 15.3.2011
https://yle.fi/aihe/artikkeli/2011/03/15/sound-rels *(Retrieved 6.10.2019)*

Thea Austin official homepage: Biography http://theaaustin.com/thea-austin-
biography/ *(Retrieved 29.6.2019)*

Tähtivaara, Sarianne : Marko "Waldo" Reijonen järkyttyi Keith Flintin kuolemasta
– Waldo's Peoplen menestyshitit syntyivät Prodigyn vaikutteista 4.3.2019 Iltalehti
https://www.iltalehti.fi/viihdeuutiset/a/d71426ba-2463-4dc0-94df-68ec23f0e1e9,
(Retrieved 12.3.2019)

Tähtivaara, Sarianne: Miisan biisit laulanut Karin Strömfelt : Hän inhosi
huijaamista. Iltalehti. https://www.iltalehti.fi/viihde/a/2016071821926247
(Retrieved 6.10.2019)

Waterfield, Bruno, Telegraph.co.uk 30.3.2007, "Eurovision entry is like my song,
claims Swede"
https://www.telegraph.co.uk/news/worldnews/1547117/Eurovision-entry-is-like-
my-song-claims-Swede.html, *(Retrieved 6.6.2019)*

Who sampled https://www.whosampled.com/

Vibe.com, Polonsky, Sarah & Wunsch, Jessica Before EDM: 30 dance tracks from
the '90s that changed the game 22.6.2013 - https://www.vibe.com/photos/edm-
30-dance-tracks-90s-changed-game *(Retrieved 6.10.2019)*

Wikipedia https://www.wikipedia.org/

Österman, Nalle: Waldo: eurodance on nykypäivän iskelmää Helsingin uutiset
verkkoversio 4.2.2014 https://www.helsinginuutiset.fi/artikkeli/253106-waldo-
eurodance-on-nykypaivan-iskelmaa *(Retrieved 6.10.2019)*

Printed:

Brewster, Bill & Broughton, Frank (2006) Last night a DJ saved my live: The
history of the disc jockey, New York : Headline Book Publishing

Bullock, Darryl W: David Bowie made me gay – 100 years of LGBT music,
Duckworth Overlook, London ISBN 978-07156-5299-2

Grönholm, Pertti: Tanssia maailmanlopun tunnelmissa - Rave-juhlat ja tekno
tainnuttavat desibeleillä artikkeli kirjassa ss 22-24.Tekno - digitaalisen
tanssimusiikin historia, filosofia ja tulevaisuus (toim. Sam Inkinen), julkaisija
Kulttuuriyhdistys Pro Arte Moderna, Oy Aquarian publications, Hämeenlinna 1994

Kling, Joni: Jokainen täällä pukeutuu mustaan ja he ovat onnellisimpia
tuntemistani ihmisistä ss. 306- 319 kirjassa Kone-Suomi toim. Kalle Kinnunen,
Kahos Publishing Oy Helsinki 2017

Larkin, Colin: The Virgin Encyclopedia Of Dance Music, Muze UK LTD London 1998
ISBN 0753502526

Larki, Colin: The Virgin Encyclopedia of Nineties Music, Muze UK LTD London 2000
ISBN 0-753504278

Mäkelä, Janne (2011) Kansainvälisen populaarimusiikin historiaa, Vaasa :
Suomen jazz & pop arkisto

Pompöös: Pompöös is my life CD albums leaflet 1994

Vanha-Majamaa, Anton: Big in Finland,ss 43-49, Rumba 4/2014

Verrina, Francesco Cataldo: The History of Italo Disco: Italian dominance on the
dance culture of 80's, copyright Kriterius Editions 2014, Printed at Lulu
International press

INTERVIEWS

Alvestad, Camilla Facebook interview (Messenger) 22.6.2019

Baskin, Shalamon Facebook interview (Messenger) 8.5.2019

Benz, Stefan e-mail interview 17.1.2020

Black, Vivian Facebook interview (Messenger) 6.7.2019

Bogaert, Jo email interview 3.9.2019

Broekhuyse, Dorian Facebook interview (Messenger) 10.7.2019

Brown, Scott email interview 26.6.2019

Catania, Tony email interview 18.6.2019

Chambers, Sandy email interview 12.2.2019

Cicero, David Facebook interview (Messenger) 2.5.2019

Cozzi,Emanuele Facebook interview (Messenger) 3.5.201 and 13.8.2019

D'Ambrosio, Maurizio Facebook interview (Messenger) 14.5.2020

Def Dames Dope email interview 11.3.2019

Detert, Thomas, email interview 8.4.2019

Digital Base Project Facebook interview (Messenger) 25.2.2019

DMN Records Facebook interview (Messenger) 4.3.2019
(wishes to stay anonymous)

Dyer, Tony Facebook interview (Messenger) 10.6.2019

Ellmer, Rolf Facebook interview (Messenger) 14.6.2019

Eskolin, Rauli email interview 29.5.2019

Fanini, Carl Facebook interview (Messenger) 15.4.2019

Farina, Mauro email interview 24.6.2019

Fenslau, Frank email interview 22.7.2019

Free 2 Night Facebook interview (Messenger) 17.4.2019

Gerhard, Nina email interview 7.5.2019

Glori, Lori Facebook interview (Messenger) 30.12.2019

Guerrini, Bruno email interview 30.1.2020

Hauss, Ingo & Lewerentz, Hayo email interview 14.4.2019

Holender, Isabelle Facebook-interview (Messenger) 10.6. and 22.6.2019

Johansson, Peter email interview 3.9.2019

Kukula, Thomas Facebook interview (Messenger) 5.9.2019 and 2.3.2020

Lagerlöf, Johan email interview 15.2.2019

Lehtonen, Ari Facebook interview (Messenger) 25.5.2019

Leigh, Lyane email interview 27.3.2019

Lindvall, Rasmus email interview 24.6.2019

Livingston, Dave email interview 27.6.2019

Lövgren, Kent email interview 26.3.2019

Mangold, Janina email interview 13.1.2020

Massiah, Zeeteah email interview 26.7.2019

McCray, Lane email interview 23.2.2019

McFarlane, Rachel Facebook interview (Messenger) 28.2.2020

Meek, Linda email interview 28.2.2019

Milton, CB email interview 28.4.2020

Mäkelä-Niemi, Kati Facebook interview (Messenger) 27.5.2019

Morgano, Franca email interview 5.2.2019

Newborn 90s Facebook interview (Messenger) 11.7.2020

Niebergall, Udo email interview 1.3.2019

Perruno, Jean Facebook interview (Messenger) 24.2.2019

Pharao, Kyra email interview 15.3.2019

Presutti, Vivian Facebook interview (Messenger) 25.3.2019

Redford, Ressu email interview 2.7.2019

Rennalls, Delroy Facebook interview (Messenger) 2.5.2019 ja 22.6.2019

Rocco, Linda email interview 25.4.2019

Rodway, Steve Facebook interview (Messenger) 24.2.2019

Rossini, Pieradis email interview 11.6.2019

Seedorf, Stacey email interview 17.5.2019

Siegel, Mimmi Facebook interview (Messenger) 19.2.2019

Simmons, Charles Facebook interview (Messenger) 13.6.2019

Sparell, Saunet Facebook interview (Messenger) 8.9.2019

Thelenius, Peter email interview 21.5.2019

Theunissen, Marcel Facebook interview (Messenger) 18.7.2019

Thomson, Patrick Facebook interview (Messenger) 17.3.2019

Wind, Jürgen email interview 20.3.2019

Winkelmann, Frank Facebook interview (Messenger) 23.7.2019

Yona, Eli Facebook interview (Messenger) 24.5.2020

Zabler, Enrico Facebook interview (Messenger) 7.7.2019

Zanetti, Roberto email interview 29.1.2019

GLOSSARY

beat = hit, unit of when measuring tempo in songs

bpm = beats per minute, tempo of the songs

bubblegum/bubblegum dance = more plastic and childish than eurodance. Lyrics were usually about things common for teenagers. The way of singing is naive. Developed from eurodance.

DJ = disc jockey, record spinner. The one who mixes the songs together. Nowadays DJ can also have successful career with his own songs.

EDM = electronic dance music. While nearly any dance music is electronic, the name has had a new meaning when electronic music started to gain more popularity in the US in the 2010's and even the biggest pop stars started to record it. Nowadays soulless and without melody, mass music.

euro = eurodance

euro house = obscure genre, has numerous subgenres, more closer to house than eurodance, artists: Livin Joy, Whigfield, Alex Party

happy hardcore = developed at rave parties in 90's. Fast, usually about 160-180 bpm, joyful. Sometimes the singing has been speeded up. Most famous artists Blümchen and Scooter in the beginning.

hi-NRG = dance music's subgenre. Fast. One of the first songs was Donna Summer's *I Feel Love*. Clear musical predecessor for eurodance.

house = dance music, with developed after disco faded away and DJ's wanted to create something similar. Drum machine and on top of it samples or keyboards. Started in the 80's. Disco and funk were the mother and father of this style, quite light sound.

italo disco = hi-NRG influenced the creation of this. Highly melodic, more electronic than disco. Bad lyrics, bad singers (some) but awesome melodies. Campy as hell. For example, Savage, Fancy, Silent Circle. One of the most important genres in creation of eurodance.

remix = Usually an alternate version of a song done by another artist, where the original parts of the song are used.

SAW= Stock, Aitken & Waterman. Producer trio Mike Stock, Matt Aitken and Pete Waterman, who were maybe the biggest hit factory in the 80's. Took its influences from hi-NRG sound. Produced many artists from Kylie Minogue to Cliff Richard.

session singer = Singer who is hired in contractual basis to provide lead or backing vocals.

techno= monotone and usually instrumental style of dance music, got started in 80's Detroit.

trance= very melodic form of dance music. Usually heavy and fast beat. Melody plays the leading part. Eurodance changed into trance pop (a heavier sound).

FOR ALL THE DANCE, DISCO AND ELECTRONIC MUSIC LEGENDS WHO AREN'T
WITH US ANYMORE:

Andrew Thomas, Bad Boys Blue (1946-2009)
Bonnie Pointer, Pointer Sisters (1950-2020)
Dag Krister Volle aka Denniz Pop, mm. Dr.Alban & E-type (1963-1998)
Dan Hartman (1950-1994)
Dardoufas, Pascal aka Pascal F.E.O.S. (1968-2020)
Dennis Fuller, London Boys (1959-1996)
Diane Charlemagne, Urban Cookie Collective (1964-2015)
Divine (1945-1988)
Donna Summer (1948-2012)
Eartha Kitt (1927-2008)
Edem Ephraim, London Boys (1959-1996
Elvira Valentine aka Goddess (1962-2002)
Fabio Frittelli, Mo-Do (1966-2013)
Florian Schneider, Kraftwerk (1947-2020)
Francisco Gutierrez, Captain Jack (1962-2005)
Frankie Knuckles (1955-2014)
Gottfried Engels (1949-2015)
Hanna-Riikka Siitonen, Taikapeili (1970-2018)
Henk Van De Wiel, Egma (?-2002)
Izora Armstead, Weather Girls (1942-2004)
James Dandu Malisiga aka Cool James (1970-2002)
Jermaine Stewart (1957-1997)
Jervis Ricardo Alfonso Lyte aka Ricardo Da Force, The KLF & N-Trance (1967-2013)
Jim Nyasani aka Jim Reeves, Sqeezer (1968-2016)
Jimmy McShane, Baltimora (1957-1995)
Johann Hölzel aka Falco (1957-1998)
John Paul Larkin, Scatman John (1942-1999)
Joseph Paquette aka Prince Ital Joe (1963-2001)
Keith Flint , The Prodigy (1969-2019)
Kirsi Hannele Sirén aka Kikka (1964-2005)
Larry Levan (1954-1992)
Laura Branigan (1952-2004)
Loleatta Holloway (1946-2011)
Louise Dean, Shiva (1971-1995)
Markus Löffel aka Mark Spoon, Jam & Spoon (1966-2006)
Melanie Appleby, Mel & Kim (1966-1990)
Melanie Thornton, La Bouche (1967-2001)
Miisa-Leena Päällysaho, Miisa (1970-2016)
Mika Kauppinen, Hausmylly (1969-2013)
Mike Staab, Mysterious Art & Magic Affair (1960-2009)
Nello Tijardovic aka Nello (1967-2001)
Patrick Cowley (1950-1982)
Paul Walden aka Guru Josh (1964-2015)
Pete Burns, Dead Or Alive (1959-2016)
Peter Rauhofer (1965-2013)
Roberto Concina aka Robert Miles (1969-2017)
Sylvester, James Jr aka Sylvester (1947-1988)
Tillmann Uhrmacher, Mysterious Art & TN'T Partyzone (1967-2011)
Tom Wilson (1951-2004)
Tony De Vit (1957-1998)

Torsten Fenslau, Culture Beat & Public Art (1964-1993)
Trevor Taylor, Bad Boys Blue (1958-2008)

And

Marie Fredriksson, Roxette (1958-2019)

Move on, move on, move your body
Move on, move on, take it easy
Move to the rhythm, it's here to stay

Anticappella: Move Your Body

Milton Keynes UK
Ingram Content Group UK Ltd.
UKHW020706220923
429186UK00016B/954